"*Investing in Hedge Funds* is the first comprehensive study of what hedge funds are and how they work. **THIS IS AN ESSENTIAL BOOK FOR ALL INVESTORS CURIOUS ABOUT ALTERNATIVE INVESTMENT STRATEGIES**. Joseph Nicholas details the range of investment strategies pursued by hedge fund managers and writes in a clear, lucid style. **I HIGHLY RECOMMEND THIS BOOK TO ACADEMICS AND PROFESSIONALS WHO WANT TO LEARN ABOUT HEDGE FUNDS**."

PROFESSOR WILLIAM N. GOETZMANN
Director, International Center for Finance
Yale School of Management

"**JOSEPH NICHOLAS PROVIDES AN EXTRAORDINARY ANALYSIS OF HEDGE FUNDS THAT CLEARLY EXPLAINS WHAT THEY ARE AND HOW THEY WORK.** This book is a must-read for anyone looking to reduce investment risks and increase performance."

WILLIAM B. NICHOLSON
Former Chairman and Chief Executive Officer
Capital Resource Advisors

INVESTING IN
HEDGE
FUNDS

Also by Joseph G. Nicholas

Hedge Fund of Funds Investing:
An Investor's Guide

Market-Neutral Investing:
Long/Short Hedge Fund Strategies

Also available from Bloomberg Press

Investing in REITs:
Real Estate Investment Trusts
Third Edition
by Ralph L. Block

The Money-Making Guide to Bonds:
Straightforward Strategies for
Picking the Right Bonds and Bond Funds
by Hildy Richelson
and Stan Richelson

The Trader's Guide to Key Economic Indicators
by Richard Yamarone

A complete list of our titles is available
at **www.bloomberg.com/books**

INVESTING IN
HEDGE
FUNDS

REVISED AND UPDATED EDITION

JOSEPH G. NICHOLAS

BLOOMBERG PRESS

NEW YORK

Revised and updated edition published 2005
3 5 7 9 10 8 6 4 2

ISBN-13: 978-1-57660-184-6

Library of Congress has cataloged the earlier printing as follows:

Nicholas, Joseph G.
  Investing in hedge funds / Joseph G. Nicholas. – Rev. and updated ed.
    p. cm.
  Summary: "Overview of the hedge fund industry and various hedge fund investment strategies. Includes industry data, graphs, and manager examples"– Provided by publisher.
  Includes bibliographic references and index.
  ISBN 1-57660-184-6 (alk. paper)
  1. Hedge funds–United States. II. Title: Hedge funds. II. Title.

HG4930.N53 2005
332.64'524–dc22

2005015773

To my parents,
Diana and George Nicholas

ACKNOWLEDGMENTS

I THANK THE FOLLOWING:

Ben Borton, Scott J. Esser, Patrick Kenary, Ken Heinz, and William Bock.

For their insightful help and comments, in good times and bad, on the various strategy chapters we would like to thank the following managers and their staffs: Dan Adler, Ray Dalio, Karen Finerman, David Fink, Kent Fleming, J.C. Frey, Richard Giacomo, Mickey Harley, Jeff James, John Kerschner, Odell Lambroza, Sam Nathans, and Seth Washburne.

INVESTING IN
HEDGE
FUNDS

INTRODUCTION

THE FIRST EDITION of *Investing in Hedge Funds* was written to provide a basic introduction to the world of hedge funds. In particular, the goal of the book was to introduce the reader to the basics of some of the most commonly followed hedge fund investment strategies. Since the publication of the first edition, there has been a significant expansion in the number of books available on the subject, many of which delve much more deeply into the subjects and strategies introduced in this book. In revising this edition, I have maintained its previous nature while updating the statistics and trade examples. For investors and those interested in learning about the hedge fund industry and its various investment approaches, this book will serve as a starting point.

From January 1990 to December 2004, the hedge fund industry's assets grew twenty-five fold, from approximately $40 billion to almost $1 trillion.[1] Over the same period, the number of hedge funds increased from 600 to more than 7,400. Many of us have read periodic reports in the press about hedge funds that generate outsized returns and losses and influence global markets. Most individuals who are familiar with the investment industry know a hedge fund manager or have a friend who does.

Despite their growing presence in world financial and investment circles, hedge funds are still enveloped in a veil of mystery. Questions abound. What are hedge funds and who runs them? What kind of investment opportunities do they offer and why should I consider them? What are the benefits and what are the risks? What kind of information do I need and where can I get it? How do I evaluate a hedge fund and how do I invest? What should I look for and what should I avoid?

Whether one ultimately decides to invest in hedge funds and the strategies they pursue, it is important to be informed in order to make an intelligent investment decision. The purpose of this book is to address these questions, share some practical insight into the industry, and provide the investor a starting point for making hedge fund investment decisions.

Money managers who distinguish themselves do so not by acting on where profit was generated in the past but where profit will be generated in the future. Those who correctly anticipate profit potential search in overlooked, complicated, or misunderstood places and employ the tools and techniques necessary to realize them. For the vast majority of investors, the traditional stock and bond investments pursued by individuals, mutual funds, and investment advisory firms represent where the investment community is now. But regulation and tradition restrict the investment approaches they employ in ways that limit the investment strategies and opportunities they can pursue. A private investment industry has advanced onto the global investment scene to profit from nontraditional opportunities. Some of the world's most sophisticated investors fund the industry, and their money is managed by a group of talented and savvy money managers who pursue a broad spectrum of alternative investment strategies. The assets are pooled and managed in private investment structures called hedge funds.

Assets are flowing to hedge funds at an increasing rate because institutions and individuals alike see hedge funds as an integral part of their overall investment approach. By providing exposures that investors may not already have, hedge funds allow these investors to further diversify their investment portfolios, protect against risks inherent in traditional investment approaches, and realize excess returns.

The specialized strategies that hedge fund managers employ provide access to markets around the globe, but they do not all pursue the same investment approach or provide the same exposures. Some offer lower-risk alternatives to traditional investments; others, through the use of leverage, take outsize risks in search of large gains. They may specialize in long-term investment approaches, arbitrage opportunities, or short-term trading strategies. Some make profits as markets rise and some as they fall. Some provide protection against market declines or neutralize certain risks. Others magnify the exposure to directional market movements.

Hedge fund managers are entrepreneurs who establish specialized money management firms. Expanding global markets provide plenty of areas where hedge fund managers can mine profits. As they expand and shift, inefficiencies emerge that create specialized opportunities for investors. Alternative investment strategies capitalize on market inefficiencies created by global economic change in a way that traditional long-term investment strategies cannot. Hedge funds are not subject to the same restrictions and use nontraditional techniques and instruments to protect against and profit from such market movements.

Most hedge fund managers are specialized to some degree and restrict themselves to a particular strategy. They attract investors by exhibiting a high level of expertise within their area of focus. Today, the majority of hedge funds are run by managers who pursue attractive, risk-adjusted returns for their clients by creating informational, statistical, or strategic advantages that allow them to turn market inefficiencies into profits.

It is no secret to the investment community that market inefficiencies represent profit opportunities. Markets always seek to become efficient, but as long as change occurs in the world, they will continue to have inefficiencies. In spite of this, the notions of perfect information, perfect competition, and theoretical equilibrium still haunt investors' thoughts, even though they are concepts that exist only in the pages of introductory economics texts. In actuality, market disequilibrium—which requires a certain level of market inefficiency —is, as George Soros once said, "inherent in the imperfect understanding of the participants." He went on to say that "financial markets are inherently unstable, and the idea of a theoretical equilibrium … is itself a product of our imperfect understanding."[2] The point is that because it takes time to communicate information, there are information gaps, or inefficiencies, that result in a difference between the "real" or potential value of an asset and its market value. Hedge fund managers use informational, statistical, or strategic advantages to make intelligent, informed estimates of the real value of assets; take positions in those assets whose market value differs from their estimate; hedge out extraneous risk; and reap the returns when information about the asset becomes more readily available and the market reacts accordingly.

A great number of factors have contributed to the rapid growth of both hedge funds and hedge fund assets. Here are four that have been the most important:

1 Opportunity. The continuing expansion of global markets and the ongoing development of new markets provide an expanding arena for investments. As long as economic conditions change and information flows imperfectly, inefficiencies will continue to be created. Markets are always striving to correct these inefficiencies because they represent a potential for profit. But while they remain, astute investment managers operating through the hedge fund investment vehicle provide investors with a way to capitalize on such opportunities.

2 Talent and expertise. As a result of the reduced cost of investment instruments, returns have become less dependent on large and costly infrastructure, and the value of talented individuals has increased. One person with a personal computer can command more informational resources and analytical power today than was possible by an investment division on Wall Street in the mid-1980s. The human factor is a key to successfully applying investment capital to current opportunities. Investment funds seek those money managers who can offer specialized knowledge, expertise, and investment talent.

3 Tools and support services. New investment instruments and brokerage services continue to evolve and to become broadly available. The technology explosion has resulted in a rapid increase in the amount of information available to investors and the timeliness of that data. Likewise, ongoing increases in computing power allow market participants to analyze and process this information more quickly and more thoroughly. At the same time the cost of such products and services has been drastically reduced.

4 Performance. Even with all other factors, the industry would not grow without producing results. With few exceptions, the investment strategies pursued by hedge fund managers have generated attractive risk-adjusted returns.

THE STRUCTURE OF THIS BOOK

This book is designed to introduce the reader to hedge funds and provide an overview of the main strategies in which hedge funds engage. Chapter 1 addresses the question: What is a hedge fund? The term has no formal definition and is used interchangeably to describe both an investment structure and an investment approach. The key to understanding hedge funds lies in separating the structure of the investment from the alternative investment strategy the fund manager employs. A hedge fund is not a static entity. It is a structure that allows the different components of the hedge fund world to interact. The most important components are the investment structure or vehicle, the investor, the fund manager, and the investment strategy. The interaction between these components forms the hedge fund dynamic.

Chapter 2 discusses the hedge fund structures that allow hedge fund managers to use a wider variety of innovative investment strategies than more traditional forms of investment. In the past, the term *hedge fund* cryptically described both an investment vehicle—a commingled investment fund—and a strategy of long and short stock investing incorporating leverage. Today, it only describes investment fund structures such as limited partnerships and offshore corporations that allow access to the various hedge fund strategies. The regulatory framework and available legal entities drive the types of investment structures that investors will use. The important features of hedge fund structures potential investors need to consider are covered in this chapter, including: legal forms, associated documentation such as limited partnership agreements, offering memorandum and subscription materials, registration and regulation, fees and expenses, investment size, lockup periods, liquidity, performance and reporting, tax issues, and ERISA (Employee Retirement Income Security Act) considerations.

Chapter 3 is an introduction to the most prominent hedge fund strategies. It introduces the elements of investing that make up these approaches. This introduction is intended to provide a framework for understanding and comparing different strategies. Many elements are not vastly different from those that make up traditional investing strategies. What is different is how the practitioners of each strategy weigh the various elements in combination with new elements and incorporate long and short exposures. Roughly, there are five important groups of elements: (1) tools and techniques, (2) instruments and markets, (3) sources of return, (4) measures for controlling risk, and (5) performance. How different strategies weight these elements determines the risk-reward characteristics that each strategy aims to produce. The second half of the chapter introduces the universe of the eleven prominent hedge fund strategies covered in more detail in later chapters. Each of the eleven strategies is described briefly and each description is accompanied by a graph illustrating the asset growth since 1990 of hedge funds employing the particular strategy and the returns those funds have produced. Following is a consideration of the universe as a whole in terms of assets under management and risk-reward profiles. By the end of this chapter, readers should have a broad sense of the spectrum of hedge fund choices and be ready for the more detailed examinations of the different approaches that follow in the individual strategy chapters.

Chapters 4 through 14 examine one hedge fund strategy each and describe how the practitioners of each strategy produce returns and control risk. Each strategy is described in terms of core strategic propositions, investment process, performance, advantages, and disadvantages. Although the overall goal of this book is to assist hedge fund investors in understanding hedge fund strategies, each strategy chapter is also designed to stand alone. The reader with interest in a particular strategy should not get lost by reading one chapter in isolation.

Chapter 15 suggests a framework for selecting hedge funds and alternative investment strategies for investment allocation. It is written for investors who want to construct a multiple-manager portfolio, but the concepts can be applied to a single manager or hedge fund as well. Three basic interrelated steps or stages in making an allocation to hedge funds are discussed: (1) planning the investment, (2) selecting the optimal structure and appropriate strategies, and (3) searching for and selecting the best managers.

Chapter 16 offers more detail on due diligence and describes three issues that affect hedge fund investors after they make an initial allocation: (1) ongoing due diligence, (2) portfolio transparency, and (3) risk monitoring. These disclosure issues have become more important as institutional investors with fiduciary responsibilities have begun to allocate assets to hedge funds. In light of the unexpected losses experienced by a number of secretive funds in 1998, prudence dictates that investors use risk monitoring systems that provide protection through some level of control over the investment.

KEYS TO
Understanding

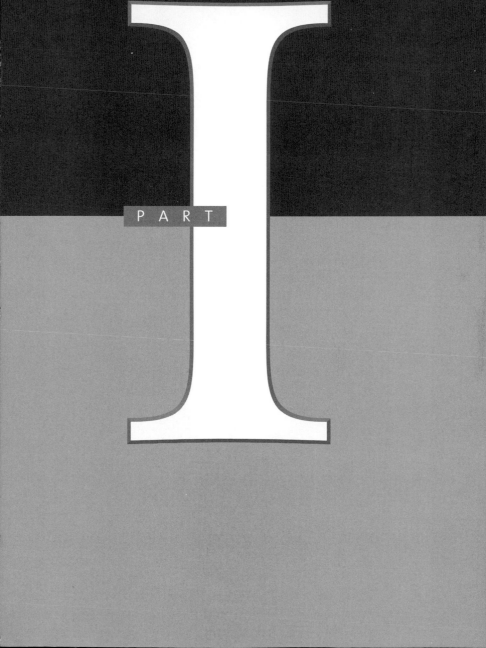

PART

I

CHAPTER

What Is a HEDGE FUND?

The term hedge fund describes an investment structure for managing a private, unregistered investment pool. Typically, this structure charges an incentive-based fee that compensates the fund manager through a percentage of the profits that the fund earns. For most hedge funds, exemption from securities registration limits the number of participants, who must also be accredited investors, qualified investors, or institutional investors. All hedge funds are not alike; managers usually specialize in one of a diverse number of alternative investment strategies operated through the hedge fund structure.

THE TERM *hedge fund* has been used to describe both an investment structure—a commingled investment fund—and a strategy—a leveraged long portfolio "hedged" by stock short sales. However, because of the diverse range of investment approaches now employed, it more accurately describes the investment structure within which a hedge fund strategy is executed. For example, a convertible arbitrage hedge fund and a distressed securities hedge fund both operate in the same type of fund structure but follow two distinct strategies. Like the term *mutual fund,* which describes only the investment structure and does not indicate whether it invests in stocks or bonds or in the United States or abroad, the term *hedge fund* alone does not tell an investor anything about the underlying investment activities. A hedge fund acts as a vehicle, helping an investor get to the ultimate investment goal: to turn market opportunities into investment returns. In this respect, a hedge fund is no different from a mutual fund. Hedge funds differ from mutual funds in the range of allowable investment approaches, the goals of the strategies that they use, and in the breadth of tools and techniques available to investment managers to achieve those goals for investors. (It should be noted that this distinction is becoming blurred. Mutual fund regulatory changes have allowed certain hedge fund strategies to operate under the mutual fund structure.)

Since the term *hedge fund* describes an investment structure and is applied to a range of strategies, in order to understand particular hedge funds it is necessary to separate the structure of the investment (its legal form and method of operations) from its investment strategy (how it invests capital in the financial markets to achieve its goals).

The investment structure is the legal entity that allows investment assets to be pooled and permits the hedge fund manager to invest them. The investment approach that the manager takes is known as the hedge fund strategy or alternative investment strategy. The structure establishes such things as the method of manager compensation, the number and type of investors, and the rights and responsibilities of investors regarding profits, redemptions, taxes, and reports. The elements that make up the strategy include how the manager invests, which markets and instruments are used, and which opportunity and return source is targeted.

HEDGE FUND STRATEGIES

There is nothing mystical about the strategies that hedge fund managers use. These strategies can be described in the same terms as those for a traditional portfolio: return source, investment method, buy/sell process, market and instrument concentrations, and risk control. The alternative investment strategies that hedge fund managers tend to use produce returns by leveraging some kind of informational or strategic advantage. Essentially, although some hedge fund strategies are complex, hedge fund investing can be understood by anyone familiar with financial markets and instruments who also has a basic working knowledge of corporate structure and finance.

Although it is important to acknowledge that most money managers who operate private investment pools using the hedge fund structure have their own styles, most of these specialized investment approaches can be categorized within the list of general strategies described in this book. The hedge fund universe is composed of managers who use a broad range of variations of these strategies. They may have little or nothing in common except that they operate under the hedge fund structure and are considered to be alternatives to traditional investment approaches.

THE JONES NOBODY KEEPS UP WITH

THERE ARE REASONS to believe that the best professional manager of investors' money these days is a quiet-spoken, seldom photographed man named Alfred Winslow Jones. Few businessmen have heard of him, although some with long memories may remember his articles in *Fortune;* he was a staff writer in the early 1940s. In any case, his performance in the stock market in recent years has made him one of the wonders of Wall Street—and made millionaires of several of his investors. On investments left with him during the five years ended last May 31 (when he closed his 1965 fiscal year), Jones made 325 percent. Fidelity Trend Fund, which had the best record of any mutual fund during those years, made "only" 225 percent. For the ten-year period ended in May, Jones made 670 percent; Dreyfuss Fund, the leader among mutual funds that were in business all during that decade, had a 358 percent gain.

The vehicle through which Jones operates is not a mutual fund but a limited partnership. Jones runs two such partnerships, and they have slightly different investment objectives. In each case, however, the underlying investment strategy is the same: the fund's capital is both leveraged and "hedged." The leverage arises from the fact that the fund margins itself to the hilt; the hedge is provided by short positions—there are always some in the fund's portfolio.

Jones's accomplishments have spawned a number of other "hedge funds."

— Carol J. Loomis
Fortune[1]

Alternative investments differ from the traditional investment approaches used in mutual funds in many significant ways. Traditional investment strategies are exclusively long. Their practitioners seek stocks or bonds that they think will outperform the market. However, alternative investment strategies invest long, short, or both, combining two or more instruments to create one investment position. Traditional strategies normally do not take advantage of leverage. Many alternative strategies do. Alternative strategies make use of hedging techniques. Unlike traditional strategies that lose money in a market decline, hedged strategies can generate profit on their hedges to offset some or all of the market losses. Hedging may take a number of forms. Some hedges seek to generate profit on an ongoing basis; others may be purely defensive or insurance against market crashes. In general, they are positions that will profit in a market decline by providing an offset, or hedge, to losses incurred on investments in the portfolio that are exposed to the market.

The returns generated by traditional long-only strategies are relative, or benchmarked, to market indexes. For example, if a traditional mutual fund invests in large-capitalization U.S. equities, its return is benchmarked to the performance of a large-capitalization stock index, and performance is judged relative to that index. Most alternative strategies, however, target absolute returns. Because the source of return for most of these strategies is not based on the directional moves of a simple market and does not relate to a particular market or index, it is not useful to compare returns with a traditional market index. Rather, returns are expected to fall within a certain range, regardless of what the markets do. The performance of these strategies will still be cyclical and subject to a variety of drivers. The recent availability of investable hedge fund indexes offered by HFR, S&P, and CSFB now provides real benchmarks for performance comparison.

The hedge fund strategies covered in this book are differentiated by the tools used and the profit opportunities targeted. The various strategies have very different risk-reward characteristics, so it is important that potential investors distinguish between them instead of lumping them together under the heading of "hedge funds." Hedge funds are heterogeneous. To render them comparable, you must categorize them by the core strategy that the fund manager uses. Some hedge fund strategies, such as macro funds, use aggressive approaches, whereas others, such as nonleveraged market-neutral funds, are conservative. Many have significantly lower risk than a traditional portfolio of long stocks and bonds for the same levels of return.

HEDGE FUND MANAGERS

Hedge fund managers are more difficult to categorize than the various strategies of the funds they manage. Their diverse backgrounds often provide them with the specialized knowledge, expertise, and skills they use to implement unique variations of general strategies.

The typical hedge fund manager is an entrepreneur who organizes a money management company and investment fund to pool his assets (often a substantial portion of his net worth) with those of family, friends, and other investors. The manager's primary efforts are directed toward the implementation of a hedge fund strategy and the management of a profitable investment portfolio. Often, the "business culture" of the manager and the money management company will reflect these primary efforts, with less emphasis on selling and investor relations when compared with traditional investment operations. Because hedge fund managers usually are investing their own assets along with those of the other investors, they are highly motivated to achieve investment returns and to reduce risk. This motivation has translated into success, as evidenced by the significant growth of the hedge fund industry and the proliferation of hedge funds and managers. Increasingly, institutions and traditional money management firms are organizing internal operations to pursue hedge fund strategies by converting traditional managers and training new ones.

HEDGE FUND INVESTORS

Hedge fund investors have traditionally been high-net-worth individuals. At times, more than half of these were from countries outside the United States. These non-U.S. investors sought to invest with the top investment talent, which in the early 1990s was almost exclusively based in the United States; today top hedge fund managers are located in financial centers around the globe. Recently, the increasing number of American and international high-net-worth individuals has been augmented by institutional investors, including pension funds, endowments, banks, and insurance companies. An infrastructure has emerged to process and make available information about hedge funds. In light of these developments, institutions have become more open to exploring allocations to alternative investment strategies. In response, many hedge funds have made changes, such as providing transparency, to accommodate the needs of institutional investors. It has been a self-reinforcing process: as funds make information about their operations available to institutions, infrastructure to support this body of information is created, and institutions are more likely to make allocations to hedge funds. These institutional investors represent a growing number of hedge fund investors that control significant assets and usually make much larger allocations than individuals; thus funds are willing to accommodate their needs.

THE HEDGE FUND DYNAMIC

As stated earlier, the hedge fund structure is an investment vehicle because it helps investors reach their ultimate goal: to turn market opportunities into investment returns. The investor brings investment capital to the industry. These assets are pooled in structures called hedge funds. The hedge fund structure gives the investor access to hedge fund managers who tap the return opportunities available from a variety of market inefficiencies. For investors, the hedge fund structure is both a method to pool their assets with those of other investors and a way to access talented hedge fund managers, the alternative investment strategies they use, and the exposures they provide. For managers, the structure enables them to pool the assets of wealthy and institutional investors, allows them to implement their particular strategies, and permits them to collect an asset-based and incentive-based fee from their investors. They combine their expertise with an alternative investment strategy to generate returns for their investors and for themselves, completing the dynamic (shown in **FIGURE 1.1**).

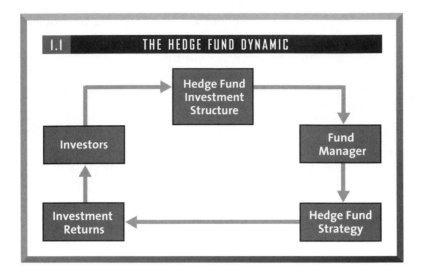

HEDGE FUND INDUSTRY CHARACTERISTICS

To understand the characteristics of the hedge fund industry, keep in mind that it is the aggregate of various strategies operating under the same general structure. The opportunities pursued by these strategies are created by market inefficiencies. The industry is dynamic in that the size, composition, and return opportunities for each strategy—and among strategies—fluctuate over time. Change also creates market inefficiencies, and the ongoing shifts in global markets and geopolitical activities continue to supply new investment opportunities to hedge fund managers.

ASSETS IN INDUSTRY/GROWTH

Assets in the hedge fund industry have grown substantially over the past fifteen years, from around $39 billion in 1990 to $973 billion in 2004 (see **FIGURE 1.2**). This growth is a result of inflows (shown as a portion of the total assets, in **FIGURE 1.3**) and performance.

Asset inflows (and outflows) have a significant impact on the growth of hedge fund assets. **FIGURE 1.4** on page 20 shows net assets flowing into hedge funds as a percentage of total

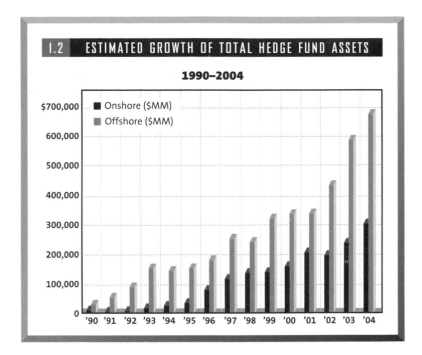

1.2 ESTIMATED GROWTH OF TOTAL HEDGE FUND ASSETS

1990–2004

■ Onshore ($MM)
■ Offshore ($MM)

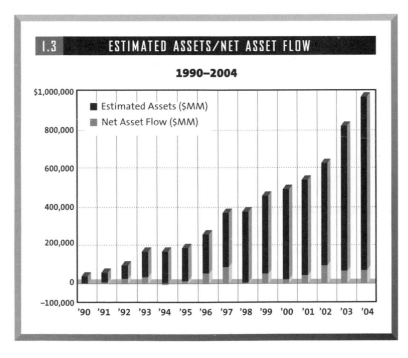

1.3 ESTIMATED ASSETS/NET ASSET FLOW

1990–2004

■ Estimated Assets ($MM)
■ Net Asset Flow ($MM)

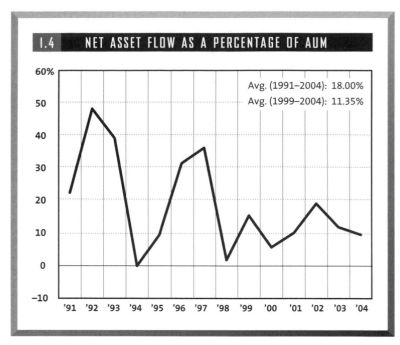

1.4   NET ASSET FLOW AS A PERCENTAGE OF AUM

Avg. (1991–2004): 18.00%
Avg. (1999–2004): 11.35%

assets under management. Over the period shown (1991 through 2004), hedge fund assets increased by an average of 18 percent each year. Year to year flows varied greatly from 22 percent in 1991 to a peak of 48 percent in 1992 before falling to zero in 1994. By 1997, flows had rebounded to 36 percent but quickly fell back to 1 percent in 1998. The large percentage swings have since subsided, with asset flow having stabilized around an 11 percent annual inflow from 1999 to 2004.

NUMBER OF FUNDS/GROWTH

FIGURE 1.5 provides annual estimates of the number of hedge funds in the industry. Not surprisingly, this measure has increased along with asset growth. Since 1990, the number of funds has increased more than tenfold from 530 to 5,782 as of 2004. Over the period from 1990 through 2000, growth in the number of hedge funds was stable and averaged 280 funds each year. In 2001, however, 569 new funds entered the market and several large additions to the number of funds in the industry followed. An average of 612

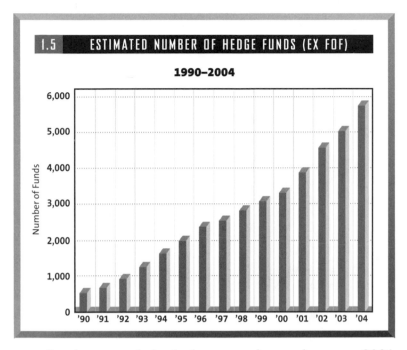

1.5   ESTIMATED NUMBER OF HEDGE FUNDS (EX FOF)

1990–2004

new funds entered the industry each year between 2001 and 2004.

ASSET SIZE OF FUNDS

The pie chart in **FIGURE 1.6** on the following page shows a grouping of hedge funds by the size of the assets they maintain under management. Nearly one-third of all funds in the industry manage between $25 million and $100 million. Funds with less than $10 million under management (22 percent) together with funds holding between $10 and $25 million (16 percent) represent more than one-third of funds as well. The remainder of the hedge fund industry is split among funds with over $100 million under management. Funds with between $100 million and $200 million and funds with between $200 million and $500 million each represent about 11 percent of the industry. Funds larger than this are still in the minority, with about 4 percent between $500 million and $1 billion, and just 3 percent with more than $1 billion under management.

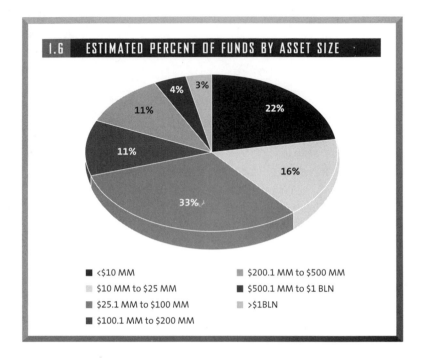

1.6 ESTIMATED PERCENT OF FUNDS BY ASSET SIZE

- ■ <$10 MM
- □ $10 MM to $25 MM
- ■ $25.1 MM to $100 MM
- ■ $100.1 MM to $200 MM
- ■ $200.1 MM to $500 MM
- ■ $500.1 MM to $1 BLN
- □ >$1BLN

AGE OF FUNDS

The chart in **FIGURE 1.7** categorizes currently active hedge funds by age. As shown, veteran funds that have existed for more than seven years represent nearly a quarter of the funds in the industry. Interestingly, nearly a third of the hedge funds are emerging funds that were launched within the past two years. Funds between 2 and 7 years of age are spread almost evenly across the remaining categories shown in the chart; an estimated 15 percent of funds have been active for between 2 and 3 three years, and 18 percent and 13 percent of funds fall into the 3 to 5 and 5 to 7 year intervals, respectively.

INDUSTRY PERFORMANCE

The hedge fund industry has provided attractive, stable returns for the past fifteen years. This is illustrated in **FIGURE 1.8**, which plots the growth of $1,000 invested in the HFRI Fund Weighted Composite Index, the MSCI World Index, and the S&P 500 index on a monthly basis from January 1990 through December 2004. Hedge funds have outperformed equities as

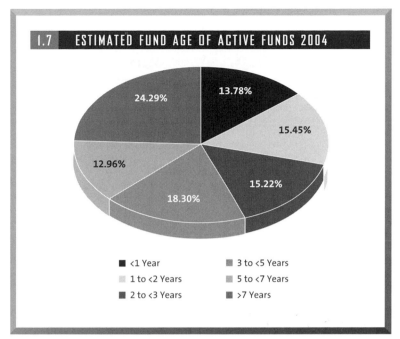

1.7 ESTIMATED FUND AGE OF ACTIVE FUNDS 2004

- ■ <1 Year
- ■ 1 to <2 Years
- ■ 2 to <3 Years
- ■ 3 to <5 Years
- ■ 5 to <7 Years
- ■ >7 Years

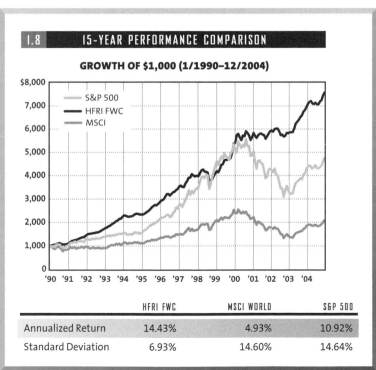

1.8 15-YEAR PERFORMANCE COMPARISON

GROWTH OF $1,000 (1/1990–12/2004)

- S&P 500
- HFRI FWC
- MSCI

	HFRI FWC	MSCI WORLD	S&P 500
Annualized Return	14.43%	4.93%	10.92%
Standard Deviation	6.93%	14.60%	14.64%

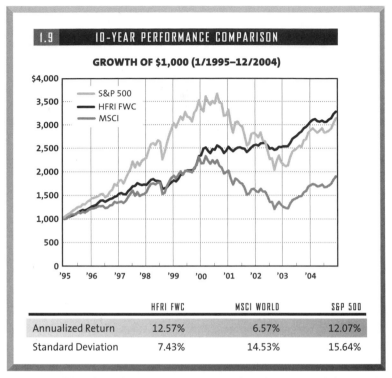

1.9   10-YEAR PERFORMANCE COMPARISON

GROWTH OF $1,000 (1/1995–12/2004)

Legend: S&P 500, HFRI FWC, MSCI

	HFRI FWC	MSCI WORLD	S&P 500
Annualized Return	12.57%	6.57%	12.07%
Standard Deviation	7.43%	14.53%	15.64%

measured by the 14.43 percent annualized return of the HFRI compared to 4.93 percent for the MSCI World and 10.92 percent for the S&P 500. During the period shown, the HFRI had less than half the volatility of each of these equity indexes at 6.93 percent compared to more than 14 percent for the MSCI World and 15 percent for the S&P 500.

FIGURE 1.9 plots the series included in Figure 1.8 for an investment beginning in January 1995. The S&P 500 outperformed the HFRI from January 1995 through its peak in August 2000. However, the subsequent downturn brought the value of an S&P investment below that of the HFRI by June 2002. Over the full ten-year period shown, the HFRI posted a return of 12.57 percent compared to 12.07 percent for the S&P and 6.57 percent for the MSCI World indexes while again generating less than half of the volatility of these indexes at 7.43 percent.

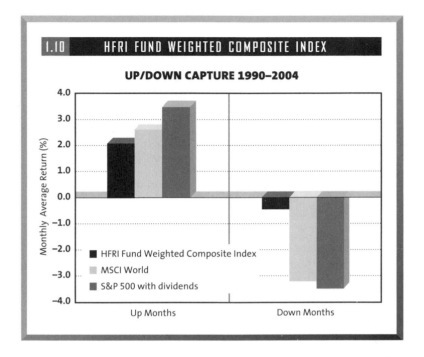

1.10 HFRI FUND WEIGHTED COMPOSITE INDEX

UP/DOWN CAPTURE 1990–2004

- HFRI Fund Weighted Composite Index
- MSCI World
- S&P 500 with dividends

WEALTH PRESERVATION

Figures 1.8 and 1.9 highlight the value of hedge funds as a wealth preserving investment. Following an upward trend for all three indexes through August 2000, the MSCI World and S&P 500 indexes lost 24 percent and 22 percent, respectively, as of September 2002. Meanwhile the HFRI Fund Weighted Composite index lost only 10 basis points for the same period.

FIGURE 1.10 depicts the monthly average returns for the HFRI, MSCI, and S&P 500 indexes during both the up and down periods of the S&P 500 from 1990 through 2004. The percentage of up months and down months is also shown for each series. The S&P 500 posted positive monthly returns for 64 percent of the period shown and its average return during these up months was 3.45 percent. For the down months, it lost an average of 3.45 percent. With fewer winning months (60 percent) and more losing months (40 percent), the MSCI World index captured 2.57 percent of the upside for the S&P 500, but lost 3.17 percent on the downside. The HFRI index,

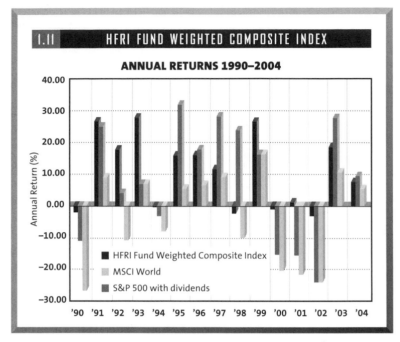

1.11   HFRI FUND WEIGHTED COMPOSITE INDEX

ANNUAL RETURNS 1990–2004

Legend:
- ■ HFRI Fund Weighted Composite Index
- ▨ MSCI World
- ■ S&P 500 with dividends

on the other hand, showed positive returns for 74 percent of the period and negative returns for just 26 percent of the period. Although it captured slightly less of the upside at 2.01 percent, its downside loss was limited to 0.44 percent.

FIGURE 1.11 shows the annual performance of the HFRI FWC compared with that of the S&P 500 and MSCI World indexes. Here we see again that hedge funds have provided an opportunity to preserve wealth during periods of drawdown in traditional equity markets. The HFRI captured much of the positive performance of the S&P 500 during up years such as 1991, 1995 to 1997, and 2003 and produced excess returns from 1991 to 1993 and in 1999. During the down years of both the S&P 500 and MSCI World indexes (1990, 2000 to 2002), the HFRI posted much smaller losses and even generated positive returns in 2001.

DRAWDOWNS

As we have seen, hedge funds have delivered attractive long-term returns with low volatility. As a group, they preserve wealth by mitigating losses. However, they do experience

1.12   HFRI FUND WEIGHTED COMPOSITE INDEX

SORTED BY MAXIMUM DRAWDOWN

DRAWDOWN START PERIOD	DRAWDOWN END PERIOD	RECOVERY	MAXIMUM DRAWDOWN	FROM MAX DRAWDOWN	FROM MAX DRAWDOWN
May 98	Mar 99	10 Months	11.42	9.62%	23.94%
Sep 00	Jan 02	16 Months	6.39	4.77%	4.99%
Jun 02	Apr 03	10 Months	5.72	3.34%	16.19%
Aug 90	Mar 91	7 Months	5.38	15.89%	29.50%
Apr 00	Aug 00	4 Months	4.75	0.15%	4.92%
Feb 94	Sep 94	7 Months	2.63	5.73%	9.43%
Oct 97	Feb 98	5 Months	2.45	5.33%	0.71%
Jan 90	Mar 90	2 Months	2.11	11.87%	10.89%
Apr 04	Sep 04	6 Months	2.0	N/A	N/A
Mar 97	May 97	2 Months	1.75	14.11%	21.60%
Oct 94	Mar 95	5 Months	1.6	13.09%	25.29%

losing periods. **FIGURE 1.12** shows multi-month losing periods, known as drawdowns, since 1990. A drawdown begins with a losing period and continues until the losses are earned back and new positive returns are achieved.

DYNAMIC NATURE OF PERFORMANCE

The hedge fund industry consists of multiple strategies. Depending on market cycles and changes, performance leadership shifts among the strategies relative to each other. **FIGURE 1.13** on the following two pages demonstrates the changing performance relationship among the strategies for each year from 1993 to 2004, ranking best to worst performing strategies as well as general market indexes. Note how the ranking changes from year to year.

1.13   HFRI INDICES ANNUAL INVESTMENT RETURNS (1993–2004)

1993	1994	1995	1996	1997	1998
HFRI Macro 53.31%	HFRI Merger Arbitrage 8.88%	HFRI Sector 39.65%	HFR Sector 30.68%	S&P 500 33.33%	S&P 500 28.59%
HFRI Sector 33.71%	HFRI Sector 7.98%	S&P 500 37.54%	HFRI Event-Driven 24.84%	HFRI Equity Hedge 23.41%	MSCI Indices US World 22.79%
HFRI Distressed Securities 32.54%	HFRI Event-Driven 6.00%	HFRI Equity Hedge 31.04%	S&P 500 22.92%	HFRI Event-Driven 21.23%	HFRI Equity Hedge 15.98%
HFRI Fund Comp. 30.88%	HFRI Fund Comp. 4.10%	HFRI Macro 29.32%	HFRI Equity Hedge 21.75%	HFRI Macro 18.82%	Lehman Gov't/Credit 12.00%
HFRI Event-Driven 28.22%	HFRI Relative Value Arbitrage 4.00%	HFRI Event-Driven 25.11%	HFRI Fund Comp. 21.10%	HFRI Fund Comp. 16.79%	HFRI Convertible Arbitrage 7.77%
HFRI Equity Hedge 27.94%	HFRI Distressed Securities 3.84%	Lehman Gov't/Credit 22.74%	HFRI Distressed Securities 20.77%	HFRI Merger Arbitrage 16.44%	HFRI Sector 7.62%
HFRI Relative Value Arbitrage 27.10%	MSCI Indices US World 3.34%	HFRI Fund Comp. 21.50%	HFRI Merger Arbitrage 16.61%	HFRI Fund of Funds Comp. 16.20%	HFRI Merger Arbitrage 7.23%
HFRI Fund of Funds Comp. 26.32%	HFRI Equity Hedge 2.61%	HFRI Convertible Arbitrage 19.85%	HFRI Convertible Arbitrage 14.56%	HFRI Relative Value Arbitrage 15.93%	HFRI Macro 6.19%
MSCI Indices US World 20.38%	S&P 500 1.32%	HFRI Distressed Securities 19.73%	HFRI Relative Value Arbitrage 14.49%	HFRI Distressed Securities 15.40%	HFRI Relative Value Arbitrage 2.81%
HFRI Merger Arbitrage 20.24%	HFRI Fund of Funds Comp. −3.48%	MSCI Indices US World 18.70%	HFRI Fund of Funds Comp. 14.39%	MSCI Indices US World 14.16%	HFRI Fund Comp. 2.62%
HFRI Convertible Arbitrage 15.22%	HFRI Convertible Arbitrage −3.73%	HFRI Merger Arbitrage 17.86%	MSCI Indices US World 11.73%	HFRI Convertible Arbitrage 12.72%	HFRI Event-Driven 1.70%
Lehman Gov't/Credit 13.20%	Lehman Gov't/Credit −4.13%	HFRI Relative Value Arbitrage 15.66%	HFRI Macro 9.32%	Lehman Gov't/Credit 9.87%	HFRI Distressed Securities −4.23%
S&P 500 10.05%	HFRI Macro −4.30%	HFRI Fund of Funds Comp. 11.10%	Lehman Gov't/Credit 3.35%	HFRI Sector 5.21%	HFRI Fund of Funds Comp. −5.11%

1999	2000	2001	2002	2003	2004
HFRI Sector 67.00%	HFRI Merger Arbitrage 18.02%	HFRI Convertible Arbitrage 13.37%	Lehman Gov't/ Credit 12.10%	MSCI Indices US World 30.82%	HFRI Distressed Securities 18.63%
HFRI Equity Hedge 44.22%	HFRI Convertible Arbitrage 14.50%	HFRI Distressed Securities 13.28%	HFRI Convertible Arbitrage 9.05%	HFRI Distressed Securities 29.70%	HFRI Event- Driven 14.18%
HFRI Fund Comp. 31.29%	HFRI Relative Value Arbitrage 13.41%	HFRI Event- Driven 12.18%	HFRI Macro 7.44%	S&P 500 28.67%	MSCI Indices US World 12.83%
HFRI Fund of Funds Comp. 26.47%	Lehman Gov't/ Credit 13.27%	Lehman Gov't/ Credit 9.40%	HFRI Relative Value Arbitrage 5.44%	HFRI Sector 28.36%	HFRI Sector 11.59%
HFRI Event- Driven 24.33%	HFRI Equity Hedge 9.09%	HFRI Relative Value Arbitrage 8.92%	HFRI Distressed Securities 5.28%	HFRI Event- Driven 25.39%	S&P 500 10.87%
MSCI Indices US World 23.54%	HFRI Event- Driven 6.74%	HFRI Macro 6.87%	HFRI Fund of Funds Comp. 1.02%	HFRI Macro 22.02%	HFRI Fund Comp. 8.91%
S&P 500 21.03%	HFRI Fund Comp. 4.98%	HFRI Fund Comp. 4.62%	HFRI Merger Arbitrage −0.87%	HFRI Equity Hedge 20.54%	HFRI Equity Hedge 7.36%
HFRI Macro 17.62%	HFRI Fund of Funds Comp. 4.07%	HFRI Fund of Funds Comp. 2.80%	HFRI Fund Comp. −1.45%	HFRI Fund Comp. 19.62%	HFRI Fund of Funds Comp. 6.67%
HFRI Distressed Securities 16.94%	HFRI Distressed Securities 2.78%	HFRI Merger Arbitrage 2.76%	HFRI Event- Driven −4.30%	HFRI Fund of Funds Comp. 11.53%	HFRI Relative Value Arbitrage 5.29%
HFRI Relative Value Arbitrage 14.73%	HFRI Macro 1.97%	HFRI Equity Hedge 0.40%	HFRI Equity Hedge −4.71%	HFRI Convertible Arbitrage 9.63%	Lehman Gov't/ Credit 4.54%
HFRI Convertible Arbitrage 14.41%	HFRI Sector 0.31%	HFRI Sector −4.90%	HFRI Sector −12.85%	HFRI Relative Value Arbitrage 9.02%	HFRI Macro 4.09%
HFRI Merger Arbitrage 14.34%	S&P 500 −9.09%	S&P 500 −11.85%	MSCI Indices US World −21.06%	HFRI Merger Arbitrage 8.12%	HFRI Merger Arbitrage 4.09%
Lehman Gov't/ Credit −2.40%	MSCI Indices US World −14.07%	MSCI Indices US World −17.83%	S&P 500 −22.09%	Lehman Gov't/ Credit 5.07%	HFRI Convertible Arbitrage 1.07%

CHAPTER

The Hedge Fund
INVESTMENT
STRUCTURE

A N INVESTOR can access a hedge fund manager by investing in an existing investment vehicle or by placing assets in a separate managed account and hiring the hedge fund manager to invest them. A hedge fund, like a mutual fund, is an investment vehicle that allows multiple investors to pool their assets and enables them to access hedge fund managers' specialized knowledge, investment expertise, and innovative trading strategies. Like the strategies that hedge fund managers use, not all hedge funds are alike. Nevertheless, many features with which an investor should be familiar before investing in a hedge fund can be usefully discussed in general terms. This chapter first discusses the differences between commingled investment vehicles and separate managed accounts. It then examines some of the features of hedge fund structures: the legal form of both domestic and offshore funds, documentation, registration and regulation, fees and expenses, investment size, lockup periods, performance reporting, tax issues, and Employee Retirement Income Security Act (ERISA) considerations.

COMMINGLED INVESTMENT VEHICLES

In the United States, most hedge funds are limited partnerships. Investors become limited partners by purchasing interests in the partnership. The general partner of a limited partnership may be an individual or corporate entity. In the case of hedge funds, the general partner is often the fund manager, who will have a large portion of her net worth invested in the fund that she manages. The general partner's liability is unlimited, but the other partners provide compensation through fees linked to the fund's performance. Typically, the manager receives 1 to 2 percent of the fund's total assets annually and 20 percent of the profits. One of the distinguishing features of hedge funds is this incentive fee structure. The partnership's profits, losses, and tax consequences "flow through" to the investors.

Four of every five hedge fund managers are based in the United States. The terms *onshore* and *offshore* are commonly used to designate where the fund is organized for legal and tax purposes (its domicile). **FIGURE 2.1** shows a percentage breakdown of the states and countries where hedge funds are domiciled. Approximately 35 percent are domiciled in the United States. Hedge funds that are organized outside the United States are called offshore funds. Offshore funds are typically established in the Caribbean tax havens, and they are usually organized as corporations. Investors purchase shares in the corporation in the same way they would purchase shares in a mutual fund; but the minimum required contribution is much higher, and many funds limit the number of contributors. The fund's gains and losses do not flow through to the investor; rather they are realized when the share price of the fund's stock appreciates or depreciates.

Neither onshore nor offshore managers typically disclose the contents of funds' portfolios to their investors, although access to this information, called transparency, is increasing and is demanded by many investors. Managers report on performance on a limited basis—for most funds, this means monthly and for some others, quarterly. In addition, some

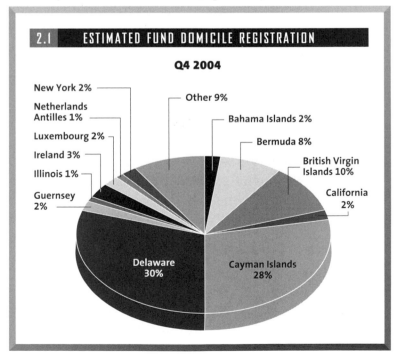

2.1 ESTIMATED FUND DOMICILE REGISTRATION

Q4 2004

New York 2%
Netherlands Antilles 1%
Luxembourg 2%
Ireland 3%
Illinois 1%
Guernsey 2%
Other 9%
Bahama Islands 2%
Bermuda 8%
British Virgin Islands 10%
California 2%
Delaware 30%
Cayman Islands 28%

fund managers require that investors "lock up" their assets for a certain period of time, which means that existing hedge fund vehicles can be illiquid investments.

Because the exemptions from registration (explained in detail in the section titled "Numbers of Investors and Minimum Investment Size," below) often limit the number of investors or require that investors meet certain standards, hedge funds usually require large minimum investments. Minimums are usually larger onshore where limits apply to U.S. investors. Minimum investment requirements range from $100,000 to $5 million and normally fall within the $500,000 to $1 million range (see **FIGURE 2.2**).

In the early stages, when a hedge fund has few investors and is trying to raise funds, it tends to have lower minimums and more flexibility to waive the minimum and accept a lesser investment amount. As the number of investors in the fund increases, the remaining slots become more valuable, and managers are less likely to waive the minimum. In many cases, the fund will actually raise the minimum for new investors and in some cases may raise the minimum for existing investors which may force out the smaller players to make room for larger allocations. Because of the more limited asset capacity of many of the hedge fund strategies, many managers also limit the size of any individual investment to ensure a diversified client base.

In general, funds accepting new investors will open on a monthly or quarterly basis. Investors who cannot meet the minimum investment size for a domestic or offshore fund sometimes participate through a feeder fund structure or wrap fee program. Basically, these arrangements enable pooling of multiple investors to meet a minimum investment size target. In a feeder fund structure, two levels of fees are imposed—one at the feeder fund level and one at the underlying fund level. As a result, fees are typically higher than in a single-tier structure. In a wrap fee program, the program sponsor compensates the individual hedge fund managers who participate. Fees paid by investors to the wrap fee sponsor include compensation to the sponsor and the compensa-

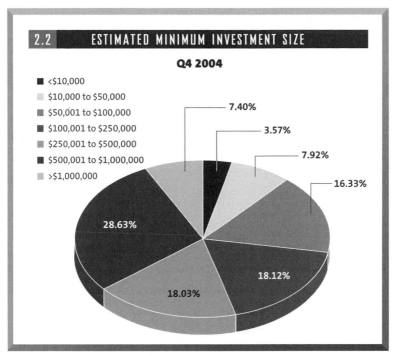

2.2   ESTIMATED MINIMUM INVESTMENT SIZE

Q4 2004

- <$10,000
- $10,000 to $50,000
- $50,001 to $100,000
- $100,001 to $250,000
- $250,001 to $500,000
- $500,001 to $1,000,000
- >$1,000,000

7.40%

3.57%

7.92%

16.33%

28.63%

18.12%

18.03%

tion that will be passed through to the hedge fund manager. As with a feeder fund, the total level of fees is higher than in a single-tier structure.

SEPARATE MANAGED ACCOUNTS

Although a managed or separate account is not a hedge fund, it is a method for accessing the investment talents of hedge fund managers. Rather than investing in an existing fund, an investor can place assets in a separate account and hire a hedge fund manager as an investment adviser to trade on a discretionary basis (see **FIGURE 2.3**). Many, but not all, hedge fund managers will do this. Multiple separate accounts create administrative burdens that the manager may or may not be willing to take on (individual reports, transparency requirements, specialized liquidity demands, trade allocation issues, individualized investment strategies). If the manager is willing to take on an individual account, the required minimum amount is usually large ($3 million to $25 million), although certain managers are set up to operate smaller accounts.

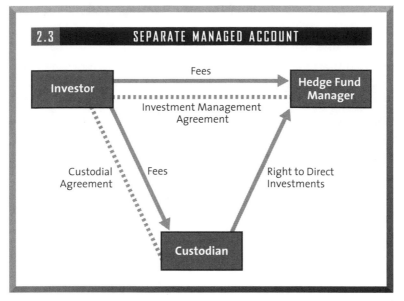

2.3   SEPARATE MANAGED ACCOUNT

Fees

Investor → Hedge Fund Manager

Investment Management Agreement

Custodial Agreement   Fees   Right to Direct Investments

Custodian

Sometimes, fund managers will prefer to use a managed account structure—for example, when the manager must develop a performance record to attract a sufficient number of investors to justify the expense of forming a fund.

A managed account is an active investment vehicle that allows the investor to retain custody and control over its assets. In contrast to the preset terms of existing structures, all aspects of the private investment-advisory relationship are potentially negotiable, allowing the investor to be very involved in the investment details. For example, an investor who proposes to make a large investment may insist on a managed account to facilitate a better fee structure and more liberal withdrawal terms than are offered to fund investors generally. Sometimes, the investor pays only an asset management fee—typically 1 to 2 percent of the net asset value (NAV) of the account. In other cases, the client also pays a performance fee based on increases in NAV—typically 10 to 20 percent. Generally, no performance fee is payable until the client has recouped past losses. In addition, existing funds usually use a single investment strategy and do not customize their operations to meet the needs of individual fund investors. Therefore, if an investor wants a different investment program than the one the fund proposes to use, such as using a higher level of leverage, a separate managed account may be preferable. In a fund, no one investor has the power to change the strategy, but managed accounts enable investors to dictate changes in the investment program over time.

The investor and the hedge fund manager will negotiate an agreement that details the nature of the separate managed account. The agreement specifies the types of investments that may be made by the manager. Some agreements are nondiscretionary—the client must approve investments. Other agreements are discretionary—the portfolio manager can make investments without client clearance, provided that he conforms to the guidelines set forth in the agreement. Investment restrictions may include, among other things: caps on the portion of the account that may be invested in a single issuer or industry or type of investment strategy (e.g., health care, emerging markets) or type of instrument (e.g., bonds, commodities, derivatives); restrictions on investment in assets in which the investor has a conflict of interest; and lists of permitted short-term investments (e.g., Treasury bills, certificates of deposit). Sometimes, the investor reserves the right to change the investment approach at any time. Usually, the investor agrees to leave the account with the manager for a fixed minimum period (lockup period) unless the manager breaches the agreement or causes more than the specified level of loss.

On the downside, the investor theoretically has unlimited liability, but this can be controlled by setting up an intermediary corporation, creating, in effect, a private fund. The investor can often choose from different investment programs or strategies that the fund manager uses, or the account may be customized to provide specific exposures. A managed account is considered quite liquid because the investor can typically terminate the account at short notice. Managed accounts are usually held with a custodian, and the trades are typically executed and cleared by independent brokers. The investor receives copies of all transactions and has full knowledge of all the account's positions. This ability to see through an investment vehicle to the contents of the portfolio is called transparency. Fully transparent managed accounts give investors a greater degree of control over their investment but also increase the amount of administrative work for the manager and fees incurred by the investor. The investor usually must pay fees to the custodian in addition to the fees that she pays to the hedge fund manager. Compared with the structure of an existing fund, a managed account offers more flexibility, the ability to negotiate the manager's fees, customized risk management, and more transparency.

CHOOSING AN INVESTMENT VEHICLE

For many investors, existing vehicles are the only option because of the high minimum contribution that fund managers require to establish a managed account. Both investment vehicles have pros and cons that the investor should carefully consider in conjunction with his overall portfolio objectives before proceeding with an investment with a particular fund manager. For example, existing funds offer limited liability, no or low organizational costs, and a lower minimum required investment. However, funds generally have limited liquidity and delayed and limited position and performance reporting, and they offer no control over investment structure and terms, such as fees and brokerage arrangements. Alternatively, a managed account offers flexibility in structure and investment terms, a high level of liquidity, and high level of position and performance reporting. However, managed accounts involve higher organizational costs and unlimited liability and require a larger minimum investment. The pros and cons of existing funds and managed accounts are summarized in **FIGURE 2.4**.

FUND OF FUNDS

One further method for accessing hedge fund managers is worth noting here: the fund of funds. Like most domestic hedge funds, fund of funds are organized as limited partnerships with a general partner who receives a management fee from the limited partners (sometimes the general partner

2.4   EXISTING FUND VERSUS MANAGED ACCOUNT

FORM OF INVESTMENT	PROS	CONS
EXISTING FUND	◆ Limited liability ◆ No up-front organizational costs ◆ Lower minimum investment	◆ Less liquidity ◆ No control over structure and terms
MANAGED ACCOUNT	◆ Immediate knowledge of managers' positions ◆ Negotiated structure and terms ◆ Higher liquidity	◆ Organizational costs ◆ Higher minimum investment ◆ No liability limitation

will also receive a performance fee). Unlike domestic hedge funds, they do not make direct investments. The manager of a fund of funds pools capital from investors and then allocates it to two or more hedge fund managers. The principle is similar to that of a mutual fund but on a larger scale. In a mutual fund, investors gain exposure to a pool of multiple securities that they otherwise could not afford. By making a single investment in a fund of funds, investors obtain access to a number of different hedge funds in which, because of the high minimum investment required by each, they could not invest individually. This approach permits them to diversify across instruments, strategies, and markets. It is a method for investors to gain exposure to a diversified group of hedge funds without incurring the high administrative and research costs that would result if they invested in the funds individually. The cost of this diversified exposure is an extra layer of fees: on top of each hedge fund manager's management and performance fees, the fund of funds manager charges a similar management fee and sometimes a performance fee as well. Fund of funds have become increasingly popular as a way to invest in hedge funds (see **FIGURE 2.5** on the following page).

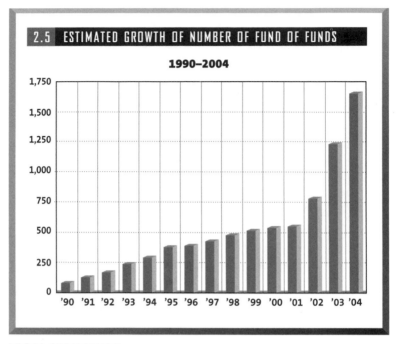

2.5 ESTIMATED GROWTH OF NUMBER OF FUND OF FUNDS

1990–2004

LEGAL STRUCTURE

Hedge fund investment structures come in a variety of legal forms depending on where they are located and the type of investor the fund organizer wishes to attract. To avoid entity-level tax, in the United States they are usually formed as limited partnerships, limited liability companies, or trusts.

Limited partnerships are organized under state law (for example, as an Illinois Limited Partnership). The general form is not unique to hedge funds but rather is used for various businesses. A limited partnership has one or more general partners and a number of limited partners. The general partner can be an individual or a corporation, is responsible for the management and operation of the partnership, and has unlimited liability. The manager will typically be the general partner but act through an entity to avoid unlimited personal liability for fund obligations.

The limited partners have liability "limited" to the amount they invest or "pay" for their limited partnership interests. Generally, they are allocated a pro rata share of all investments and expenses of the fund. The limited partnership interests are not traded and cannot be sold to any other prospective investor. They can be sold back to the partnership or "redeemed" only under the procedures established in the partnership agreement.

Offshore funds present a second legal form. Offshore funds are funds organized outside of the United States, usually in an offshore tax haven such as the Cayman Islands, Bermuda, the British Virgin Islands, or the Bahamas. Typically, a corporate structure is used, but because of the tax haven, no entity-level tax is imposed. Instead of a general partner, these structures have a management company. Investors purchase shares, and, as is the case with domestic funds, their liability is limited to the amount they invest. For tax reasons, offshore funds typically comprise primarily non-U.S. investors. However, many managers of offshore funds permit tax-exempt U.S. investors, such as pension plans, endowments, and charitable trusts, to participate. Sometimes, fund managers create both a domestic fund and a parallel offshore fund. In that case, the manager may offer one or both options to tax-exempt investors. (Sometimes the manager will prefer to keep all tax-exempt investors in the offshore fund, in order to avoid using up participant openings, or "slots.")

NUMBERS OF INVESTORS AND MINIMUM INVESTMENT SIZE

Hedge funds are usually private investment vehicles. In the United States they are most often structured to fall within one of the several exemptions from SEC registration provided in the Investment Company Act of 1940, as amended. Until 1997, the most common exemption that was followed, known as 3(c)(1), limited participants to ninety-nine accredited investors. An accredited investor is (1) an individual who has made $200,000 a year in income for the past two years and has a reasonable expectation of doing so in the future; (2) one who, together with a spouse, has an income of $300,000 per year; or (3) one who has a net worth of $1 million, excluding home and automobile. A 3(c)(1) fund cannot offer securities publicly.

In 1997, under the National Securities Markets Improvements Act (NSMIA), a further exemption, known as 3(c)(7), was enacted. It created a new exclusion from the definition of an "investment company" for investment pools if all investors are "qualified purchasers," with no limit on the number of investors. A qualified purchaser is

1 an individual holding at least $5,000,000 in investments,

2 a family company that owns not less than $5,000,000 in investments,

3 a person, acting for her own account or for the accounts of other qualified purchasers, who owns and invests on a discretionary basis at least $25,000,000 in investments,

4 a company, regardless of the amount of such company's investments, if each beneficial owner of the company's securities is a qualified purchaser, or

5 a trust if each of the trustee(s) and settlor(s) is a qualified purchaser.

Both the 3(c)(1) and 3(c)(7) exemptions require that the sale of securities not be made by way of a public offering. Most U.S. state securities laws (blue sky laws) also contain exemptions from registration for limited or private offerings.

Hedge fund managers are investment advisers. However, many are also exempt from registration with the SEC because they have a limited number of investors and do not advertise themselves as investment advisers. A growing number of hedge fund managers nonetheless are registering in response to investor and business demands and as of this writing, the SEC has passed a rule requiring hedge fund managers to register as advisories by the year 2006.

REPORTING AND DISCLOSURE

Hedge funds have historically calculated and reported performance on a monthly or quarterly basis. In response to increased investor demand, some funds now report weekly, and even daily, estimates, but the industry as a whole normally provides monthly performance results. Furthermore, there is no standard reporting format. Some hedge funds provide faxes of percentage profit or loss. Others send detailed statements to each investor with a letter describing the fund's investment activities and results. Most managers, however, provide monthly returns for the previous period within two weeks by fax, mail, or e-mail. Audits and the K1s (partner tax statements) are sent to investors annually. Hedge fund investors, except those who invest in separate managed accounts, are dependent on underlying managers for performance reporting.

Reporting of portfolio exposure information is less uniform than performance reporting, with practices ranging from no disclosure to full position transparency. The trend is clearly toward more transparency, with managers increasingly making at least summary exposure information available for their funds.

LIQUIDITY

In a hedge fund context, liquidity refers to the timing and notice period required for investors to redeem their investment and have their money returned from the fund. For example, quarterly liquidity means that an investor can take money out of the funds at the end of each calendar quarter, and monthly liquidity means that an investor can get out at the end of each month. One mistake that many investors make is not factoring in the "notice period" they are required to give before they can redeem their investments. Some hedge funds cannot generate cash for investor redemptions on short notice and require notice periods that range from thirty to ninety days. For example, for a fund that allows redemption at the end of each calendar quarter and requires a sixty-day notice, an investor wishing to redeem on June 30 must notify the fund in writing by April 30. An investor waiting until May to notify the fund cannot get out until September 30.

The redemption provisions also specify what time frame a fund has to actually pay the investor back in full. In the above example, the fund might have thirty days to pay 90 percent of the investment. The remaining 10 percent is held back until the fund's year-end audit is completed, which may mean that final payment will be received by the investor in March or

April of the following year. This holdover provision generally only applies to investors who redeem the full amount of their investment.

Hedge funds may not be required to make payment in cash. Certain funds generally, and many funds in extreme circumstances such as liquidation, may make payment in securities rather than in cash. This is particularly true for funds holding private or illiquid securities, such as those of bankrupt companies. But it is not the case for all hedge funds, and some hedge fund managers make all efforts to accommodate investors by returning their capital as early as possible in cash. A fund's offering memorandum will specify its ability to make payments in cash or securities.

LOCKUP

A lockup period is the length of time that investors must remain invested before their investment can be redeemed or becomes subject to the standard liquidity provision. The lockup period for hedge funds ranges from a few months to one or more years, but usually the lockup in U.S. funds is one year. It works like this: If the liquidity is quarterly and the lockup is one year, then an investor who invests on January 1 cannot redeem until December 31 of the same year. Once a year has passed, liquidity becomes quarterly, so the next date when a redemption would be allowed is March 31 of the following year.

DOCUMENTATION

The three main documents investors encounter when investing in hedge funds organized as limited partnerships are the offering memorandum, the limited partnership agreement, and the subscription agreement. Offshore hedge funds usually offer shares, so their documents will not include a limited partnership agreement (see **FIGURE 2.6**). The offering memorandum for offshore funds usually contains less disclosure than that for onshore funds.

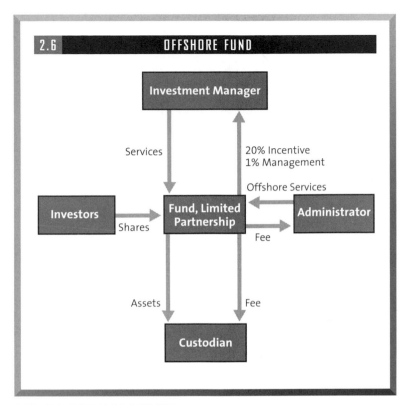

2.6 — OFFSHORE FUND

Investment Manager

Services

20% Incentive
1% Management

Offshore Services

Investors → **Fund, Limited Partnership** ← **Administrator**

Shares

Fee

Assets

Fee

Custodian

OFFERING MEMORANDUM

The offering memorandum may also be called the private placement memorandum, disclosure document, prospectus, or any of a number of other variations. It provides a general discussion of the securities that the hedge fund is selling, a summary of the limited partnership agreement, fee structures, redemption provisions, background information on the manager and key personnel, a discussion of risks and conflicts of interest and taxation, and other information essential to making an investment decision.

LIMITED PARTNERSHIP AGREEMENT

The limited partnership agreement is the contract that the investor enters into as a limited partner to the partnership. It specifies the rights and obligations of the limited and general partners and how the partnership will be operated. As the partnership is organized under a state act, specific law that applies to the limited partnership is not described in the agreement.

SUBSCRIPTION AGREEMENT

The subscription agreement is an application for acceptance as a limited partner that includes investor information and representations of the investor's suitability for inclusion in the partnership. It is a signed offer to invest accompanied by a check or wire transfer of the investment amount. If it is accepted by the general partner, then the assets are placed in the fund and the investor becomes a limited partner and investor. Usually, the only further evidence of the transaction is a letter from the manager to the investor confirming that the investor was accepted.

FEES AND EXPENSES

Hedge funds typically charge two fees: a management fee and an incentive fee. The management fee is based on a percentage of the assets in the fund, usually 1 or 2 percent each year. It is paid monthly or quarterly and may be due at the beginning or end of each period. The fee is automatically deducted pro rata from each investor's account. The incentive fee or "carried interest" is the hedge fund manager's share in the fund's profits. Usually this is 20 percent and is paid annually in the United States, but it may be calculated monthly or quarterly offshore. Two terms should be noted when reviewing incentive fees: *hurdle rate* and *high water mark*. A hurdle is the return that must be earned each year before the manager starts participating in the profits. Often, the Treasury bill rate is used. Use of a high water mark requires a manager to attain performance above the highest previous level before earning additional incentive fees. In other words, the investor does not pay for covering the same ground twice because losses must be made up before the manager begins participating in profits. Most hedge funds have high water marks but not hurdles. Specifics on how fees are calculated are described in the offering materials and fund documentation.

The fund also pays legal, audit, administrative, and other expenses, all of which should be described in the fund documentation.

TAX ISSUES

The tax consequences incurred by a hedge fund vary widely from strategy to strategy and for each manager's approach within each strategy. The impact varies from structure to structure as well, so investors should consult experts to determine the tax implications of a specific fund. Some general comments can be made here. As mentioned earlier, most U.S.-based hedge funds are organized as limited partnerships that allow tax consequences to pass through to the investor. This means tax-related activities such as profits, losses (long-term and short-term), and consequences of leverage to tax-exempt institutions such as UBTI (unrelated business taxable income) will figure into each investor's tax calculation. Investment programs can generate UBTI if (1) they use leverage or (2) they involve receipt of trade or business income, such as advisory or breakup fees. Some tax-exempt investors are unwilling to tolerate any UBTI. Others will accept UBTI provided that the net return is sufficiently high to offset the tax consequences.

Assuming that the fund is structured as a corporation rather than a pass-through entity such as a partnership, pass-through trust, or limited liability company, an offshore corporation is generally considered to cut off tax consequences by delivering profit or loss through the appreciation or depreciation of the shares purchased by the investor. Therefore, offshore funds are often offered so that tax-exempt investors may invest in leveraged programs. Taxable investors do not care about UBTI. Therefore, if a domestic fund includes both taxable and nontaxable investors, there is a conflict of interest as to whether the manager considers investments based on pre-UBTI or post-UBTI returns. Managed accounts and offshore funds avoid this issue. In general, tax-exempt investors are not otherwise concerned about the level of taxable income generated by a fund for its taxable investors. However, both taxable and tax-exempt investors aim to avoid funds that pay tax at the entity level and need to consider liability for taxes in foreign jurisdictions. Sometimes, taxable investors are able to receive tax credits for withholding taxes paid to other jurisdictions that are not available to tax-exempt investors. Another tax impact worth noting here is that offshore funds have withholding obligations on dividends that may range from a few basis points (1/100 of a percentage point) to a few percentage points, depending on the investment strategy. It is one of the reasons (slightly higher fees offshore being another) that the performance of offshore funds tends to underperform onshore "sister" funds.

ERISA CONSIDERATIONS

ERISA directly affects the pension policies of corporations and unions. If benefit plan investors constitute less than 25 percent of the aggregate commitments to a hedge fund, the fund is not deemed to hold plan assets and is not subject to ERISA restrictions on transactions with prohibited persons nor to ERISA fee limits. Additionally, the plan fiduciary does not have liability with respect to the disposition of those assets by the fund (although the fiduciary may be held liable with respect to the decision to place the assets in the fund). If a managed account structure is used by an ERISA plan, the account will constitute plan assets. For liability reasons, ERISA plans often insist on investing only with RIAs or, if a manager is not registered with the SEC, using an RIA to recommend making the investment. Depending on the investment strategy (e.g., investments in derivatives), it may be necessary for the manager to become a qualified professional asset manager, which, among other things, requires that the manager have at least $50 million in assets under management and $750,000 in equity, and that no pension plan can constitute 20 percent of the manager's assets under management. Some ERISA investors create in-house asset managers to facilitate the making of investments in unregistered entities without incurring the expense of an independent adviser. The in-house asset manager is registered as an investment adviser. As a result of recent amendments to securities laws, it generally is no longer possible for a manager to register as an investment adviser under federal law unless the adviser has at least $25 million under discretionary management. Advisers controlling smaller amounts will usually register with the states. For a limited time, state-registered investment advisers provide the same level of protection to the ERISA fiduciary as do federally registered advisers.

INVESTING

With Knowledge

PART

I

CHAPTER

3

Hedge Fund
STRATEGIES

A BROAD RANGE OF STRATEGIES are operated under the hedge fund structure. This spectrum includes nonleveraged hedged styles and highly leveraged directional approaches.[1]

To comprehend these strategies, an investor must understand the different elements of investing of which they are composed. This knowledge builds a framework from which to compare the different approaches. Although some elements are not vastly different from those that constitute traditional investing methods, others are unique to hedge fund strategies. This chapter discusses five important groups of elements: tools and techniques, instruments and markets, performance, sources of return, and measures for controlling risk.

TOOLS AND TECHNIQUES

LEVERAGE

Leverage refers to taking on investment exposures that exceed the amount of assets managed. For example, a hedge fund with $100 million in assets might have $150 million in investments. This can be accomplished through borrowing funds to increase the amount invested in a particular position or through the use of derivatives. Investors use leverage with the belief that the return on the leveraged exposures will exceed the cost of the leverage. Investors who use leverage increase the risk of their investment; therefore, they usually try to use it where they perceive low-risk situations that can benefit from low-cost funding. Sometimes, managers use leverage to enable them to put on new, favorable positions without having to take off other positions prematurely. Managers who target very small price discrepancies or spreads will often use leverage to magnify the returns from these discrepancies.

SHORT SELLING

Short selling is selling a security that the manager does not own. The security is borrowed from another holder, such as a bank, an insurance company, or a major brokerage firm. To borrow the security, the fund manager needs some form of collateral, such as other equities or U.S. Treasury bills (T-bills). After borrowing the security, the manager immediately sells it on the open market with the intention of buying it back later at a lower price and returning it to the lender. Until that future date, the proceeds from the short sale usually earn interest in a money market account. If the price of the security sold short declines, then the short seller will realize profits equal to the difference between the price at which he sold the security and the price at which he buys it back, plus the interest earned on the short sale proceeds. Alternatively, if the price of the security sold short appreciates, then the manager will realize losses equal to the difference between the price at which she must buy the security and the price at which she sold it, less any interest earned on the short sale proceeds.

Different strategies use short selling in different fashions. Some use it as a trading technique from which to derive profits, and others use it as a hedge against market declines. Managers must always consider whether a security is available to sell short. The securities of larger, more liquid companies tend to be more readily available to sell short than those of smaller, less liquid entities.

HEDGING

Hedging is taking a secondary position with the express purpose of counterbalancing a known risk involved with a primary position. This can be accomplished by taking positions in specifically related securities for specific risks or by purchasing index options for market risks. These positions are taken to offset changes in economic conditions other than the core investment idea, such as a change in the overall level of stock market prices, a change in interest rates, or a change in foreign exchange rates. The basic hedging technique is to purchase a primary long position and a secondary short position in a similar security to offset the effect that any changes in the overall level of the financial market or sector will have on the long position. For example, if an investor's rationale for buying a bond is that he thinks that the market has mispriced the credit risk of the issuing company, he would hedge against interest rate changes by buying a long position in the bond and a short position in a similar bond. If interest rates change, then any adverse effect on the long position will be offset by a positive effect on the short position. The process is reversed if a manager is trying to hedge against price increases. Alternatively, a manager can purchase index options to hedge movements in overall price levels. Hedging is a way in which an investor can neutralize the effects of systemic changes in market conditions.

ARBITRAGE

Arbitrage is the simultaneous purchase and sale of a related or similar security to profit from an expected change in the pricing relationship—for example, purchasing an undervalued convertible bond (a bond that can be converted to common stock, in which the conversion component is mispriced) and selling short the underlying common stock.

INVESTMENT INSTRUMENTS AND MARKETS

INSTRUMENTS

The assets that are available for purchase in financial markets are called investment instruments. These include stocks and bonds and all levels of financial derivatives. Derivatives are securities whose value is based on or is derived from the value of another instrument. For instance, the value of derivatives such as futures and options is based on the future value of a stock market index or the future value of Eurodollar deposits.

One way to distinguish different investment strategies is by the instruments in which they invest. Many hedge fund strategies invest in instruments avoided by traditional investment funds, such as futures; options; asset-backed securities; or the bonds, bank debt, or trade claims of companies with low credit ratings or in bankruptcy proceedings. Some hedge funds also invest in complex financial derivatives, such as interest-rate swaps, swaptions, and credit default swaps. These instruments allow for a larger degree of flexibility in hedging various risks than is available to traditional asset managers.

MARKETS

A market can refer to geography or asset classes. The grouping can be based on criteria such as an asset or instrument type (e.g., the stock market or the futures market), or on geographic location (e.g., Asian emerging market or Russian market). The term can be confusing because it is used on many different levels, but at base it refers to a mechanism by which investors and suppliers who are interested in a group of assets that share some underlying characteristic are brought together.

RISK CONTROL

Risk, quite simply, is exposure to uncertainty. There are two components of investment risk: uncertainty and exposure to that uncertainty. To control risk, managers must reduce uncertainty about future events and/or reduce the exposure of their portfolio to uncertainty about the future. Many of them will use hedging strategies to do so. Other common techniques follow.

RESEARCH

Research refers to the gathering, analysis, interpretation, and interpolation of information. Since markets act on information, a manager who obtains better or earlier information, or superior interpretation of it, has an edge on the market. Good research allows managers to take positions in instruments that are mispriced, in an absolute or relative sense, before the market reacts. The most common techniques for identifying such securities are in-depth fundamental and technical analysis.

DIVERSIFICATION

Diversification is the creation of variations in a portfolio through positions to reduce the adverse impact of a loss in any one position. Investment managers diversify their holdings to reduce exposure to risks associated with any one position, industry, sector, or type of instrument.

The logic of diversification can be implemented on many levels. Investment managers will diversify their holdings across industries, sectors, instruments, time horizons, and even investment styles.

POSITION LIMITS

Many investment managers limit the size of positions in their portfolios to restrain the damage that any individual position can cause. Position size may be based on a percentage of assets or on a specified maximum loss on each position. This ensures a certain level of diversification.

BUY/SELL TARGETS

Many investment managers perform their analyses relative to a market and estimate the value at which they think a security in which they have a position should be trading. Once it reaches that estimate, they liquidate the position because they believe the profit opportunity has run its course. Targets quantitatively articulate the investment disciplines imposed by the manager.

STOP-LOSS LIMITS

Many investment managers will not keep a security in their portfolio if it declines past a predetermined point. A stop-loss limit identifies the maximum loss a manager is willing to take on a position.

PERFORMANCE

The performance of hedge fund strategies is often presented and evaluated in terms of absolute return and risk-adjusted return. Unlike traditional investments that can be compared to, or benchmarked against, market indexes, most hedge fund strategies are not directly related to the direction of a specific market and therefore cannot be evaluated in that manner.

Increasingly, their performance is compared to indexes representing managers pursuing the same or a similar strategy.

HEDGE FUND STRATEGIES

The following paragraphs summarize the eleven hedge fund strategies covered in this book. In addition, this chapter includes charts that show how the amount of assets each strategy controls has changed from 1990 to 2004 in relation to the average annual returns of those funds. These graphs allow readers to note the relationship between assets controlled and fund performance. As might be expected, funds tend to follow performance. However, this is by no means a one-to-one relationship.

For example, there are presently more event-driven funds than there are macro funds, but the macro funds control about three times as many assets. When a strategy is producing high returns, not only are there ample investment profits that are increasing assets, but allocations from new investors will increase assets as well. New funds will be created to share in the profits and attract some of the new allocations. When the amount of assets allocated to a strategy increases, it is usually some combination of these factors. The process is reversed when a strategy is producing poor results.

FIXED-INCOME ARBITRAGE

Fixed-income strategies are "alternative" approaches to traditional, long-only fixed-income investments, and include arbitrage and opportunistic strategies. Arbitrage strategies involve investing in one or more fixed-income securities and hedging against underlying market risk by simultaneously investing in another fixed-income security. Managers seek to capture profit opportunities presented by what are usually small pricing anomalies, while maintaining minimum exposure to interest rates and other systemic market risks. In most cases, managers take offsetting long and short positions in similar fixed-income securities that are mathematically or historically interrelated when that relationship is temporarily distorted by market events, investor preferences, exogenous shocks to supply or demand, or structural features of the fixed-income market. These positions could include, for example, corporate debt, U.S. Treasury securities, U.S. agency debt, sovereign debt, municipal debt, or the sovereign debt of emerging markets countries. Trades often involve swaps and futures. Trading managers realize a profit when the skewed relationship between the securities returns to a normal range, or "converges."

Managers often try to neutralize interest-rate changes and derive profit from their ability to identify similar securities that are mispriced relative to one another. Because the prices of fixed-income instruments are based on yield curves, volatility curves, expected cash flows, credit ratings, and special bond and option features, managers must use sophisticated analytical models to identify pricing disparities. The strategy often involves significant amounts of leverage. Opportunistic fixed-income strategies may be long or short in a variety of fixed-income instruments, essentially offering what a manager considers a "best of" the fixed-income markets.

FIGURE 3.1 shows how the returns and total assets of fixed-income arbitrage funds have changed from 1990 to 2004. The amount of assets under management grew as the number of fixed-income arbitrage funds grew. From 1996 to 2001, the amount of assets under management actually declined before increasing significantly from 2002 to 2004. Fixed-income arbitrage funds had their worst year, performance-wise, in 1998, showing relatively stable returns in the following years.

EQUITY MARKET-NEUTRAL (STATISTICAL ARBITRAGE)

Equity market-neutral strategies strive to generate consistent returns in both up and down markets by selecting equity positions with a total net portfolio exposure of zero. Managers hold a number of long equity positions and an equal, or close to equal, dollar amount of offsetting short positions for a total net exposure close to zero. A zero net exposure is referred to as *dollar neutrality* and is a common characteristic of all equity market-neutral managers. By taking long and short positions in equal amounts, the conservative equity-market-neutral managers seek to neutralize the effect that a systemic change

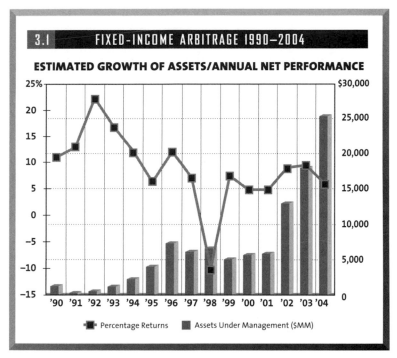

3.1 FIXED-INCOME ARBITRAGE 1990–2004

ESTIMATED GROWTH OF ASSETS/ANNUAL NET PERFORMANCE

■ Percentage Returns ■ Assets Under Management ($MM)

will have on values of the stock market as a whole. Most, but not all, equity-market-neutral managers extend the concept of neutrality to risk factors or characteristics such as beta, industry, sector, investment style, and market capitalization. In all equity-market-neutral portfolios, stocks expected to outperform the market are held long, and stocks expected to underperform the market are sold short. Returns are derived from the long/short spread, or the amount by which long positions outperform short positions.

FIGURE 3.2 on the following page shows how the returns and total assets of equity-market-neutral funds changed from 1990 to 2004. Assets peaked in 2001 following strong performance in 2000, and from 2002 to 2004, performance was below the historical averages.

CONVERTIBLE ARBITRAGE

Convertible arbitrage involves taking a long security position and hedging market risk by taking offsetting positions, often in different securities of the same issuer. A manager may,

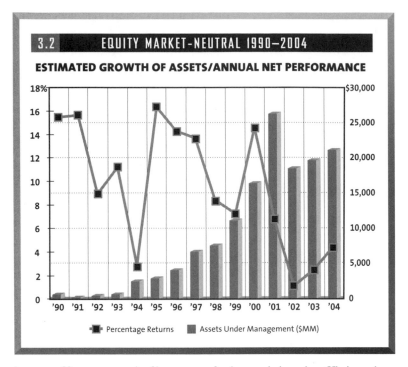

3.2   EQUITY MARKET-NEUTRAL 1990–2004

ESTIMATED GROWTH OF ASSETS/ANNUAL NET PERFORMANCE

Percentage Returns   Assets Under Management ($MM)

in an effort to capitalize on relative pricing inefficiencies, purchase long positions in convertible securities, generally convertible bonds or warrants, and hedge a portion of the equity risk by selling short the underlying common stock. A manager may also seek to hedge interest-rate or credit exposure under some circumstances. For example, a manager can be long convertible bonds and short the underlying issuer's equity, and may also use futures to hedge out interest-rate risk or credit default swaps to hedge default risk. Timing may be linked to a specific event relative to the underlying company, or a belief that a relative mispricing exists between the corresponding securities.

FIGURE 3.3 shows how the returns and total assets of convertible arbitrage funds changed from 1990 to 2004. This strategy has shown a significant growth in assets since 1999, though performance has declined, most notably in 2004.

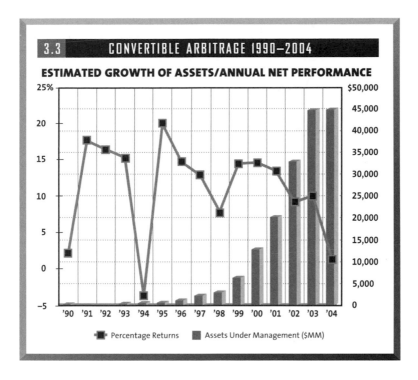

3.3 CONVERTIBLE ARBITRAGE 1990–2004

ESTIMATED GROWTH OF ASSETS/ANNUAL NET PERFORMANCE

Legend: ■ Percentage Returns ■ Assets Under Management ($MM)

MERGER (RISK) ARBITRAGE

Merger arbitrage, also sometimes known as risk arbitrage, involves investing in securities of companies that are the subject of some form of extraordinary corporate transaction, including acquisition or merger proposals, exchange offers, cash tender offers, leveraged buyouts, proxy contests, recapitalizations, restructurings, or other corporate reorganizations. These transactions generally involve the exchange of securities for cash, other securities, or a combination of cash and other securities. Typically, a manager might purchase the stock of a company being acquired or merging with another company and sell short the stock of the acquiring company. A manager engaged in merger arbitrage transactions derives profit (or loss) by realizing the price differential between the price of the securities purchased and the value ultimately realized from their disposition. The success of this strategy usually depends on the consummation of the proposed merger, tender offer, or exchange offer. Managers may use equity options as a low-

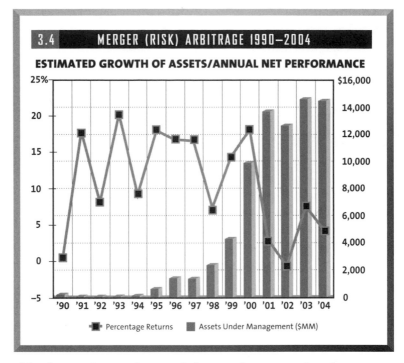

3.4   MERGER (RISK) ARBITRAGE 1990–2004

ESTIMATED GROWTH OF ASSETS/ANNUAL NET PERFORMANCE

Percentage Returns   Assets Under Management ($MM)

risk alternative to the outright purchase or sale of common stock. In certain cases where the outcome of a merger is very doubtful, the manager may short the deal by reversing the positions and going short the target and long the acquiring firm.

FIGURE 3.4 shows how the returns and total assets of merger arbitrage funds changed from 1990 to 2004. Assets under management spiked up during 2000 and 2001 followed by a sharp decline in returns due to the lack of merger activity and a scarcity of return opportunities.

DISTRESSED SECURITIES

Distressed securities managers invest in and may sell short the securities of companies in which the security's price has been, or is expected to be, affected by a distressed situation. A *distressed security* may be defined as a security or other obligation of a company that is encountering significant financial or business difficulties, including companies that

1 may be engaged in debt restructuring or other capital transactions of a similar nature while outside the jurisdiction of federal bankruptcy law,

2 are subject to the provisions of federal bankruptcy law, or

3 are experiencing poor operating results due to unfavorable operating conditions, overleveraged capital structure, catastrophic events, extraordinary write-offs, or special competitive or product-obsolescence problems.

These managers seek profit opportunities arising from inefficiencies in the market for such securities and other obligations.

Negative events, and the subsequent announcement of a proposed restructuring or reorganization to address the problem, may create a severe market imbalance as some holders attempt to sell their positions at a time when few investors are willing to purchase the securities or other obligations of the troubled company. If a manager believes that a market imbalance exists and the securities and other obligations of the troubled company may be purchased at prices below their value, he may purchase them. Increasingly, distressed securities managers have looked to complement long positions with short positions in companies headed for financial distress. Profits in this sector result from the market's lack of understanding of the true value of deeply discounted securities as well as mispricings within a distressed company's capital structure.

FIGURE 3.5 on the following page shows how the returns and total assets of distressed securities funds changed from 1990 to 2004. Assets have increased steadily since 2000, coinciding with the increase in distressed opportunities and associated performance.

EVENT-DRIVEN STRATEGIES

Event-driven investment strategies, or "corporate life cycle investing," are based on investments in opportunities created by significant transactional events, such as spin-offs, mergers and acquisitions, industry consolidations, liquidations, reor-

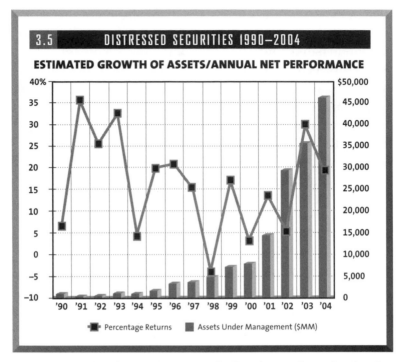

3.5   DISTRESSED SECURITIES 1990–2004

ESTIMATED GROWTH OF ASSETS/ANNUAL NET PERFORMANCE

Percentage Returns   Assets Under Management ($MM)

ganizations, bankruptcies, recapitalizations, share buybacks, and other extraordinary corporate transactions. Event-driven trading involves attempting to predict the outcome of a particular transaction as well as the optimal time at which to commit capital to it. The uncertainty about the outcome of these events creates investment opportunities for managers who can correctly anticipate them. As such, event-driven trading embraces merger arbitrage, distressed securities, value with a catalyst, and special situations investing.

Some event-driven managers utilize a core strategy whereas others opportunistically make investments across the range when different types of events occur. Dedicated merger arbitrage and distressed securities managers should be seen as stand-alone options, whereas event-driven is a multistrategy approach. Instruments include long and short common and preferred stocks, as well as debt securities, warrants, stubs, and options. Managers may also utilize derivatives such as index put options or put option spreads to leverage returns and hedge out interest-rate and/or market risk. The success

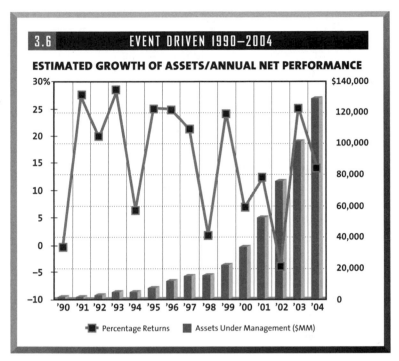

3.6   EVENT DRIVEN 1990–2004

ESTIMATED GROWTH OF ASSETS/ANNUAL NET PERFORMANCE

Percentage Returns   Assets Under Management ($MM)

or failure of this type of strategy usually depends on whether the manager accurately predicts the outcome and timing of the transactional event. Event-driven managers do not rely on market direction for results; however, major market declines, which would cause transactions to be repriced or to break apart and risk premiums to be reevaluated, may have a negative impact on the strategy.

FIGURE 3.6 shows how the returns and total assets of event-driven funds changed from 1990 to 2004. Total assets under management grew steadily from 1999 to 2004. Although corporate activity associated with economic recovery drove return opportunities from 2003 to 2004, performance was choppy.

MACRO INVESTING

Macro strategies attempt to identify extreme price valuations in stock markets, fixed-income markets, interest rates, currencies, and commodities and make bets on the anticipated price movements in these markets, sometimes in a leveraged fashion. Trades may be designed as an outright directional bet on an asset class or geographical region (e.g., long Japanese equities), or be designed to take advantage of geographical imbalances within an asset class (e.g., German 10-years relative to U.S. 10-years). To identify extreme price valuations, managers generally employ a top-down global approach that concentrates on forecasting how global macroeconomic and political events affect the valuations of financial instruments. These approaches may be either systematic or discretionary.

The strategy has a broad investment mandate, with the ability to hold positions in practically any market with any instrument. In general, managers try to identify opportunities with a definable downside and favorable risk-reward characteristics. Profits are made by correctly anticipating price movements in global markets and having the flexibility to use any suitable investment approach to take advantage of extreme price valuations. Managers may use a focused approach or diversify across approaches. They often pursue a number of base strategies to augment their selective large directional bets.

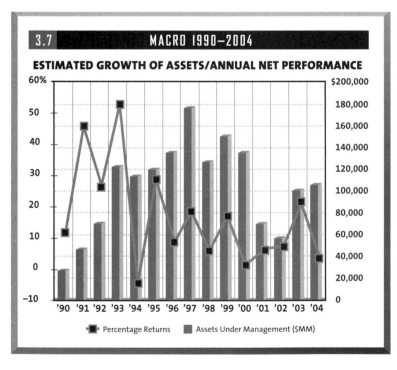

3.7   MACRO 1990–2004

ESTIMATED GROWTH OF ASSETS/ANNUAL NET PERFORMANCE

- ■ Percentage Returns   ■ Assets Under Management ($MM)

FIGURE 3.7 shows how the returns and total assets of macro funds changed from 1990 to 2004. Asset levels peaked in 1997 and bottomed in 2002 following a declining performance trend. That trend reversed in 2003, though performance for 2004 was well below historical averages.

SECTOR

Sector strategies combine core long holdings of equities with short sales of stock or sector indexes within a group of companies or segments of the economy that are similar either in what they produce or who their market is. Managers combine fundamental financial analysis with industry expertise to identify the best profit opportunities in the sector. Net exposure of sector portfolios may range anywhere from net long to net short depending on market and sector-specific conditions. Managers generally increase net long exposure in bull markets for the sector and decrease net long exposure, or may even be net short, in bear markets for the sector.

Generally, the short exposure is intended to generate an ongoing positive return in addition to acting as a hedge against a general sector decline. In a rising market for the sector, sector managers expect their long holdings to appreciate more than the sector and their short holdings to appreciate less than the sector. Similarly, in a declining market, they expect their short holdings to fall more rapidly than the sector falls and their long holdings to fall less rapidly than the sector. Profits are made when long positions appreciate and stocks sold short depreciate. Conversely, losses are incurred when long positions depreciate and/or the value of stocks sold short appreciates.

FIGURE 3.8 on the following page shows how the returns and total assets of sector funds changed from 1990 to 2004. There was substantial asset growth from 2000 to 2004, though performance followed the general equity markets into negative territory in 2001 and 2002, before recovering in 2003 and 2004.

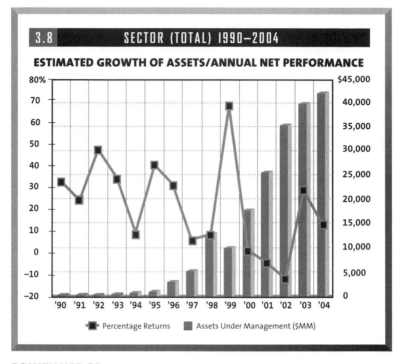

3.8   SECTOR (TOTAL) 1990–2004

ESTIMATED GROWTH OF ASSETS/ANNUAL NET PERFORMANCE

Percentage Returns ■ Assets Under Management ($MM)

EQUITY HEDGE

Equity hedge, also known as long/short equity, combines core long holdings of equities with short sales of stock, stock indexes, or derivatives related to equity markets. Net exposure of equity hedge portfolios may range anywhere from net long to net short, depending on market conditions. Managers generally increase net long exposure in bull markets and decrease net long exposure, or may even be net short, in bear markets. Generally, the short exposure is intended to generate an ongoing positive return in addition to acting as a hedge against a general stock market decline. Stock index put options or exchange-traded funds are also often used as a hedge against market risk.

In a rising market, equity hedge managers expect their long holdings to appreciate more than the market and their short holdings to appreciate less than the market. Similarly, in a declining market, they expect their short holdings to fall more rapidly than the market falls and their long holdings to fall less rapidly than the market. Profits are made when long positions appreciate and stocks sold short depreciate. Conversely, losses are incurred when long positions depreciate and/or the value of stocks sold short appreciates. The source of return of equity hedge is similar to that of traditional stock-picking trading strategies on the upside, but it uses short selling and hedging to attempt to outperform the market on the downside. Some equity hedge managers are value oriented, others are growth oriented, while a third category is opportunistic, depending on market conditions.

Equity nonhedge strategists use a strategy that is similar to traditional, long-only strategies but with the freedom to use varying amounts of leverage. Although most of them reserve the right to sell short, short sales are not an ongoing component of their investment portfolios, and many have not carried short positions at all. Equity nonhedge is treated as a variation of the equity hedge strategy. At heart, these are both concentrated stock-picking strategies, one that hedges market risk by augmenting core long positions with short positions and the other that forgoes that short exposure. The freedom to use leverage, take short positions, and hedge long positions is a strategic advantage that differentiates equity hedge strategists from traditional, long-only equity investors.

FIGURES 3.9 and **3.10** on the following page show how the returns and total assets of equity hedge and equity nonhedge funds changed from 1990 to 2004. Equity hedge fund assets have grown steadily since 1997 whereas equity nonhedge fund growth peaked in 1999 and declined through 2002. Performance for both peaked in 1999 and declined along with the general equity markets, bottoming in 2002. Note that in the recovery performance in 2003, equity nonhedge almost doubled the performance of equity hedge.

EMERGING MARKETS

Emerging markets strategies involve primarily long investments in the securities of companies in countries with developing, or emerging, financial markets. Managers make particular use of specialized knowledge and an on-the-ground presence in markets where financial information is often

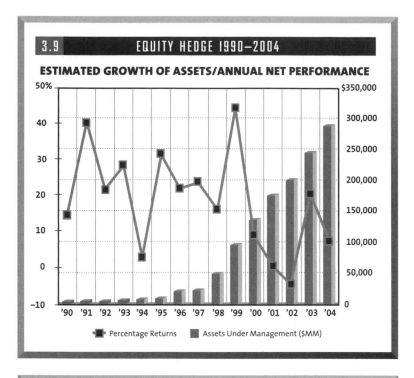

3.9   EQUITY HEDGE 1990–2004

ESTIMATED GROWTH OF ASSETS/ANNUAL NET PERFORMANCE

Percentage Returns   Assets Under Management ($MM)

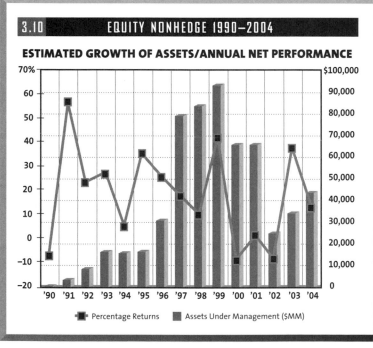

3.10   EQUITY NONHEDGE 1990–2004

ESTIMATED GROWTH OF ASSETS/ANNUAL NET PERFORMANCE

Percentage Returns   Assets Under Management ($MM)

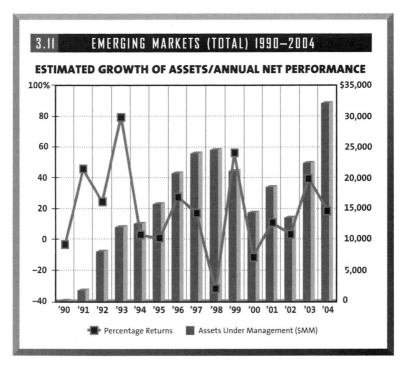

3.11 EMERGING MARKETS (TOTAL) 1990–2004

ESTIMATED GROWTH OF ASSETS/ANNUAL NET PERFORMANCE

■ Percentage Returns   ■ Assets Under Management ($MM)

scarce. Such knowledge and presence creates an informational edge that allows them to take advantage of mispricings caused by emerging markets inefficiencies. They make profits by mining these markets for undervalued assets and purchasing them before the market corrects itself. Because of the less developed and less liquid nature of these markets, emerging markets securities are generally more volatile than securities traded in developed markets. Managers can be differentiated by country exposures and types of instruments used.

FIGURE 3.11 shows how the returns and total assets of emerging markets funds changed from 1990 to 2004. Assets managed by such funds has grown from a very small amount in 1990 to more than $30 billion at year-end 2004, reflecting the ever-increasing interest of managers and investors alike in the opportunities offered by newly created markets. Assets under management had a peak in 1998, the same year performance collapsed, although the strategy posted a powerful recovery in 1999. Performance was strong in 2003 and 2004 coinciding with AUM reaching a new high in 2004.

SHORT SELLING

Short selling strategies seek to profit from a decline in the value of stocks. The strategy involves selling a security the investor does not own in order to take advantage of a price decline the investor anticipates. Managers borrow the securities from a third party in order to deliver them to the purchaser. Managers eventually repurchase the securities on the open market in order to return them to the third-party lender. If the manager can repurchase the stock at a lower price than for what it was sold, a profit is made. In addition, managers earn interest on the cash proceeds from the short sale of a stock. If the price of the stock rises, then the manager incurs a loss. This strategy is seldom used as a stand-alone investment. But because of its negative correlation to the stock market, it tends to produce outsized returns in negative environments and can serve as "disaster insurance" in a multimanager allocation. Some managers may take on some long exposure but remain net short, or short biased. Short bias strategies are much less volatile than pure short selling exposure, but they do not provide as much upside in severely negative equity markets.

FIGURE 3.12 at right shows how the returns and total assets of short selling funds changed from 1990 to 2004. Asset levels more than tripled in 2002 following strong positive performance from 2000 to 2002. Assets under management reached a new high in 2004, even though the strategy posted negative returns in 2003 and 2004.

UNIVERSE OF HEDGE FUND STRATEGIES

Hedge fund managers sometimes speak of a universe of stocks or bonds that they consider for investment. The universe of hedge fund strategies described in this book will give investors insight into the majority of investment approaches practiced by hedge fund managers. Although some strategies have been omitted, the eleven covered in this book now account for about 90 percent of all hedge fund assets. To be fair to the hedge fund managers, each one has a unique approach.

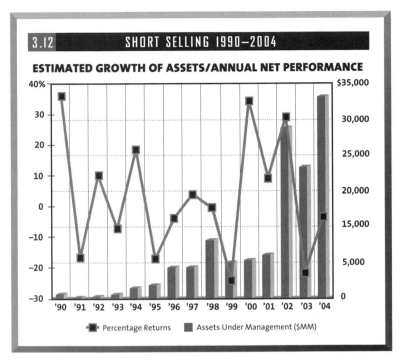

3.12 SHORT SELLING 1990–2004

ESTIMATED GROWTH OF ASSETS/ANNUAL NET PERFORMANCE

- Percentage Returns
- Assets Under Management ($MM)

However, this book places the methodologies in categories, focusing on their similarities. Funds that do not fit formally into these categories are most likely using similar investing principles. In the future, new approaches will inevitably be created that combine elements of investing in ways not corresponding to the categories discussed here. In fact, new strategies are added every year. However, the universe of hedge fund strategies covered in this book gives investors a useful point of reference for considering present and future investment approaches used by hedge fund managers.

FIGURES 3.13 and **3.14** on the following page show the percentage of total hedge fund assets (AUM) controlled by each of the strategies at the end of 1990 and again at the end of 2004. The graphs clearly illustrate the changes that have taken place in the industry. All the strategies grew in assets in the 1990s, but some grew faster than others. In addition, some strategies started with far fewer assets. For example, macro strategies have grown in assets but at the same time have lost overall market share, declining from the majority of assets

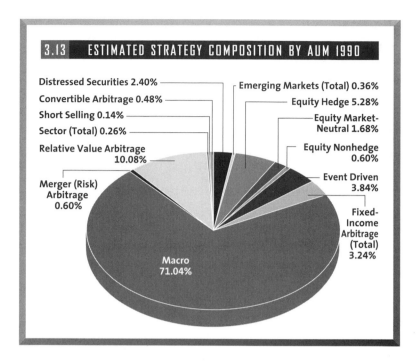

3.13   ESTIMATED STRATEGY COMPOSITION BY AUM 1990

Distressed Securities 2.40%

Convertible Arbitrage 0.48%

Short Selling 0.14%

Sector (Total) 0.26%

Relative Value Arbitrage 10.08%

Merger (Risk) Arbitrage 0.60%

Emerging Markets (Total) 0.36%

Equity Hedge 5.28%

Equity Market-Neutral 1.68%

Equity Nonhedge 0.60%

Event Driven 3.84%

Fixed-Income Arbitrage (Total) 3.24%

Macro 71.04%

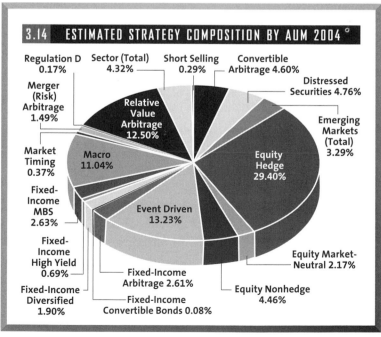

3.14   ESTIMATED STRATEGY COMPOSITION BY AUM 2004 °

Regulation D 0.17%

Sector (Total) 4.32%

Short Selling 0.29%

Convertible Arbitrage 4.60%

Merger (Risk) Arbitrage 1.49%

Distressed Securities 4.76%

Relative Value Arbitrage 12.50%

Emerging Markets (Total) 3.29%

Market Timing 0.37%

Macro 11.04%

Equity Hedge 29.40%

Fixed-Income MBS 2.63%

Event Driven 13.23%

Fixed-Income High Yield 0.69%

Fixed-Income Arbitrage 2.61%

Equity Market-Neutral 2.17%

Fixed-Income Diversified 1.90%

Fixed-Income Convertible Bonds 0.08%

Equity Nonhedge 4.46%

in the industry to 11 percent. Niche and specialist strategies have gained ground as a percentage of overall industry assets. Today, equity hedge funds represent the largest percentage of industry assets. These changes cannot be attributed to any single factor, but reflect a trend toward more specialization and less aggressive returns. The strategy weightings will continue to change in response to the changing opportunities that the market offers and the shifting makeup of the investor base. There are two key points to observe: First, that the hedge fund industry is comprised of a variety of investment strategies. Second, the industry is dynamic, not static. Strategies, as well as the assets within strategies, change based on performance and opportunity and so the overall composition of the industry shifts over time.

RISK-REWARD SPECTRUM

The various hedge fund strategies have very different risk-reward characteristics and should be evaluated individually rather than in a group. Hedge funds are heterogeneous, which explains why it's important to categorize them by the core strategy that the fund manager uses. Some hedge fund strategies are aggressive in nature, such as macro funds. Others, such as nonleveraged market-neutral funds, are conservative. Many have significantly lower risk than a portfolio of long stocks and bonds for the same levels of return. Overall, hedge fund strategies, except for short selling, have performed well on a risk-adjusted basis at all points on the risk-reward spectrum. **FIGURE 3.15** on the following page plots the average annualized return of each strategy against its annualized standard deviation. The risk-reward profiles of T-bills and the S&P 500 index of blue-chip stocks provide a basis of comparison. The capital market line drawn through the T-bills and the S&P 500 represents a rough estimate of the expected trade-off between risk and return for traditional investments. Notice that the risk-reward profile of every hedge fund strategy except short selling is above the line. Keep this spectrum in mind as you read the different strategy chapters. Think of how it reflects the market environment

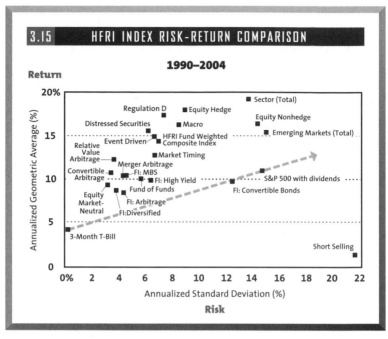

3.15   HFRI INDEX RISK-RETURN COMPARISON

1990–2004

since 1990, and how it might change when market conditions shift.

Each of the strategy chapters discusses the core strategy principles, the investment process, the advantages and disadvantages of the strategy, and its performance since 1990. The short version of the strategy is reprinted at the beginning of each chapter to introduce the most important elements to look for in the chapter. For those readers looking strictly for numbers, the performance section includes month-by-month and summary statistics for each strategy. The most important concepts from the chapter are highlighted in the Summary Points section that follows the performance statistics. Finally, key words and concepts in bold type are defined in the Key Terms section at the end of each chapter.

CHAPTER 4

Fixed-Income
ARBITRAGE

FIXED-INCOME STRATEGIES are alternative approaches to traditional, long-only fixed-income investments and include arbitrage and opportunistic strategies. **ARBITRAGE STRATEGIES** involve investing in one or more fixed-income securities and hedging against underlying market risk by simultaneously investing in another fixed-income security. Managers seek to capture profit opportunities presented by what are usually small pricing anomalies, while maintaining minimum exposure to interest rates and other systemic market risks. In most cases, managers take offsetting long and short positions in similar fixed-income securities that are mathematically or historically interrelated when that relationship is temporarily distorted by market events, investor preferences, exogenous shocks to supply or demand, or structural features of the fixed-income market. These positions could include, for example, corporate debt, U.S. Treasury securities, U.S. agency debt, sovereign debt, municipal debt, or the sovereign debt of emerging-markets countries. Trades often involve swaps and futures. Trading managers realize a profit when the skewed relationship between the securities returns to a normal range, or "converges."

Managers often try to neutralize interest-rate changes and derive profit through their ability to identify similar securities that are mispriced relative to one another. Because the prices of fixed-income instruments are based on yield curves, volatility curves, expected cash flows, credit ratings, and special bond and option features, managers must use sophisticated analytical models to identify pricing disparities. The strategy often involves significant amounts of leverage. Opportunistic fixed-income strategies may be long or short in a variety of fixed-income instruments, essentially offering what a manager considers a best-of list of the fixed-income markets.

Over time, new fixed-income instruments and their derivatives have evolved to meet suppliers' need and investors' demand for more diverse investment options. Consequently, the universe of fixed-income issues has expanded to tailor cash flows and modify various categories of risk to investors' preferences. It now includes everything from Treasury bills to corporate bonds to swaps to asset-backed securities. Even though they behave differently from more traditional fixed-income instruments under certain circumstances, when these newer instruments are mispriced, they provide fixed-income arbitrageurs with the same kind of arbitrage profit opportunities.

Because of the proliferation of fixed-income instruments, there are enough slight variations of the basic fixed-income arbitrage strategy to fill an entire book. The nuances of fixed-income instruments are the subject of other books. The focus of this book is alternative investment strategies, so this chapter concentrates on the core strategy principles practiced by most fixed-income arbitrageurs.

CORE STRATEGY

Fixed-income arbitrageurs take offsetting long and short positions in similar fixed-income securities whose values are mathematically or historically interrelated but in which that relationship is believed to be temporarily out of sync. These positions could include corporate debt, sovereign debt, municipal debt, or the sovereign debt of emerging-markets countries. Many times, trades will involve swaps and futures. When a bond or its derivative is sold short, the seller borrows that security and sells it immediately on the market with the intention of buying it back later at a lower price. By purchasing cheap fixed-income securities and selling short an equal amount of expensive fixed-income securities, fixed-income arbitrageurs attempt to protect themselves from changes in interest rates.

If they select instruments that respond to interest-rate changes similarly, then an interest-rate rise that adversely affects the long position will have an offsetting positive effect on the short position. They realize a profit when the skewed relationship between the securities returns to normal. Rather than try to guess in which direction the market will move, they neutralize interest-rate changes and derive profit entirely from their ability to identify similar securities that are mispriced relative to one another.

Arbitrageurs use sophisticated analytical models to identify true pricing disparities. They will assign probabilities to the different scenarios that they think can affect the pricing relationship, such as different interest-rate environments or an international financial crisis, to narrow the universe of possible or likely outcomes. The complexity of fixed-income pricing is actually essential to fixed-income arbitrageurs. They rely on investors less sophisticated than they to over- and undervalue securities by failing to value explicitly some feature of the instrument (e.g., a call option) or the probability of a possible future occurrence (e.g., a political event) that will affect the valuation of the instrument.

One way that fixed-income arbitrageurs compare different bond issues is by looking at their **YIELDS** and **YIELD CURVES**. A yield curve is a graphic representation of the yield to maturity at a given point in time for a variety of equally risky bonds differing in maturity. Because U.S. Treasuries are nearly risk free, the Treasury rate is used as a benchmark. Corporate bonds of comparable maturity and coupon rates will have higher yields than the Treasuries to reflect greater default risk, so their yields are often quoted as a **SPREAD** above the Treasury rate. The more risky the bond issue is, the larger the spread. Spreads are measured in basis points. One basis point equals 1/100 of a percent.

An example of a spread relationship is the Treasury-to-Eurodollar (TED) spread. U.S. Treasury bills, notes, and bonds are guaranteed and therefore are extremely low risk. Even though the European banks have very high credit ratings, and the U.S. government and the European banks are chasing the same dollars, the European banks have to pay a higher yield because their bonds are not guaranteed. Thus, when world financial markets are relatively stable and investors perceive the risk of European bank defaults to be extremely low, they will loan their dollars to European banks in exchange for the higher yield. As this happens, the TED spread will tighten. When conditions become unstable and investors do not perceive the spread to be large enough to compensate for the risks involved, then the same dollars will make their way back to safer U.S. Treasury instruments. If this state of affairs persists, then the TED spread will widen as the European banks offer more attractive yields to try to attract dollar deposits.

INVESTMENT PROCESS

Fixed-income arbitrageurs analyze fixed-income instruments' current yields and potential for capital appreciation to try to find valuation discrepancies. When they are able to determine a significant relationship between the yields of two or more bonds, establish that the relationship is out of sync, and determine that the probabilities are in their favor that the relationship will return to normal or shift in a way that they anticipate, they will simultaneously buy the undervalued security and sell short the overvalued security. After the positions are put on, the trade is monitored and then liquidated when the instruments reach their expected values. If they do not behave as expected, the positions will be reconsidered. Often, fixed-income arbitrageurs identify spread relationships that are only a few basis points from where they should be. To make a significant amount of money on the trade, arbitrageurs will apply a large amount of leverage to these positions. Because the downside risk on any one trade is small, the use of leverage does not increase risk dramatically.

MANAGER EXAMPLE

Let us revisit the TED spread. Suppose the price of a U.S. Treasury bill is 94.30 (implied yield of 5.70 percent) and the Eurodollar future is trading at 93.10 (implied yield of 6.90 percent). The TED spread is 94.30 – 93.10 = 1.20. The spread would be quoted as 120 (basis points). A fixed-income arbitrageur analyzes this spread and determines that it will widen further to 130 because of international financial worries. He would then buy T-bill futures and sell Eurodollar futures, expecting T-bill futures to outperform the market and Eurodollar futures to underperform it. This is known as buying the spread. Such a trade would unfold as follows:

Buy 10 T-bill futures contracts @ 94.30
Sell short 10 Eurodollar futures contracts @ 93.10
Spread = 120 basis points

As the fixed-income arbitrageur's analysis predicted, the spread widens to 130, with T-bills now trading at 94.25 and Eurodollars at 92.95:

Sell 10 T-bill contracts @ 94.25
Buy 10 Eurodollar contracts @ 92.95
Spread = 130 points

Profit (from Eurodollars) = 15 basis points x $25 per basis point
                           x 10 contracts = $3,750
Loss (from T-bills) = 5 basis points x $25 per basis point
                           x 10 contracts = $1,250
Net Profit = $2,500

MORTGAGE-BACKED SECURITIES

One of the newer additions to the universe of fixed-income securities is **MORTGAGE-BACKED SECURITIES** (MBS). Like other fixed-income instruments, MBSs have certain properties of which fixed-income arbitrage strategies try to take advantage.

A mortgage-backed security represents an ownership interest in mortgage loans made by financial institutions such as savings and loans, commercial banks, or mortgage companies to finance the borrower's purchase of a home. Commercial banks, government agencies such as the Government National Mortgage Association (GNMA or Ginnie Mae), and government-sponsored enterprises such as the Federal National Mortgage Association (FNMA or Fannie Mae) will pool mortgage loans in a trust and issue securities that represent a direct ownership in that trust. Like traditional bonds, MBSs have an interest and a principal component. Unlike traditional bonds, MBSs have uncertain maturity dates because every mortgagee in the pool has the option to refinance or prepay the mortgage. Like traditional bonds,

MBSs' prices fluctuate in response to interest rates. However, interest rates have an additional effect on them. Generally, when interest rates decline, **PREPAYMENTS** accelerate beyond the initial pricing assumptions, which causes the average life and expected maturity of the MBS to shorten. However, when interest rates rise, prepayments slow down beyond the initial pricing assumptions and can cause the average life and expected maturity of the MBS to increase and its market value to decline. When prepayments increase because of a drop in interest rates, the principal of the security may have to be invested at a lower interest rate than the coupon of the security.

Although prepayments are a function of interest rates, they do not have a one-to-one relationship with new rates. Other prepayment factors, such as housing turnover, are much less influenced by interest rates than are refinancings. Thus, prepayment risk can be difficult to quantify. Because the borrower can choose to prepay the mortgage, MBSs contain an embedded option. The price that an investor must be paid to accept this option increases as the propensity to refinance increases. However, these securities are often mispriced because it is so difficult to predict prepayments exactly. Generally, MBSs have higher yields than traditional bonds because of prepayment risk.

Although MBSs may seem very different from traditional fixed-income instruments, fixed-income investors are looking for the same things in both. At the end of the day, investors must judge whether the reward that an instrument offers (coupon) at the price it is being offered (price of the security) is worth the risk associated with that instrument (whether it is credit risk, market risk, or prepayment risk). When the market over- or undervalues a security, an opportunity for arbitrage profits exists.

RISK CONTROL

As discussed earlier, many fixed-income arbitrageurs try to insulate themselves from market risk by taking offsetting long and short positions in similar securities that are historically or statistically interrelated but for which the spread relationship is temporarily out of sync. "Statistically interrelated" refers to **DURATION**.

Duration demonstrates how sensitive a bond's price is to a shift in interest rates. It is a measure of the average (cash-weighted) term to maturity of a bond. For example, if a bond has a duration of three years, then the bond's value will decline approximately 3 percent for each 1 percent increase in interest rates or rise 3 percent for each 1 percent fall in interest rates. Such a bond is less risky than a bond with a six-year duration, which will decline in value 6 percent for each 1 percent increase in interest rates and rise 6 percent for each 1 percent decrease. In general terms,

$$\text{Duration} = \frac{\text{(Change in price)/Price}}{\text{Change in interest rates}}$$

Duration is measured in years because it is equal to the average maturity of bonds for which that particular price/yield relationship holds. Bonds with longer maturities will be more affected by a change in interest rates because that change will be felt over a longer period of time. For example, if someone has a two-year bond with a coupon rate of 7 percent and a five-year bond with a similar rate of 7 percent, and interest rates rise 1 percent, then both bonds are less attractive than they were at the time of purchase because the same interest rate is available now for less money. The price of the two-year bond reflects only the present value of its now less favorable rate over two years, whereas the five-year bond reflects the present value over five years. Accordingly, the price of a bond with a longer maturity will be more sensitive to changes in interest rates.

Fixed-income arbitrageurs often will buy a bond and sell short another bond with similar duration. That way, if interest rates change, the effect on the long position will be offset by the short position because both bonds respond the same way to the change. If the total duration of the long side of a portfolio is equal to the total duration of the short side of the portfolio, then the portfolio is said to have zero duration. Arbitrageurs will often try to eliminate market risk by structuring their trades and portfolios to be at or near zero duration. They can hedge out foreign currency risk in a similar fashion. In addition, they will usually minimize credit risk by dealing only in issues with high credit ratings. Finally, fixed-income arbitrageurs will usually maintain a diversified basket of trades so that the portfolio is not dependent on any one position. For the most part, they try to hedge away all the known risks. What is left is the risk that the mathematical relationship that they identify does not behave as they expected or was not out of sync in the first place.

MANAGER EXAMPLE

FIGURE 4.1 on the following page illustrates a trade in two very similar, highly liquid mortgage-backed fixed-income instruments. The two securities provide comparable absolute yields as well as comparable spreads over U.S. Treasury securities; however, by trading one bond against the other, the manager is able to extract a profit from the mispricing of the option imbedded in the fixed-income security.

In the example, the manager purchases the 5 percent coupon Low Loan Balance 15-Year FNMA bond and sells short the 5 percent coupon Generic 15-Year FNMA bond. At inception, the spread trade is approximately carry neutral, with the Low Loan Balance costing the manager 102.125, while the manager receives 102 for the short in the Generic. Under the scenario where rates increase by 1 percent, both bonds are expected to experience a highly similar price performance decline to approximately 98.25. However, in the scenario where rates decline by 1 percent, the Low Loan Balance is expected to significantly outperform the Generic security, rising to a price of 104.5, while the other security experiences a smaller price increase, rising to approximately 104.

This asymmetric risk-return continuum is a result of the market mispricing of the option in one of the securities relative to the price of the other, represented graphically as a lower option cost in the following example. One security exhibits a

4.1   LOW LOAN BALANCE MBS POOLS

Description of Security: Conventional MBS pools where the maximum loan size for any and all individual loans within the pool is $85,000.

Long Low Loan Balance 15-Year FNMA 5.0
Short Generic 15-Year FNMA 5.0

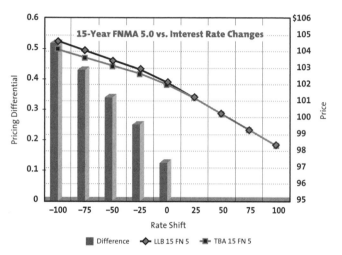

SMITH BREEDEN OAS ANALYSIS

Low Loan Balance 15-Year FNMA 5.0s = $102.125 vs.

Generic 15-Year FNMA 5.0s = $102.00

LOW LOAN BALANCE 15-YEAR FNMA 5.0%

Yield	4.70%
Option Cost	0.30%
Comparable Treasury	3.80%
OAS	**0.60%**

GENERIC 15-YEAR FNMA 5.0%

Yield	4.70%
Option Cost	0.60%
Comparable Treasury	3.80%
OAS	**0.30%**

All information is provided for informational purposes only and should not be deemed as a recommendation to buy the securities mentioned. The above information represents securities that may be traded in accounts managed in accordance with Smith Breeden's mortgage investment strategy. Smith Breeden cannot guarantee the success of the investment strategy and uses non-performance-based criteria to select the securities noted above. The securities were selected for conceptual illustration only. December 2004.

SOURCE: TRADE EXAMPLE PROVIDED BY KENT FLEMING, SMITH BREEDEN ASSOCIATES

superior convexity profile of the rate of change in the price for a corresponding change in the prevailing market yield. These trades in highly liquid securities can be implemented on a dollar neutral basis, or as described can be a slight negative carry at inception with an attractive risk-return trade-off relative to the overall cost of the trade. Or, these trades can be supplemented by selling options through other fixed-income instruments that can provide higher risk-return profiles, for example, call options on U.S. Treasuries. [1]

ADVANTAGES/DISADVANTAGES

Practitioners of fixed-income arbitrage can achieve consistently high returns without exposure to the ebb and flow of interest rates. The strategy has performed in a variety of economic conditions because it ferrets out trading anomalies rather than attempting to time interest-rate changes. It is consistent and normally exhibits very low volatility. On the downside, identifying trading anomalies is no easy task considering the complexity of fixed-income instrument pricing. The need to sell securities short limits arbitrageurs to those markets where short selling is an option. Consequently, they tend to trade very liquid issues with high credit ratings that have very low default risk and can easily be sold short. These are the most efficient fixed-income markets; therefore the pricing relationships are less apt to be far out of sync. This means that these traders often must identify small discrepancies and apply heavy leverage to them.

The use of leverage also magnifies the risk of the position as well as creating additional risk. This was dramatically illustrated by Long-Term Capital Management as well as by other highly leveraged hedge funds when theory met reality in 1998. Among other issues, highly leveraged bets on the relationship between government and corporate bonds went against expectations when the collapse of the Russian market helped trigger a market sell-off and flight to quality from corporate into government bonds.

PERFORMANCE

From January 1990 to December 2004, fixed-income arbitrage funds registered average annualized returns of 8.45 percent, with an annualized standard deviation of 4.33. These returns are well above traditional fixed-income investments at a comparable level of risk. The high year was 1992 at 22.13 percent, and the low year was 1999 with a loss of 10.29 percent. As shown in **FIGURE 4.2**, though the strategy has not produced a return above 10 percent since registering an 11.89 percent return in 1996, the stability and low risk of fixed-income arbitrage funds has attracted assets that have more than quadrupled the strategy's asset size since 1997. As evidenced by a correlation statistic of −0.06, fixed-income arbitrage has very little sensitivity to stock market prices in general. The low correlation to market indexes is expected because fixed-income arbitrageurs target pricing discrepancies rather than market movements.

FIGURE 4.3 shows the total strategy assets and net asset flows per year from 1990 to 2004 for fixed-income arbitrage. The year-end asset total equals the previous year's asset size plus

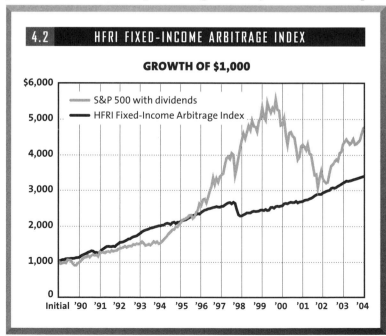

4.2   HFRI FIXED-INCOME ARBITRAGE INDEX

GROWTH OF $1,000

S&P 500 with dividends
HFRI Fixed-Income Arbitrage Index

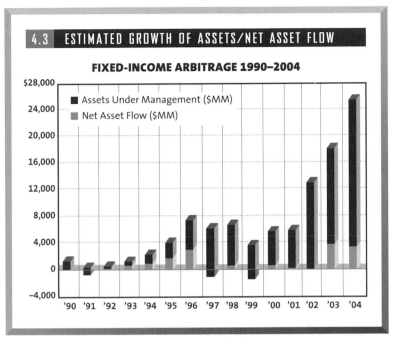

4.3 ESTIMATED GROWTH OF ASSETS/NET ASSET FLOW

FIXED-INCOME ARBITRAGE 1990–2004

■ Assets Under Management ($MM)
■ Net Asset Flow ($MM)

annual performance plus net asset flows. Since the end of 2001, approximately $14 billion in net inflows has increased the strategy's total assets under management almost five-fold to over $25 billion at the end of 2004.

FIGURE 4.4 on the following page shows the return distribution for fixed-income arbitrage compared to the overall hedge fund industry, stocks, and bonds. Note that performance in this strategy is focused in the 0 to –2 percent per month range which results in its consistently low volatility performance.

FIGURE 4.5 shows the average upside and downside capture since 1990 for fixed-income arbitrage funds. Note that the strategy's performance is virtually the same in up months as it is in down months, again showing its low volatility and low correlation to the major stock markets.

SUMMARY POINTS

PROFIT OPPORTUNITY

◆ Arbitrage is the practice of buying securities in one market and reselling similar securities simultaneously in another to profit from a discrepancy in the price of the asset in the two markets.

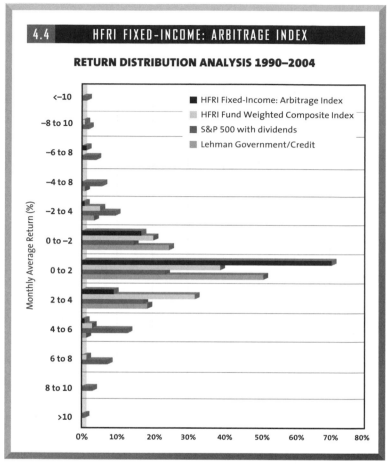

4.4   HFRI FIXED-INCOME: ARBITRAGE INDEX

RETURN DISTRIBUTION ANALYSIS 1990–2004

◆ Because the prices of fixed-income instruments are based on yield curves, volatility curves, expected cash flows, credit ratings, and special bond and option features, the fixed-income arbitrageur must use sophisticated analytical models to identify true pricing disparities. The complexity of fixed-income pricing is what provides arbitrage opportunities.

◆ Practitioners of fixed-income arbitrage can achieve consistently high returns without exposure to the ebb and flow of interest rates. The strategy should work equally well in most economic conditions because it ferrets out trading anomalies rather than attempting to time interest-rate changes. The high degree of leverage that is often used, however, can result in significant losses when abrupt market shifts collapse liquidity.

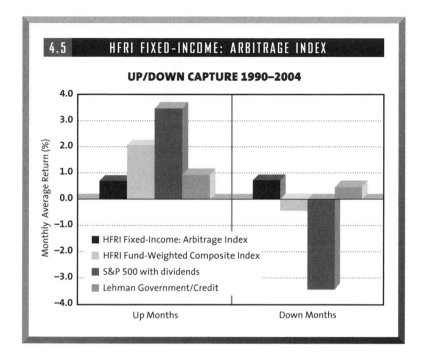

4.5 HFRI FIXED-INCOME: ARBITRAGE INDEX

UP/DOWN CAPTURE 1990–2004

- HFRI Fixed-Income: Arbitrage Index
- HFRI Fund-Weighted Composite Index
- S&P 500 with dividends
- Lehman Government/Credit

SOURCE OF RETURN

◆ Fixed-income arbitrageurs take offsetting long and short positions in similar fixed-income securities whose values are mathematically or historically interrelated but temporarily are out of sync.

◆ Fixed-income arbitrageurs realize a profit when the skewed relationship between the securities behaves as they expect.

◆ Often fixed-income arbitrageurs identify spread relationships that are only a few basis points from where they should be. To make a significant amount of money on the trade, they will apply a large amount of leverage to these positions.

INVESTMENT PROCESS

◆ When fixed-income arbitrageurs are able to determine a significant relationship between the yields of two or more bonds, establish that the relationship is out of sync, and determine that the relationship will change in a way that they anticipate, they will simultaneously buy the undervalued security and sell short the overvalued security.

◆ Fixed-income arbitrageurs will buy a bond and sell short another bond with similar duration. That way, if interest rates change, then the effect on the long position will be offset by the short position, because both bonds respond the same way to the change.

◆ On the downside, identifying trading anomalies is no easy task, considering the complexity of fixed-income instrument pricing. The need to sell securities short limits fixed-income arbitrageurs to those markets in which short selling is an option.

KEY TERMS

Arbitrage. The simultaneous purchase and sale of a security or pair of similar securities to profit from a pricing discrepancy.

Duration. A measure of how sensitive a bond's price is to a shift in interest rates. In general terms,

$$\text{Duration} = \frac{(\text{Change in price})/\text{Price}}{\text{Change in interest rates}}$$

Fixed-income securities. Securities that entitle the holder to a series of fixed payments at predetermined future dates.

Mortgage-backed securities. Securities that represent an ownership interest in mortgage loans made by financial institutions (such as savings and loans, commercial banks, or mortgage companies) to finance the borrower's purchase of a home.

Prepayments. When mortgages are paid early, usually due to refinancing by the homeowner, investors receive principal payments ahead of the scheduled repayment date.

Spread. Corporate bonds of a comparable maturity and comparable coupon rates to Treasuries will have higher yields to reflect greater default risk, so their yields are often quoted as a spread above the Treasury rate. The more risky the bond issue, the larger the spread. Spreads are measured in basis points. One basis point equals 1/100 of a percent.

Yield. The single investment rate that sets the present value of all a bond's future cash payments equal to the price of the bond.

Yield curves. The relationship between the interest rate and term of a bond which typically appears as a curve when plotted.

CHAPTER

5

Equity Market
Neutral
(STATISTICAL ARBITRAGE)

E QUITY-MARKET-NEUTRAL strategies strive to generate consistent returns in both up and down markets by selecting equity positions with a total net portfolio exposure of zero. Managers hold a number of long equity positions and an equal, or close to equal, dollar amount of offsetting short positions for a total net exposure close to zero. A zero net exposure is referred to as **DOLLAR NEUTRALITY** and is a common characteristic of all equity-market-neutral managers. By taking long and short positions in equal amounts, the conservative equity-market-neutral managers seek to neutralize the effect that a systemic change would have on values of the stock market as a whole. Most, but not all, equity-market-neutral managers extend the concept of neutrality to risk factors or characteristics such as beta, industry, sector, investment style, and market capitalization. In all equity-market-neutral portfolios, stocks expected to outperform the market are held long, and stocks expected to underperform the market are sold short. Returns are derived from the long/short spread, or the amount by which long positions outperform short positions.

EQUITY MARKET-NEUTRAL can be a deceptive name. Equity-market-neutral strategies are not without risk; they merely neutralize one kind of risk in favor of another. In equity portfolios, there are two primary sources of risk: stock selection and the market. Selecting stocks involves uncertainty about the fate of a particular stock. **MARKET RISK** is exposure to uncertainty about what the stock market as a whole will do next. Because they think they can predict the fate of a particular stock better than the direction of the market as a whole, equity-market-neutral specialists try to neutralize systemic risks associated with the market in favor of exposure to **STOCK SELECTION RISK**. They do so by taking a large number of long positions in stocks that they think will outperform the market and an offsetting amount of short positions in stocks that they think will underperform the market. Most practitioners of the strategy rely on quantitative, computer-run models. Equity-market-neutral specialists use these quantitative models to create a statistical advantage in picking stocks and a strategic advantage in controlling exposure to systemic risk. This approach is designed to produce consistent returns with very low volatility in a variety of market environments.

CORE STRATEGY

Equity-market-neutral strategists will hold a large number of equity positions and an offsetting amount of short positions. They use sophisticated quantitative and qualitative models to pick stocks. Stocks expected to outperform the market are held long, and stocks expected to underperform the market are sold short. Equity-market-neutral strategists try to keep market exposure to a minimum. A simplified version of the formula that they use to calculate market exposure is shown below:

$$\text{Market exposure} = \frac{\text{Long exposure} - \text{Short exposure}}{\text{Capital}}$$

Equity-market-neutral strategists may extend this logic across sectors, industries, and investment styles. For example, if they take a long position in an information technology stock that they think is undervalued, then they will take an offsetting short position in an information technology stock that they think is overvalued. By being long and short in equal amounts, the equity-market-neutral strategist insulates the portfolio from any systemic turn of events that affects the information technology sector as a whole and emphasizes the ability of the chosen model to pick over- and undervalued stocks.

At the heart of most equity-market-neutral strategies is a proprietary multifactor model (econometric or otherwise) of equity risk and return that constructs an optimal portfolio while neutralizing systemic risks. Equity-market-neutral strategists capitalize on the power of these quantitative models to analyze financial data for large numbers of stocks over multiple factors. Because quantitative models can analyze such large amounts of data once they are constructed, equity-market-neutral strategists sometimes use the entire breadth of the market to protect themselves from its caprices. They take

large numbers of positions because they believe that their statistical advantage in picking stocks is similar to the advantage
that the house enjoys in blackjack: any one bet may go against
it, but in the long run the odds are statistically in its favor.

INVESTMENT PROCESS

First, equity-market-neutral specialists define a universe of
stocks to be considered. This universe is usually made up of
large, very liquid names because smaller, less liquid stocks
are not always available to borrow and sell short, and equity-
market-neutral portfolios experience high turnover. Furthermore, equity-market-neutral specialists consider a broad
range of large-capitalization stocks because their quantitative
models are not limited by the need to analyze each firm individually. Once their models are developed, they can look at
any number of firms.

Next, an equity-market-neutral specialist applies a model to
the defined universe of stocks. This model does two things: it
identifies the most relatively overvalued and relatively undervalued stocks in the universe and defines the risk factors of
owning those particular stocks. The model evaluates companies by using a set of indicators or factors. The **INDICATORS**
that are plugged into the model are usually based on publicly available information and conceptually sound and stable
economic ideas about value, they possess a good historical
forecasting record, and have a low correlation with other indicators in the model. Indicators with more forecasting ability
will be appropriately weighted in the model. A similar model
is used to evaluate **SYSTEMIC RISK FACTORS**.

After evaluating the defined universe of stocks for both
value and risk, the equity-market-neutral specialist creates the
optimal bundle of equal amounts of undervalued and overvalued stocks while maintaining as close to a net zero exposure
to the systemic risk factors as possible.

MANAGER EXAMPLE

A conservative implementation of equity-market-neutral
investing can be seen by looking at some well-known stocks.

The illustration offers examples of "paired" equity-market-neutral and "iterative" equity-market-neutral portfolio-construction strategies.

General Motors (GM) and Ford offer a simple illustration of a paired equity-market-neutral strategy. From a risk perspective, they both make autos and have finance subsidiaries and international operations. If the investment selection process ranks Ford highly and General Motors poorly, the investor can go long Ford and short GM. It is easy to have equal dollar-weighted positions of these very liquid stocks. By replicating this long/short construction process in each of the other sectors, you have built a paired long/short strategy.

Paired strategies are understandable, but the opportunity for execution is limited. In reality, there are very few combinations of liquid stocks with opposite performance expectations and identical risk profiles in the same industry.

Consider the challenge presented by a favorable investment selection ranking of General Electric (GE). Holding this company as a long position could require many other firms to be sold short to maintain industry neutrality. GE is in a wide variety of businesses and does not fit into one industry. Its businesses include jet engine manufacturing, leasing, appliances, investment management, electrical distribution, industrial controls, plastics, broadcasting, and our friend the light bulb.

A manager who wants to be as close to neutral as quantifiably possible must offset a variety of market and industry risk factors. This calls for an iterative approach to portfolio construction. Rather than pairing a series of companies together in a portfolio, the long and short portfolios are viewed holistically. The key concern is that the risk characteristics of the long and short portfolios are mirror images. Quantitative risk characteristics can be used to create a risk sensitivity measure for each controlled factor. The long portfolio is built relative to the short portfolio, while the short portfolio is built relative to the long portfolio.[1]

MANAGER EXAMPLE

One obvious way to neutralize the portfolio is to offset stocks on an industry or sector basis. Go long the most attractive stock in the industry, and short the least attractive. This is a simple way to combine attractive return potential with risk minimization.

More comprehensively, this can be done at the portfolio level. The risk characteristics of the long and the short portfolio can be matched (beta risk, economic risk, interest-rate risk, and so forth) while building the optimal strategy.

An example from our history is fairly recent. Some stock selection models that are fundamental in orientation analyze price-to-earnings ratios in order to determine whether a stock is undervalued or overvalued. From 2002 to 2004, small-cap stocks greatly outperformed big-cap stocks, leaving the model biased towards big caps, which looked more attractive compared to their small-cap counterparts. Meanwhile, the concurrent slide of the dollar against overseas currencies caused companies that generate much of their business overseas to outperform the market, and thus appear unattractive from a P/E ratio standpoint. The portfolio manager must balance the trading strategy's predilection for high alpha stocks with the need to neutralize the overall portfolio's exposure to market-capitalization and currency risks. He must decide on the importance of these attributes relative to each stock, balance the risk profile of each stock, and balance the transaction cost associated with each stock. Because of these complex interactions, computer algorithms are used to fully balance the portfolio.

The quantitative nature of equity-market-neutral strategies creates an image of a black box that, once established, runs of its own accord. In fact, equity-market-neutral specialists expend a great deal of time and resources on constantly improving and refining their models. At the trading level, they will rebalance their portfolios continuously to reflect the model's changing opinions of individual stocks and to maintain neutrality over the chosen risk factors. In addition, equity-market-neutral specialists must develop state-of-the-art trading systems that allow them to implement their model-driven strategies in a cost-effective manner.[2]

RISK CONTROL

Equity-market-neutral specialists construct portfolios that consist of approximately equal dollar amounts of offsetting long and short positions to render the portfolio insensitive to market risk. The positions are based on a variety of risk-production factors such as industry sectors, market capitalization, P/E ratio, or beta. They emphasize small position size and widespread diversification to limit the damage any one position can have on the portfolio as a whole. They take positions in larger, more liquid companies to control short squeezes and liquidity risks. Most equity-market-neutral specialists actively manage risk in terms of stop-loss levels and target prices for individual positions to reduce the impact of any single position on the portfolio.

SHORT SELLING

Equity-market-neutral specialists, by definition, actively engage in short selling. As always, the major disadvantage of short selling is a limited upside and a theoretically infinite downside. When an investor borrows a stock and sells it short, she makes a profit when the price of the stock declines and loses money if it appreciates. Because the price of a stock can decline only to zero, the maximum profit on a short sale is the full price of the stock at the time that it is sold short. However, the price of the stock can theoretically appreciate an infinite amount.

In many markets, all stocks are not available to short. Equity-market-neutral specialists try to get around this difficulty by screening the liquidity of stocks in their investment universe to eliminate stocks that are or will be in short supply. Another worry for equity-market-neutral specialists is getting caught in a short squeeze. They try to avoid short squeezes by taking short positions in stocks in which investors have shown little interest. A positive feature of short selling is the interest that is collected after the borrowed stock is sold and before it is bought back, which is called the short interest rebate. Nevertheless, short selling is a complicated trading process that requires resources to implement. Equity-market-neutral specialists try to build these implementation costs into their models.

ADVANTAGES/DISADVANTAGES

Equity-market-neutral strategies leverage manager skills and the predictive power of quantitative models. Because the approach is designed to pick both good and bad stocks rather than time investment styles or industries, it is expected to work equally well in all economic environments; however, performance will depend in part on which factors have or have not been neutralized. It offers the chance to make positive investment returns in a down market, and theoretically eliminates the risk of substantive losses stemming from market decline. Equity-market-neutral specialists argue that it would be virtually impossible to construct a scenario where a large diversified portfolio of large, liquid U.S. stocks could decline substantially in price without a similar significant price decline taking place in the offsetting short positions within the same factor groups. In a worst-case scenario, the value of every stock in the United States would go to zero for a loss of 100 percent on the long positions and a similar gain of 100 percent for the short positions. The portfolio would still achieve a positive return if the money from the short sales earned interest, discounting for margin interest.

Equity-market-neutral strategies generate returns on both the long and short sides; these returns have a low correlation to the returns of long-only market indexes. Because of its low correlation to other asset classes, an equity-market-neutral strategy can provide diversification relative to those other asset classes.

PERFORMANCE

As shown in **FIGURE 5.1**, on a risk-adjusted basis, equity-market-neutral funds have performed very well since 1990. From January 1990 to December 2004, equity-market-neutral funds

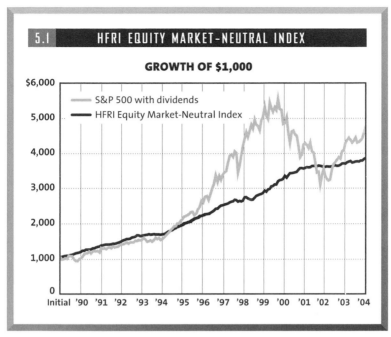

5.1   HFRI EQUITY MARKET-NEUTRAL INDEX

GROWTH OF $1,000

- S&P 500 with dividends
- HFRI Equity Market-Neutral Index

registered average annualized returns of 9.35 percent with an annualized standard deviation of 3.19. This low standard deviation is comparable with volatility measures for investment-grade fixed-income instruments and is almost unheard of in an equity-only portfolio. Equity-market-neutral funds registered similarly low volatility on a month-to-month basis. Though equity-market-neutral funds seem to have struggled with performance since 2001, averaging only 3.59 percent annually, they have still faired better than the S&P 500, which has averaged an annual loss of 0.52 percent over the same period. In addition, equity-market-neutral funds have showed positive monthly performance in almost 82 percent of all months since 1990, while the S&P 500 has reflected positive performance in only 64 percent of months during that time span.

FIGURE 5.2 shows the total strategy assets and net asset flows per year from 1990 to 2004 for equity market neutral. The year-end asset total equals the previous year's asset size plus annual performance plus net asset flows. Since the end of 1998, approximately $10 billion in net inflows has increased

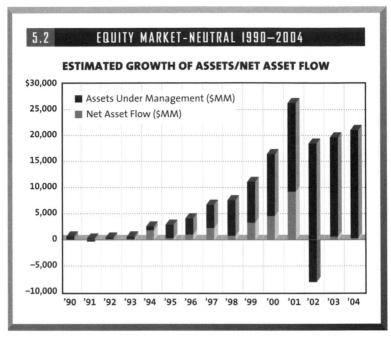

5.2   EQUITY MARKET-NEUTRAL 1990-2004

ESTIMATED GROWTH OF ASSETS/NET ASSET FLOW

- ■ Assets Under Management ($MM)
- ■ Net Asset Flow ($MM)

the strategy's total assets under management almost three-fold to over $21 billion at the end of 2004.

FIGURE 5.3 shows the return distribution for equity market neutral compared to the overall hedge fund industry, stocks, and bonds. Note that performance in this strategy is focused in the 0 to 2 percent per month range which results in its consistent low-volatility performance.

FIGURE 5.4 shows the average upside and downside capture since 1990 for equity-market-neutral funds. Note that the strategy's performance beats the total hedge fund industry, stocks, and bonds during down months. This example of downside protection reflects the essence of market-neutral investing.

SUMMARY POINTS

PROFIT OPPORTUNITY

◆ Equity-market-neutral specialists use both long and short quantitative models to create a statistical advantage in picking stocks and a strategic advantage in controlling exposure to systemic risk by balancing the long and short exposure across a variety of market factors.

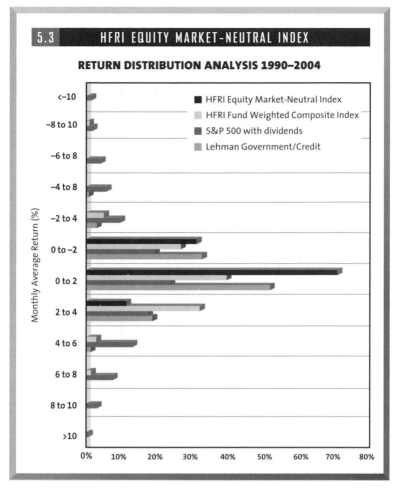

5.3   HFRI EQUITY MARKET-NEUTRAL INDEX

RETURN DISTRIBUTION ANALYSIS 1990–2004

■ HFRI Equity Market-Neutral Index
▨ HFRI Fund Weighted Composite Index
■ S&P 500 with dividends
▨ Lehman Government/Credit

◆ They capitalize on the power of these quantitative models to analyze financial data for large numbers of stocks over multiple factors.

SOURCE OF RETURN

◆ Returns are generated from long positions in stocks that will outperform the market and short positions in stocks that underperform the market.

◆ Large numbers of positions are taken to benefit from the statistical advantages identified in the statistical models.

◆ Because the strategy is designed to pick both good and bad stocks rather than to time investment styles or industries, it should work

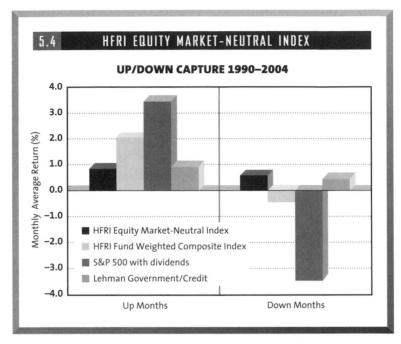

5.4   HFRI EQUITY MARKET-NEUTRAL INDEX

UP/DOWN CAPTURE 1990–2004

Legend:
- HFRI Equity Market-Neutral Index
- HFRI Fund Weighted Composite Index
- S&P 500 with dividends
- Lehman Government/Credit

Y-axis: Monthly Average Return (%)
X-axis: Up Months, Down Months

equally well in most economic environments. It offers the chance to make investment returns in a down market and theoretically eliminates the risk of substantive losses stemming from market decline.

INVESTMENT PROCESS

◆ A large number of long positions in stocks expected to outperform the market and an equal number of offsetting short positions in stocks expected to underperform the market are selected based on statistical models. These selections are then screened for elements that might be missed by the models before the positions are put on. Positions are reevaluated and rebalanced on a regular basis.

KEY TERMS

Dollar neutrality. A zero net exposure that characterizes all equity-market-neutral managers.

Equity-market-neutral portfolio. A portfolio composed of balanced exposure to long stock positions and offsetting short stock positions.

Indicators. Financial data used to forecast the future performance of a company.

Market exposure. The amount of a portfolio exposed to market risk because it is not matched by an offsetting position.

Short selling. The practice of borrowing a stock on collateral and immediately selling it on the market with the intention of buying it back later at a lower price.

Stock selection risk. Exposure to uncertainty about the future valuation of a particular stock.

Systemic or market risk. Exposure to uncertainty about systemic rises and falls in stock market prices that affect the prices of all stocks in a market or sector.

Systemic risk factors. Factors, such as interest rates or the price of oil, that have the ability to affect the valuation of a whole range of securities, or an entire market, if they change.

CHAPTER

Convertible
ARBITRAGE

CONVERTIBLE ARBITRAGE involves taking a long security position and hedging market risk by taking offsetting positions, often in different securities of the same issuer. A manager may, in an effort to capitalize on relative pricing inefficiencies, purchase long positions in convertible securities, generally convertible bonds or WARRANTS, and hedge a portion of the equity risk by selling short the underlying common stock. A manager may also seek to hedge interest-rate or credit exposure under some circumstances. For example, a manager can be long convertible bonds and short the issuer's underlying equity, and may also use futures to hedge out interest-rate risk or credit default swaps to hedge default risk. Timing may be linked to a specific event relative to the underlying company, or a belief that a relative mispricing exists between the corresponding securities.

CORE STRATEGY

Investment managers identify mispriced convertible bonds that they judge to have a favorable total-return profile. A favorable total-return profile means that the convertible bond's price will decline less rapidly than the underlying stock's in a falling equity market and will mirror the price of the stock more closely in a rising equity market (see **FIGURE 6.1**).

In this example, the total-return profile of the convertible bond is favorable because it captures most of the upward movement of the underlying equity but escapes a significant amount of the downside.

The example simplifies the pricing relationships of which convertible arbitrage specialists try to take advantage. Before delving deeper, it's important to examine the basic elements

6.1	TOTAL-RETURN PROFILE		
CHANGE IN PRICE OF UNDERLYING EQUITY	UP 20%	UNCHANGED	DOWN 20%
Price of Equity	+20%	0%	−20%
Price of Convertible	+14%	+1%	−12%

constituting the peculiar features of the convertible bond that make these arbitrage opportunities available.

CONVERTIBLE BOND BASICS

A **CONVERTIBLE BOND** is a corporate bond issued with a conversion feature that allows the holder to convert the bond into a fixed number of shares of the issuing company's underlying common stock at any time prior to maturity or redemption of the bond. Like a bond, a convertible bond has a **COUPON** or guaranteed interest payment and a **MATURITY DATE** (on which the issuer will redeem the bond at **PAR VALUE**). Some convertible bonds have a **CALL FEATURE** that, after the call date, allows the issuer to redeem the bond at its discretion, but at specified prices, before the stated maturity date.

Because convertible bonds combine bond features with stock features, their valuation is also a hybrid of stock and bond valuations. The value of the bond component of a convertible is known as the **INVESTMENT VALUE**. The price of the convertible will not normally fall below its investment value because even if the stock component falls to zero, the convertible still has value as a bond due to its claim against company assets senior to stockholders. The stock conversion component of a convertible bond is called its latent warrant. The value of the convertible bond if it were to be converted to common stock is called its **CONVERSION VALUE**. Because the holder of a convertible bond can convert it into a predetermined number of shares of the issuer's common stock, the value of the convertible bond often strongly correlates with the value of the underlying equity. Thus, as the price of the common stock appreciates or depreciates, the convertible bond's valuation usually follows. The degree to which such a change in the value of the underlying equity is reflected in the value of the convertible bond depends on the convertible bond's premium over conversion value.

For example, if a bond trading at $1,000 (normal par value) can be converted into fifty shares of a $14 stock, then the conversion value would be $700 (50 × 14). The premium is the difference between the market or purchase price and the conversion value, or $300 (1,000 – 700). The conversion premium is usually expressed as a percentage of the conversion value. Thus, in this example the convertible bond had a 42.9 percent conversion premium (300/700). Generally, the higher a convertible bond's conversion premium, the less the price of the convertible bond will correlate with the price of the underlying common stock. Various factors affect a convertible bond's conversion premium, such as, convertibles with higher yields will have a higher conversion premium because the convertible acts more like a bond as it trades closer to the level at which the issuer could issue nonconvertible debt. Thus, in such cases, investors pay more for the yield component than the equity component, regardless of what price the common stock may trade for.

Because it is a hybrid security, a convertible bond will respond to different market forces than its underlying common stock will. In fact, there is almost never a one-to-one correspondence between the price of a convertible bond and the price of its underlying common stock. For example, the price of a convertible bond will tend to move inversely to changes in interest rates because of its bond characteristics, whereas its underlying common stock will react to the perceived macroeconomic causes and effects of such interest-rate fluctuations. There is no single formula for calculating the movement of an underlying security as a function of its corresponding convertible bond, only a range of factors that have varying levels of predictive value. Convertible bond specialists make arbitrage profits by identifying pricing disparities between convertible bonds and their underlying equity and tightly monitoring the factors that will change these relationships.

INVESTMENT PROCESS

Convertible bond specialists screen hundreds of convertible bonds to identify ones that are undervalued or mispriced relative to their underlying common stock. They may look at company fundamentals to identify future potential and the credit aspects of the bond. Some of the factors they consider may be premium-to-conversion ratio, call provisions on the bond, creditworthiness of the issuer (probability of default), yield advantage, and the company's earnings momentum. When they identify an undervalued or mispriced convertible bond, they will purchase the convertible and sell short the underlying common stock, creating a neutral position that can make money in a number of market conditions.

When a stock is sold short, the seller borrows that stock and immediately sells it on the market with the intention of buying it back later at a lower price. The cash proceeds from the sale are held in a money market account earning interest. This interest is known as a **SHORT INTEREST REBATE**. If the stock pays a dividend, the convertible arbitrage specialist must pay the dividend. If the price of the stock falls, the convertible arbitrage specialist makes profits equal to the amount of the price decline multiplied by the number of shares sold short. Conversely, if the price of the stock rises, the convertible arbitrage specialist will realize losses equal to the amount the stock appreciates multiplied by the number of shares sold short.

When convertible arbitrage specialists sell short the underlying equity of a convertible bond, they hedge against a decline in the price of the stock. The amount of stock sold short is nearly always less than the full conversion amount, because this allows the position to retain profit potential on the upside. The number of shares sold short depends on how much market exposure is desirable. In a bear market approach, these specialists will sell a large percentage of the conversion amount short, forgoing any upside potential so that they can make profits in a falling equity market. In a bull market approach, they will sell less than is required for risk neutrality, allowing them to make more profits from equity appreciation. The number of shares they decide to sell short out of the total number possible is called the **HEDGE RATIO**. A hedge ratio that does not add exposure to up or down markets is called a neutral hedge. To determine the hedge ratio that will achieve the risk-reward characteristics they seek to attain, convertible arbitrage specialists look at stock prices, yield curve shifts, dividend yield, and volatility of the stock.

MANAGER EXAMPLE

A convertible arbitrage specialist purchases $10,000 of a 6 percent convertible bond on ABC company. In the convention for bond price quotes, 100 equals $1,000 of face value, so 10 bonds at 100 equals $10,000. The bond's coupon is 6 percent (each bond pays $60 per year, for a total of $600 for the 10 bonds). The current price of the common stock is $16. The interest rate for funds held in a money market account (the short rebate interest rate) is 2.25 percent. The common stock does not pay dividends. The conversion ratio is 40, entitling an investor to exchange each security for 40 shares of stock in ABC company. In this example, the investor will receive 400 shares of stock (40 shares per bond). Since the equity price is $16 a share, the conversion value will be $640 per bond (40 × $ 16 = $640).

In this example, the convertible arbitrage specialist maintains an approximately neutral hedge ratio of 75 percent. For example, if the stock moves by $1, it is assumed that the convertible will move by approximately 75 cents. To set up the neutral hedge, the arbitrageur purchases $10,000 of convertible bonds and sells short 480 stock shares (640 shares × 0.75). FIGURE 6.2 on the following page shows how stock price changes can affect the overall return to a convertible arbitrage position.

In column A, although the stock price declines by 50 percent to $8, the convertible bond price declines by only 33 percent to $67, because the valuation favors the bond component as the stock component decreases in value. The decline in the price of the bond results in a loss of $3,300. However, the short sale of stock more than offsets this loss by generating a profit of $3,800. Therefore, the net trading profit in this scenario is $500. In all the scenarios, the static return remains constant at $772.80. The total return on the position in scenario A is $1,272.80 or 12.73 percent (1,272.80/10,000).

In scenario B, neither the price of the stock nor the price of the convertible bond changes. Therefore, the profit comes solely from the static returns of $772 or 7.2 percent (772/10,000).

In scenario C, the stock price increases by 50 percent to $24. Because convertible bonds have a tendency to move more in line with the prices of their underlying stocks as the stock price increases, the price of the convertible bond increases by 42 percent to $142. The increase in the price of the bond results in a profit of $4,200. In addition, the loss on the short sale of stock is only $3,840 because only 75 percent of the warrant was sold short. The net trading profit in this scenario is $360. The total return on the position in scenario C is $1,132.80 or 11.33 percent (1,132.80/10,000).

In scenario D, the stock and convertible bond prices do not move in relation to one another as the convertible arbitrage

6.2 CONVERTIBLE ARBITRAGE EXAMPLE

THE STRATEGIES

Bonds Purchased	10 @ 100 = $10,000
Coupon	6% ($60 x 10) = $600
Conversion Ratio	40 shares per bond @ $16
Hedge Ratio	75% (480 x $16) = $7,680
Short Rebate	2.25% of $7,680 = $172.80

THE SCENARIOS

	PURCHASE PRICE	PRICE CHANGE OVER TWELVE MONTHS			
		A	B	C	D
Stock	$16.00	$8.00	$16.00	$24.00	$17.00
Convertible Bond	$100.00	$67.00	$100.00	$142.00	$95.00
Bond Coupon	$600.00	$600.00	$600.00	$600.00	$600.00
Short Rebate	$172.80	$172.80	$172.80	$172.80	$172.80
Static Profit/Loss		$772.80	$772.80	$772.80	$772.80
Bond Profit/Loss		–$3,300.00	0.00	$4,200.00	–$500.00
Stock Profit/Loss		$3,800.00	0.00	–$3,840.00	–$480.00
Trading Profit/Loss		$500.00	0.00	$360.00	–$980.00
TOTAL PROFIT/LOSS		$1,272.80	$772.80	$1,132.80	–$207.20
as a Percentage of Capital		12.73%	7.73%	11.33%	–2.07%

specialist expected (this can occur due to events such as the announcement of an LBO offer or a special dividend). The price of the convertible bond drops by 5 percent to $95 due to factors other than a decline in the value of the underlying stock, while the price of the stock increases to $17. This event-risk produces a trading loss on both the convertible bond and the short sale of the underlying stock that totaled $980. The net loss after the static return is $207.20 or 2.07 percent (207.20/10,000).[1]

RISK CONTROL

Convertible arbitrage specialists try to invest in convertible bonds whose prices will decline less rapidly than the underlying stock in a falling equity market and will mirror the price of the stock more closely in a rising equity market. When they can identify such securities, they can make nice investment returns with little to no risk. However, this is not always possible because the pricing relationship does not always hold.

Two factors may disrupt the pricing relationship: the market or an issue specific to the company. At the market level, shifts in stock market volatility, interest-rate changes, foreign exchange relationships, and political events can affect the relationship that the convertible arbitrage specialist expected would hold between the convertible bond and its underlying stock. Market risk is controlled by constructing portfolios that will stand up to a variety of different scenarios. At the company level, improving or weakening credit quality, short stock buy-ins, call features, dividend increases that reduce the cash flow component of the convertible bond, and corporate events such as takeovers and recapitalizations can alter the relationship between the convertible bond and its underlying stock. Issue-specific risks are controlled by diversifying the portfolio, doing in-depth credit analyses of each company, and actively hedging positions.

ADVANTAGES/DISADVANTAGES

Convertible arbitrage allows an investment manager to benefit from a bond yield and stock and bond price movements, regardless of market direction. It provides a **STATIC RETURN** from its coupon and the short interest rebate, regardless of stock and bond price movements. These returns can be augmented by trading returns if the convertible arbitrage specialist can identify undervalued or mispriced securities and successfully predict the future relationship between the price of these convertible bonds and their underlying stock. Hedging with common stock allows the convertible arbitrage specialist to design a strategy that has the ability to meet a wide range of investment objectives. Depending on what kind of hedge is preferred (bearish, neutral, bullish), the investment manager can create anything from a high-performance alternative to money markets to a conservative alternative to owning common stock to a low-risk alternative to short selling.

If the expected price relationships do not hold, the convertible arbitrage specialist can lose both on the bond and on the stock component of a convertible bond. This is a very real possibility because there is almost never a one-to-one correspondence between the price of a convertible bond and the price of its underlying common stock. In addition, for small-cap stocks, not all stocks are available to short so the universe of convertibles securities to choose from is somewhat limited.

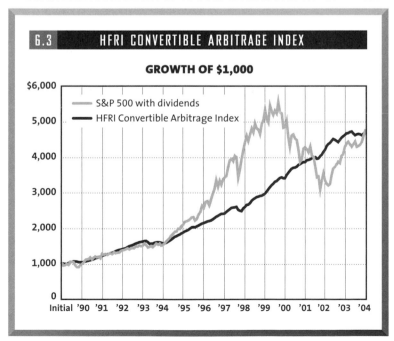

6.3 HFRI CONVERTIBLE ARBITRAGE INDEX

GROWTH OF $1,000

S&P 500 with dividends
HFRI Convertible Arbitrage Index

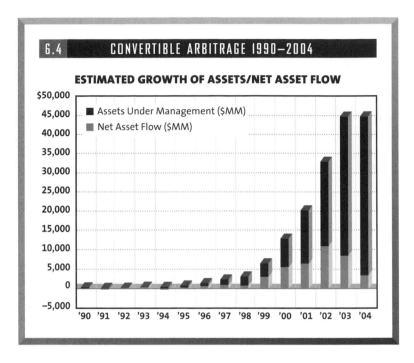

6.4   CONVERTIBLE ARBITRAGE 1990–2004

ESTIMATED GROWTH OF ASSETS/NET ASSET FLOW

■ Assets Under Management ($MM)
■ Net Asset Flow ($MM)

'90 '91 '92 '93 '94 '95 '96 '97 '98 '99 '00 '01 '02 '03 '04

PERFORMANCE

As shown in **FIGURE 6.3**, convertible arbitrage funds have produced very steady, low-risk returns since 1990, registering average annualized returns of 10.80 percent with an annualized standard deviation of 3.39. This encouragingly compares to the S&P 500 index, which produced virtually the same annualized return, but at a risk more than 11 percent higher than that of convertible arbitrage funds. Because of the consistent performance of the strategy over the past several years, convertible arbitrage has attracted more than $37 billion in assets since 1999. Also, as evidenced by the low correlation to the S&P 500 of 0.29, convertible arbitrage has very little sensitivity to stock market prices in general.

FIGURE 6.4 shows the total strategy assets and net asset flows per year from 1990 to 2004 for convertible arbitrage. The year-end asset total equals the previous year's asset size plus annual performance plus net asset flows. Since the end of 1999, more than $34 billion in net inflows has helped increase the strategy's total assets under management seven-fold to almost $45 billion at the end of 2004.

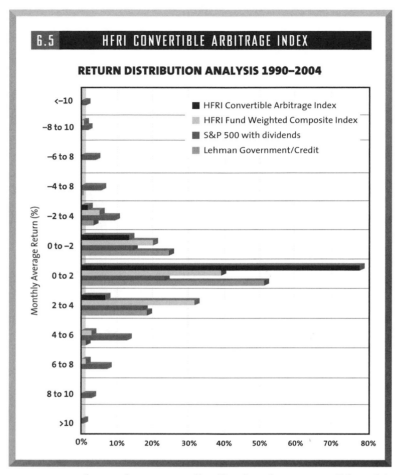

6.5   **HFRI CONVERTIBLE ARBITRAGE INDEX**

RETURN DISTRIBUTION ANALYSIS 1990–2004

FIGURE 6.5 shows the return distribution for convertible arbitrage compared to the overall hedge fund industry, stocks, and bonds. Note that performance in this strategy is strongly focused in the 0 to 2 percent per month range. Such results have become commonplace for this strategy; indeed more than 78 percent of historical monthly returns have fallen under this range, resulting in consistent low-volatility performance.

FIGURE 6.6 shows the average upside and downside capture since 1990 for convertible arbitrage funds. Note that the strategy's performance beats the total hedge fund industry, stocks, and bonds during down months. Convertible arbitrage has received a reputation for providing excellent downside protection during volatile market spans.

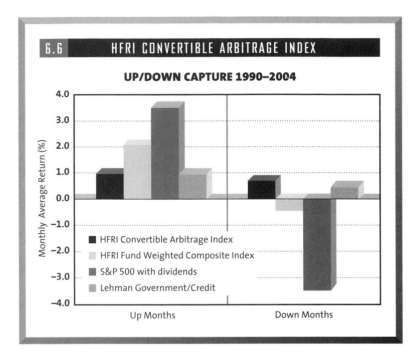

SUMMARY POINTS

PROFIT OPPORTUNITY

◆ Convertible bonds are hybrid securities that have features of a bond and of stock, and therefore their valuations reflect both types of instruments.

◆ Arbitrage opportunities arise when pricing discrepancies exist between the bond and the underlying equity. Such opportunities can be exploited by buying the convertibles and selling short the underlying common stock.

SOURCE OF RETURN

◆ Convertible bond specialists make arbitrage profits by identifying pricing disparities between convertible bonds and their underlying equity and tightly monitoring the factors that will change these relationships.

◆ Positive carry from interest rates

◆ Trading profits from adjusting equity hedges

◆ Embedded credit spread exposure

INVESTMENT PROCESS

◆ When convertible bond specialists identify an undervalued or mispriced convertible bond, they will purchase the convertible and sell short the underlying common stock, creating a neutral position that can make money in a number of market conditions.

◆ When a convertible arbitrage specialist sells short the underlying equity of a convertible bond, he hedges against a decline in the price of the stock.

◆ The number of shares sold short (the hedge ratio) depends on how much exposure to the market the convertible arbitrage specialist wants.

KEY TERMS

Convertible arbitrage. The simultaneous purchase of a convertible bond and sale of the underlying common stock to profit from a pricing discrepancy.

Call feature. A feature that allows the issuer to redeem the bond before it matures.

Conversion value. The value of the convertible bond if it were to be converted to common stock.

Convertible bond. A corporate bond issued with a conversion feature that allows the holder to convert the bond into a fixed number of shares of the issuing company's common stock.

Coupon. A bond's fixed-interest payment.

Hedge ratio. The number of shares that the convertible arbitrage specialist decides to sell short out of the total number possible.

Investment value. The value of the bond component of a convertible bond.

Maturity date. The date on which a bond is redeemed (a five-year bond comes to maturity five years after it is issued).

Par value. The face value of a bond, or the amount for which it is redeemed at maturity.

Short interest rebate. The interest earned on the cash proceeds of a short sale of stock.

Static return. The interest income from coupon payments and short interest rebates that is unaffected by price fluctuations of convertible bonds and their underlying stock.

Warrant. The stock conversion component of a convertible bond.

CHAPTER 7

Merger (Risk)
ARBITRAGE

MERGER ARBITRAGE, also sometimes known as risk arbitrage, involves investing in securities of companies that are the subject of some form of extraordinary corporate transaction, including acquisition or merger proposals, exchange offers, cash tender offers, **LEVERAGED BUYOUTS**, proxy contests, recapitalizations, restructurings, or other corporate reorganizations. These transactions generally involve the exchange of securities for cash, other securities, or a combination of cash and other securities. Typically, a manager purchases the stock of a company being acquired or merging with another company and sells short the stock of the acquiring company. A manager engaged in merger arbitrage transactions derives profit (or loss) from the differential between the price of the securities purchased and the value ultimately realized from their disposition. The success of this strategy usually depends on the consummation of the proposed merger, tender offer, or exchange offer. Managers may use equity options as a low-risk alternative to the outright purchase or sale of common stock. In certain cases where the outcome of a merger is very doubtful, the manager may short the deal by reversing the positions and going short the target and long the acquiring firm.

When a merger is pending, uncertainty about the outcome creates a pricing disparity between the price of the acquiring company's stock and the price of the target company's stock. If the announced deal is completed, the two stocks will eventually represent ownership interests in the same company. Until the deal is consummated, there is typically a **SPREAD** between the prices of the two stocks that reflects both the market's uncertainty about whether the deal will occur and the time value of money.

Because their outcomes are uncertain, mergers and acquisitions provide a particular kind of arbitrage opportunity. Traditional investment funds can profit from these opportunities only in a cursory way because they are restricted from short selling. However, merger arbitrage specialists use hedging strategies and specialized knowledge of merger and acquisition processes to extract arbitrage profits from the pricing discrepancies that result when potential mergers or acquisitions are announced.

CORE STRATEGY

In stock swap mergers, risk or merger arbitrage specialists buy the common stock of a company being acquired or merging with another company and hedge the position by selling short the stock of the acquiring company. In a cash transaction, hedging may be done indirectly or not at all. During negotiations, the target company's stock will typically trade at a discount to its value after the merger is completed because all mergers involve some risk that the transaction will not occur. If the transaction fails, then the price of the target company's stock usually declines. Profits are made by capturing the spread between the current market price of the target company's stock and the price to which it will appreciate when the deal is completed.

Merger arbitrage specialists do not try to anticipate possible mergers. Instead, they research announced mergers and acquisitions to reduce uncertainty about possible outcomes. They will try to ascertain the probability of new bidders for the target company after the announcement. Before taking a position, merger arbitrage specialists will consider public corporate documents, analyst reports, standard media releases, and conversations with company and industry contacts. If the reward outweighs the risk of the deal failing, then they may invest in the situation. Generally, they will add to positions as more information becomes available and the outcome of the transaction becomes more certain. They will liquidate an investment position either when the rewards do not offset the perceived risks or when the transaction is consummated.

INVESTMENT PROCESS

The simplest example of a merger arbitrage opportunity is a company being acquired for cash, or a **CASH MERGER**. The target company's stock will typically trade at slightly less than the price proposed by the acquiring company, reflecting the market uncertainty of the transaction being completed.

An investor who purchases the target company's stock will receive this discount when the deal is completed.

In what are known as **STOCK-FOR-STOCK MERGERS**, the holders of the target company's stock receive shares of the acquiring company's stock rather than cash. In a normal stock-for-stock merger situation, a merger arbitrage specialist will sell the acquiring company's stock short and purchase a long position in the target company in the ratio of the proposed transaction to lock in the spread. If the purchasing firm is offering one half share of its stock for every share of the target company, then the specialist will sell half as many shares of the purchasing firm as she buys of the target company.

Merger transactions are often complex, such as when the exchange ratio is based on the price of the acquiring company's stock when the deal is closed, but they generally combine elements of cash purchases and stock swaps. Typically, the outcome of more complex mergers is less certain, and therefore the spread is larger in these cases. Hostile takeovers and multiple bidder situations also make for larger spreads.

MANAGER EXAMPLE
The Cash Deal
On February 17, 2004, Cingular Wireless, the second-largest provider of cellular phone service in the United States (a joint venture between SBC Communications and BellSouth), announced the acquisition of AT&T Wireless, the third-largest provider of cellular phone service in the United States, that would make Cingular the largest provider of cellular phone service in the United States. Each AT&T Wireless shareholder, upon completion of the acquisition, would be paid $15 cash for each share held. On the final day, AT&T Wireless rose to $13.77, offering the opportunity to earn $1.23 per share if the merger was completed, an 8.9 percent gross return. Risks included denial of the merger by antitrust or regulatory authorities, and, if approved, how long this would take. The merger closed October 31, 2004, resulting in an annualized return of 12.0 percent.

The Stock-for-Stock Deal[1]

On January 15, 2004, JPMorgan Chase, the third-largest bank holding company in the United States with $793 billion in assets, announced the acquisition of BankOne, the sixth-largest bank holding company in the United States with $290 billion assets, which would make JPMorgan Chase the second-largest bank holding company in the United States. Each BankOne share, upon completion of the acquisition, would be converted into 1.32 shares of JPMorgan Chase. On the first day after the announcement, BankOne rose to $50.65, a discount of $0.73 to the implied value of 1.32 JPMorgan Chase shares ($51.38), which traded that day at $38.92, offering a 1.4 percent gross return, and based on an estimated 5.5 months to close, a 3.1 percent annualized return. Managers also received interest on the proceeds of the JPMorgan stock sold short of roughly 1 percent per annum, increasing the return to 4.1 percent annualized (BankOne increased its dividend to parity with JPMorgan so dividends did not affect the return). The merger closed July 1, 2004 as expected, providing a 4.1 percent return for a very low risk investment.

ADVANTAGES/DISADVANTAGES

Merger arbitrage is mainly event driven rather than market driven. Merger arbitrage returns, therefore, are not strongly correlated to overall stock market movement. A group of merger arbitrage specialists can achieve high returns over time based on the ability to anticipate the probable outcome of specific transactions as opposed to the far more random nature of most directional investment strategies.

Although they are not correlated to overall stock market movements, merger arbitrage returns still depend on the overall volume of merger activity, which has historically been cyclical in nature. Because merger activity can be cyclical, merger arbitrage specialists may have a hard time diversifying their portfolios during down periods. Often, merger arbitrage is used as one component of a more general event-driven strategy.

PERFORMANCE

As shown in **FIGURE 7.1**, from January 1990 to December 2004, merger (risk) arbitrage averaged an annualized rate of return of 10.41 percent, with an annual standard deviation of 4.28. This is a slightly lower rate of return than the S&P 500 index of blue-chip stocks, which averaged more than 10.92 percent for the same period, although merger arbitrage funds produced such a return with substantially lower risk. The S&P 500 had an annualized standard deviation of 14.64, whereas the HFRI Merger Arbitrage Index deviated from its mean by only 4.28. Merger arbitrage produced an annualized 6.33 percent return during the recession years of 2000 to 2002, while the S&P 500 lost more than 14.50 percent during the same period. In addition, the HFRI Merger Arbitrage Index registered a correlation to the S&P 500 of 0.46 since 1990, which means that the index had a low sensitivity to changes in the prices of the stock market as a whole.

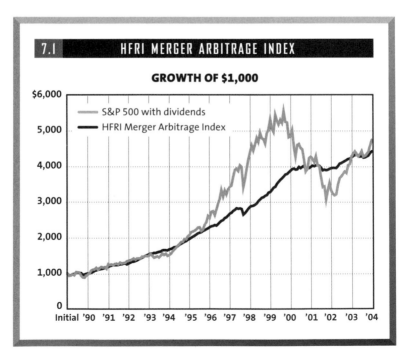

7.1   **HFRI MERGER ARBITRAGE INDEX**

GROWTH OF $1,000

S&P 500 with dividends
HFRI Merger Arbitrage Index

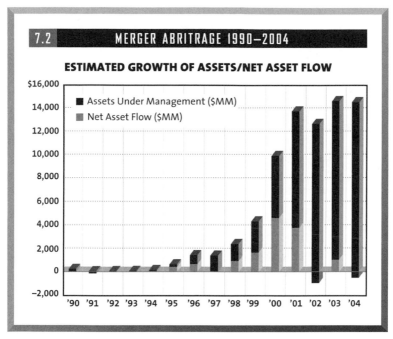

7.2   **MERGER ABRITRAGE 1990–2004**

ESTIMATED GROWTH OF ASSETS/NET ASSET FLOW

- ■ Assets Under Management ($MM)
- ■ Net Asset Flow ($MM)

FIGURE 7.2 shows the total strategy assets and net asset flows per year from 1990 to 2004 for merger arbitrage. The year-end asset total equals the previous year's asset size plus annual performance plus net asset flows. Since the end of 1999, the almost $8 billion in net inflows has helped triple the strategy's total assets under management to more than $14 billion as of the end of 2004.

FIGURE 7.3 on the following page shows the return distribution for merger arbitrage compared to the overall hedge fund industry, stocks, and bonds. It is interesting to note that fund performance in this strategy is strongly focused in the 0 to 2 percent per month range. In fact, since 1990, three out of every four months' net return has fallen under this range.

FIGURE 7.4 shows the average upside and downside capture since 1990 for merger arbitrage funds. Note that the strategy's net returns outperform the total hedge fund industry and stock market during down months, while keeping pace with the consistent, low-volatility returns of the bond market.

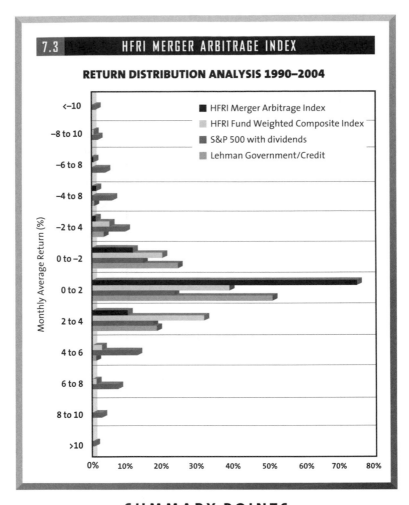

7.3   HFRI MERGER ARBITRAGE INDEX

RETURN DISTRIBUTION ANALYSIS 1990–2004

- ■ HFRI Merger Arbitrage Index
- ▨ HFRI Fund Weighted Composite Index
- ■ S&P 500 with dividends
- ▨ Lehman Government/Credit

SUMMARY POINTS

PROFIT OPPORTUNITY

◆ Financial traders profit from discrepancies in the market's pricing of an asset or two interrelated assets.

◆ Practitioners of merger arbitrage use specialized knowledge of merger and acquisition processes and hedging strategies to extract arbitrage profits from the pricing discrepancies that result when potential mergers or acquisitions are announced.

SOURCE OF RETURN

◆ Merger arbitrage specialists profit by capturing the spread between the current market price of the target company's stock and the price

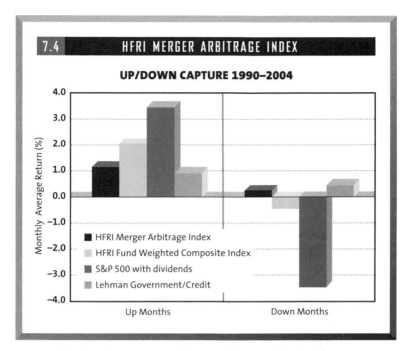

7.4 HFRI MERGER ARBITRAGE INDEX

UP/DOWN CAPTURE 1990–2004

- ■ HFRI Merger Arbitrage Index
- ■ HFRI Fund Weighted Composite Index
- ■ S&P 500 with dividends
- ■ Lehman Government/Credit

to which it will appreciate if the deal is completed.

◆ If the spread is favorable, merger arbitrage specialists buy the common stock of a company being acquired or merging with another company and, when appropriate, sell short the stock of the acquiring company.

◆ Merger arbitrage profits are dependent on the overall volume of these types of transactions rather than market direction (event driven rather than market driven).

INVESTMENT PROCESS

◆ Merger arbitrage specialists analyze the possible outcomes of announced deals rather than attempt to anticipate or identify companies to be involved in future mergers.

◆ In a normal stock swap merger situation, a merger arbitrage specialist sells the acquiring company's stock short and purchases a long position in the target company in the ratio of the proposed transaction to lock in the spread.

◆ Typically, the outcomes of more complex mergers are less certain, and therefore the spread will be larger.

KEY TERMS

Cash merger. A deal in which the acquiring company pays cash for the target company.

Leveraged buyout. An often hostile situation in which the acquiring company buys out the target company by using borrowed funds.

Spread. The difference between the current market price of the target company's stock and the price to which it will appreciate if the deal is completed.

Stock-for-stock merger, or **stock swap merger.** A deal in which the holders of the target company's stock receive shares of the acquiring company's stock rather than cash.

CHAPTER

Distressed
SECURITIES

D ISTRESSED SECURITIES MANAGERS both invest in and sell short the securities of companies wherein the security's price has been or is expected to be affected by a distressed situation. A distressed security may be defined as a security or other obligation of a company that is encountering significant financial or business difficulties, including companies that (1) may be engaged in debt restructuring or other capital transactions of a similar nature while outside the jurisdiction of federal bankruptcy law, (2) are subject to the provisions of federal bankruptcy law, or (3) are experiencing poor operating results due to unfavorable operating conditions, overleveraged capital structure, catastrophic events, extraordinary write-offs, or special competitive or product obsolescence problems. These managers seek profit opportunities arising from inefficiencies in the market for such securities and other obligations.

Negative events, and the subsequent announcement of a proposed restructuring or reorganization to address the problem, may create a severe market imbalance as some holders attempt to sell their positions at a time when few investors are willing to purchase the securities or other obligations of the troubled company. If a manager believes that a market imbalance exists and the securities and other obligations of the troubled company may be purchased at prices below their value, he may purchase them. Increasingly, distressed securities managers have looked to complement long positions with short positions in companies headed for financial distress. Profits in this sector result from the market's lack of understanding of the true value of the deeply discounted securities as well as mispricings within a distressed company's capital structure.

The securities of a company suffering from financial difficulties often trade below their intrinsic value because of uncertainty about the future of the company. Moreover, traditional investment funds are often limited in their ability to hold these potentially undervalued securities by policy restrictions and regulatory constraints that do not now allow them to own securities with very low credit ratings. Hedge fund managers who specialize in distressed securities combine specialized knowledge of the bankruptcy process and fundamental analysis of companies and industries to extract investment returns from the pricing distortions engendered by sound companies with bad capital structures. Their investment mandate and willingness to tolerate long periods of illiquidity allows them to cope with the vagaries of distressed securities.

CORE STRATEGY

Distressed securities specialists find investment opportunities in companies undergoing financial or operational difficulties. Usually, the distressed company is in some stage of negotiating a financial corporate reorganization or has filed for bankruptcy. There are three major sources of these financial problems: operational disorder, significant legal liability, or major management upheaval. If the company has a strong core business, its management and creditors will try to deleverage the balance sheet. As a consequence of the reorganization, investors generally exchange their existing debt for a combination of equity and debt, with the new debt carrying a lower interest rate than the original debt. Distressed securities specialists will buy the securities if they believe that the company will return to historical profit levels after the reorganization because management will be free to focus on operations, which will reduce uncertainty about the future of the company. Although the turnaround time can be several years, they believe that a combination of new management, appropriate capital reinvestment, and a less onerous debt structure will encourage an upward evaluation of the company. The recovery process generally involves several major steps. Each one of these steps can provide an investment opportunity when an exit catalyst, an event that may change the market's perception of (and therefore the value of) the distressed company, leads to higher valuations of the company's securities. An **EXIT CATALYST**, in this context, usually involves the company passing a significant milestone on its path to recovery.

CORPORATE FINANCE AND BANKRUPTCY BASICS

To grow, companies need capital. They raise capital through either debt or equity financing. To the extent that a company is engaged in a speculative or risky business venture, it will have to pay a higher yield to attract bond purchasers. A company is said to be **HIGHLY LEVERAGED** if its ratio of debt payments to cash flow is high. When a company can no longer pay the principal or interest due to its bondholders (a process known as **SERVICING DEBT**), it is said to be in default. Companies with otherwise successful business operations go into default primarily for two reasons: bad capital structure and adverse outside events. In the first case, the company simply takes on more debt than it can service. In the second case, the company is pushed into default by an outside event such as a large cash award against it in a liability lawsuit. In either case, the company must make an arrangement with its creditors.

If the company reorganizes, it usually operates under Chapter XI of the U.S. Bankruptcy Code. If the company liquidates, it operates under Chapter VII of the U.S. Bankruptcy Code. In a liquidation scenario, the proceeds from the sale are allocated to the holders of the company's securities, with preferential payments made in order of seniority. The total proceeds generated by a **LIQUIDATION** are significantly less than the value of the enterprise if the company can continue to operate. Therefore, creditors often have a financial incentive to allow a company that has defaulted to reorganize. The company can work out an arrangement with its creditors outside the bankruptcy or within it. Within bankruptcy, the bankruptcy code (Chapter XI) protects a company from its creditors, which allows the company to reorganize its capital structure in a way that enables it to become profitable again. The new capital structure can take many forms, but usually debt is converted into equity.

INVESTMENT PROCESS

Distressed situations provide the opportunity to buy securities at a greatly discounted price because of **STRUCTURAL ANOMA- LIES**. Many institutions will not hold a company's bonds when that company is in financial difficulty. As the credit quality of a distressed company deteriorates, the price of its securities often reflects selling pressures created by investment policy restrictions, regulatory constraints, and window dressing for year-end investment holdings. Such artificial selling pressure distorts the bonds' prices.

Distressed securities specialists make investment returns on mispricings in two types of valuation: **FUNDAMENTAL** or **INTRINSIC VALUE**, which is the actual value of the company that the security represents; and **RELATIVE VALUE**, which is the value of the security relative to the value of other securities of the same company. When the market price of a company's security is lower than its fundamental value because the company is experiencing temporary financial difficulties, distressed securities specialists will take core positions in these securities and hold them through the restructuring process, because they believe that the security will approach its "real" value after the restructuring is complete. While a company is restructuring, the prices of its different financial instruments can become mispriced relative to one another. This is an opportunity for what distressed securities specialists call **INTRACAPITALIZATION** or **CAPITAL STRUCTURE ARBITRAGE**. They will purchase the undervalued security and take short trading positions in the overpriced security to extract arbitrage profits.

Distressed securities specialists are better equipped than other investors to take advantage of these opportunities, because they can combine financial analysis of the fundamental value of distressed companies with specialized knowledge of the bankruptcy process that allows them to predict, and when necessary take steps to influence, the outcome of bankruptcies and reorganizations. They use information drawn from Wall Street research, marketplace contacts, publications, databases, financial and legal due diligence, and their own valuation models to estimate the fundamental value of distressed companies.

The greatest advantage that distressed securities specialists have over other investors in distressed situations is their specialized knowledge of the bankruptcy and out-of-court restructuring processes. When a company restructures in a typical Chapter XI situation, some of its debt is converted into equity. Therefore, the various involved parties must negotiate how to value that equity. Moreover, the bankruptcy code requires that the most senior creditors be repaid in full before any payment is provided to junior creditors. Consequently, the senior creditors' normal negotiating strategy is to (1) seek cash, (2) obtain the majority of their claim in new securities, or (3) demand new equity ownership based on current performance. They often succeed because the company is being valued at the bottom of the business cycle. Distressed securities specialists have intimate knowledge of these kinds of negotiating and restructuring processes and can assess whether the company's problems can be resolved outside bankruptcy and how the company must restructure its capital. They also know the major players in the processes: bankruptcy lawyers, accountants, turnaround managers, and distressed securities investors. Their industry expertise allows them to forecast the outcome of specific restructurings and judge whether a given company's securities are overvalued or undervalued.

PHASES OF THE BANKRUPTCY PROCESS

Distressed securities specialists choose to invest at different phases of the bankruptcy cycle depending on their risk-reward tolerance. Much of this decision is dictated by how willing they are to become involved in the bankruptcy process. The early stages of bankruptcy tend to be chaotic. Traditionally, the courts have extended almost exclusive control of the process to the company's existing management for at least six months to one year. During that time, the company's cash flow rises because management controls receipts and can postpone payments to creditors. However, during this initial period the management must propose plans for reorganization. The holders of the company's securities critically review these plans. Thus, the early stages of bankruptcy are contentious and unpredictable.

On a selective basis, distressed securities specialists often play an active role in restructuring distressed companies. In such cases, they may join the company's creditors committee or the board of directors. Before getting involved, they determine what the likely exit catalyst in the restructuring process will be. If they can add value by creating or facilitating an exit catalyst, then they will play an active role if the value that is added outweighs the opportunity cost of getting involved. Restructurings are very time intensive, so the manager who is involved will need to allocate time away from other aspects of business, such as finding new investments. Also, the manager cannot trade the company's securities while on the committee, due to the privileged nature of the information provided to committee members. The distressed securities specialist weighs these disadvantages against the sometimes overwhelming advantages of being able to control and influence a situation to maximize potential returns. Manager involvement indicates a long-term commitment; it is essential that the manager have a large pool of committed capital so that liquidity is not a problem.

LEVEL OF THE CAPITAL STRUCTURE

A distressed company's securities fall along a risk spectrum that runs from the least risky (bank debt and senior corporate debt) to the most risky (common stock). Positions are sometimes hedged by taking a position long senior debt securities and at the same time short the equity of the same company. The core strategy is to buy the securities that provide the most attractive risk-reward ratio. Sometimes, distressed securities specialists will roll down a company's capital structure from **SENIOR DEBT** to preferred or common equity as the company's financial situation improves and clarifies.

RISK CONTROL

Distressed securities specialists control risk through portfolio diversification, hedging techniques, and little, if any, use of leverage. In fact, brokers generally will not lend against bankrupt security holdings. Portfolios are diversified across assets and industries and over business cycles. Most managers cap the amount of their portfolio that can be held in any one position. They monitor risk by defining specific events that they anticipate and a valuation target and revisiting the investment if events do not transpire as anticipated or the target valuation is reached. Market risk may be hedged with index options, but it is generally a long strategy. Event risk can be hedged by having long and short holdings, but often the price volatility of an instrument is accepted as a risk that should not be managed. For clients who require certain levels of liquidity, the specialist will also monitor the overall liquidity of the portfolio.

MANAGER EXAMPLE

Seitel, Inc. is a leading provider of seismic data and related geophysical expertise to the petroleum industry onshore, offshore, the transition zone of the U.S. Gulf of Mexico, onshore East Texas, and Canada. Seitel owns an extensive library of proprietary onshore and offshore seismic data, accumulated since 1982, which it offers for license to a wide range of oil and gas companies. Its customers use the data, in part, to assist their identification of new geographical areas where subsurface conditions are favorable to oil and gas exploration, to determine the size, depth, and geophysical structure of previously identified oil and gas fields, and to optimize the development and production of oil and gas reserves.

The manager's investment thesis is that Seitel has a valuable seismic library, which is a distinguishing characteristic of the company, and that a global environment of rising energy prices makes Seitel's services an attractive proposition. Its library of onshore seismic data is one of the largest available for licensing in the United States and Canada. It also has ownership in a library of offshore data covering parts of the U.S. Gulf of Mexico shelf and certain deep-water areas in the western and central U.S. Gulf of Mexico. On January 17th, 2004, Seitel filed its Reorganization Plan with the U.S. bankruptcy court with the support of the Official Committee of Equity Holders of Seitel, Inc., Berkshire Hathaway Inc., and Ranch Capital L.L.C., the holders of approximately $255 million aggregate principal amount of the firm's senior unsecured notes and Seitel's largest creditors. The Plan was confirmed by the bankruptcy court on March 18, 2004.

The manager learned of the filing from the *Daily Bankruptcy Review* and determined that Seitel had three attractive characteristics: (1) it was "under the radar" of the big distressed investing players, (2) it had a high-profile investor, and (3) it had a solid business. When researching the event, it was discovered that Seitel had a good core business (seismic data libraries) and had expanded into businesses it did not understand (oil and gas production and an Internet business). It was also discovered that Warren Buffett bought 100 percent of Seitel's debt and offered $0.40 per share to the shareholders. The manager then acted by contacting the Seitel Board directly and persuading them that there was a better alternative for the shareholders than Buffett's offer.

In structuring the trades, the manager then began buying shares at $0.30 per share, helped organize shareholders into a shareholders' committee, and helped company management create a restructuring plan that included buying out Buffett, selling its oil and gas division, closing its Internet division, cutting staff, and recapitalizing the balance sheet. The manager continuously monitored the post-trade and exit strategy. The manager is currently seeking to place shares and warrants (at $6.60 per share) with a private placement in order to lock in gains and to set up a sale of the company as an exit strategy (shares at this writing were trading at the equivalent of $6.60 per share after 6:1 split).[1]

ADVANTAGES/DISADVANTAGES

Distressed securities investment strategies are event driven. Thus, they can provide opportunities in almost any economic environment because investment returns are dependent on specific corporate events rather than market conditions. Even during a recession or rising interest-rate environment, a distressed security can perform well when the issuer reorganizes successfully. Because the strategy generates core returns based on events specific to the distressed company, such as bankruptcy filing, the outcome of intercreditor negotiations, or the amount of asset divestiture proceeds, its investment returns tend to have a low correlation to general financial markets.

However, investments in distressed securities are illiquid, which means that they do not lend themselves well to annual or more frequent liquidity windows. The length of a bankruptcy proceeding is notoriously hard to forecast and the outcome is always uncertain, both of which make the maturity of any particular investment in a distressed situation unpredictable. The prices of distressed securities are volatile during the bankruptcy process because useful information on the company becomes unavailable during this period. Investment managers who participate on creditor and equity committees must commit a large amount of time and must freeze their holdings until an arrangement is reached. Finally, distressed securities specialists need to find defaulted securities of companies that have strong core operations.

PERFORMANCE

As shown in **FIGURE 8.1**, from January 1990 to December 2004, distressed securities strategies averaged an annualized rate of return of 15.60 percent with an average annual standard deviation of 6.14 percent. As could be expected, the recession years, 1998, 2000, and 2002, were off years for distressed specialists with returns of −4.23, 2.78, and 5.28 percent, respectively. These recessions led to a number of good companies running into financial difficulties, which meant that there were ample

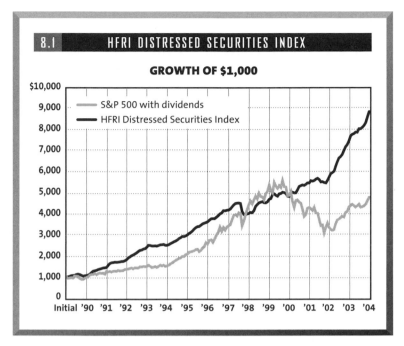

8.1   HFRI DISTRESSED SECURITIES INDEX

GROWTH OF $1,000

- S&P 500 with dividends
- HFRI Distressed Securities Index

distressed opportunities in the year that immediately followed each recession year. Case in point, the distressed securities strategy registered 16.94, 13.28 and 29.56 percent returns in 1999, 2001, and 2003, respectively. These figures are evidence of the cyclical nature of distressed investing. In addition, the event-driven nature of distressed investing is made obvious by a correlation statistic of 0.39 since 1990, which means that changes in the prices of the market as a whole have little effect on distressed-investing returns.

FIGURE 8.2 on the following page shows the total strategy assets and net asset flows per year from 1990 to 2004 for distressed securities. The year-end asset total equals the previous year's asset size plus annual performance plus net asset flows. Since the end of 2000, nearly $25 billion in net inflows has led to the almost six-fold increase of the strategy's total assets under management, to more than $46 billion as of the end of 2004.

FIGURE 8.3 shows the return distribution for distressed securities compared to the overall hedge fund industry, stocks, and bonds. Since 1990, half of the strategy's monthly perfor-

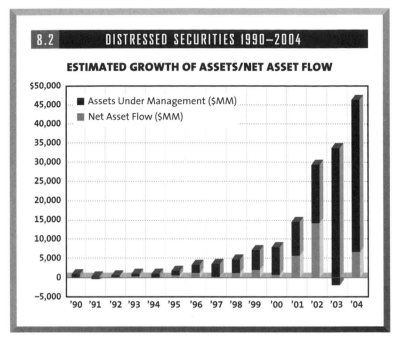

8.2   DISTRESSED SECURITIES 1990–2004

ESTIMATED GROWTH OF ASSETS/NET ASSET FLOW

- ■ Assets Under Management ($MM)
- ■ Net Asset Flow ($MM)

mance falls under the 0 to 2 percent return range, while more than 27 percent of the monthly performance returns have registered from 2 to 4 percent, the highest percentage of any hedge fund strategy.

FIGURE 8.4 shows the average upside and downside capture since 1990 for distressed securities funds. The strategy's net returns outperform the total hedge fund industry and stock market during down months, while maintaining similar performance to the bond market.

SUMMARY POINTS

PROFIT OPPORTUNITY

◆ Distressed securities specialists invest in the securities of companies that are experiencing financial or operational difficulties.

◆ Because regulatory or policy constraints prevent many traditional investors from owning bankrupt or near-bankrupt companies, the securities of these companies are often priced significantly below distressed securities specialists' estimates of their "real" value.

◆ Distressed securities investment strategies are event driven, which means they provide opportunities in almost any economic environ-

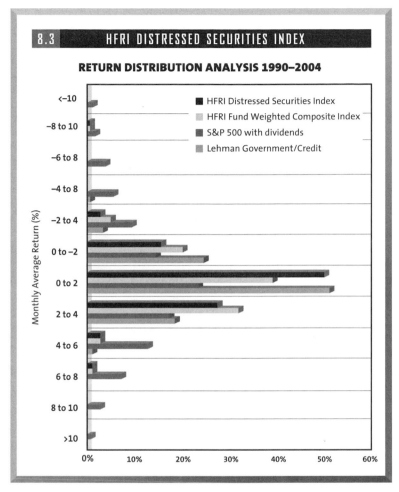

8.3 **HFRI DISTRESSED SECURITIES INDEX**

RETURN DISTRIBUTION ANALYSIS 1990–2004

- HFRI Distressed Securities Index
- HFRI Fund Weighted Composite Index
- S&P 500 with dividends
- Lehman Government/Credit

Monthly Average Return (%) categories (y-axis): <–10, –8 to 10, –6 to 8, –4 to 8, –2 to 4, 0 to –2, 0 to 2, 2 to 4, 4 to 6, 6 to 8, 8 to 10, >10

x-axis: 0%, 10%, 20%, 30%, 40%, 50%, 60%

ment because investment returns are dependent on specific corporate events rather than market conditions.

SOURCE OF RETURN

◆ Distressed securities specialists make investment returns on two kinds of mispricings: the fundamental value of securities and their value relative to the distressed company's other debt instruments.

◆ Distressed securities specialists combine financial analysis of the fundamental value of distressed companies with specialized knowledge of the bankruptcy process that allows them to predict, and when necessary take steps to influence, the outcome of bankruptcies and reorganizations.

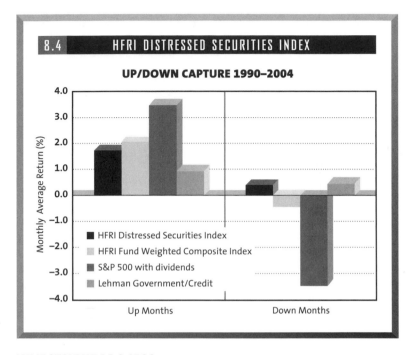

8.4   HFRI DISTRESSED SECURITIES INDEX

UP/DOWN CAPTURE 1990–2004

- ■ HFRI Distressed Securities Index
- ■ HFRI Fund Weighted Composite Index
- ■ S&P 500 with dividends
- ■ Lehman Government/Credit

INVESTMENT PROCESS

◆ Distressed securities specialists identify companies with strong operations that are overleveraged (good operating companies with excessive debt). They buy those companies' securities at a discount to their intrinsic value and anticipate the timing and consequence of major events, or "exit catalysts," that will lead to higher valuations.

◆ Companies with otherwise successful business operations go into default for two reasons: bad capital structure and adverse outside events.

◆ When they design a new capital structure, bankrupt companies will usually convert debt into equity, lower the interest costs, and extend the maturity on the remaining debt.

◆ The later in the bankruptcy cycle that an investor takes a position in a distressed company, the more certain is the outcome of the restructuring process. Because there is less risk in the later stages, the returns are usually also lower.

◆ The expertise of distressed securities specialists allows them to forecast the outcome of specific restructurings and judge whether a given company's securities are overvalued or undervalued.

◆ The specialist who can add value by creating or facilitating the exit catalyst will play an active role if the value added outweighs the opportunity cost of becoming involved.

KEY TERMS

Distressed securities. The securities of companies that are experiencing financial or operational difficulties. Distressed situations include reorganizations, bankruptcies, distressed sales, and other corporate restructurings.

Exit catalyst. An event on the horizon that the distressed securities specialist expects will change the market's perception of (and therefore the value of) the distressed company.

Fundamental value. The intrinsic or "real" value of a security, which reflects both tangible and intangible company assets.

Highly leveraged company. A company that has too large an amount of debt relative to its ability to service that debt.

Intracapitalization or **capital structure arbitrage**. A trade where a manager goes long one security and short another security within the capital structure of a single issuer.

Liquidation. The sale of assets for cash, sometimes to pay off debt.

Relative value. The value of a particular security relative to that of other similar or related instruments, such as the same company's other debt instruments.

Senior debt. A class of debt securities whose holders a company is obligated to pay off before the holders of its other securities, in the case of bankruptcy.

Servicing debt. Paying the interest and principal due to bondholders.

Structural anomalies. Structural features of financial markets including investment policies, which can cause forced selling of securities of companies experiencing financial distress.

CHAPTER

9

Event-Driven
STRATEGIES

EVENT-DRIVEN INVESTMENT STRATEGIES, or "corporate life cycle investing," are based on investments in opportunities created by significant transactional events, such as spin-offs, mergers and acquisitions, industry consolidations, liquidations, reorganizations, bankruptcies, recapitalizations, share buybacks, and other extraordinary corporate transactions. Event-driven trading involves attempting to predict the outcome of a particular transaction as well as the optimal time at which to commit capital to it. The uncertainty about the outcome of these events creates investment opportunities for managers who can correctly anticipate them. As such, event-driven trading embraces merger arbitrage, distressed securities, value with a catalyst, and special-situations investing.

Some event-driven managers utilize a core strategy while others opportunistically make investments across the range when different types of events occur. Dedicated merger arbitrage and distressed securities managers should be seen as stand-alone options, whereas event driven is a multistrategy approach. Instruments include long and short common and preferred stocks, as well as debt securities, warrants, stubs, and options. Managers may also utilize derivatives such as index put options or put option spreads to leverage returns and hedge out interest-rate and/or market risk. The success or failure of this type of strategy usually depends on whether the manager accurately predicts the outcome and timing of the transactional event. Event-driven managers do not rely on market direction for results; however, major market declines, which would cause transactions to be repriced or to break apart, and risk premiums to be reevaluated, may have a negative impact on the strategy.

Proponents of event-driven investment strategies argue that by focusing on corporate events rather than market direction, these strategies will produce more consistent returns through various market environments than traditional approaches that depend on general trends in market price levels. Because corporate events are cyclical in nature, the prevailing corporate event activity fluctuates over time. For example, there are more mergers during periods of economic expansion and more bankruptcies during economic downturns. Event-driven strategists use specialized knowledge of all the significant events in the corporate life cycle and the flexibility to invest in the outcomes of a variety of corporate events to extract investment profits from the mispricings caused by uncertainty about the outcomes of these events.

CORE STRATEGY

Investors who use event-driven investment strategies focus on the outcomes of the significant events that occur during a corporation's life cycle. Generally, these extraordinary corporate events fall into three categories: risk arbitrage opportunities, distressed securities situations, and special situations. Risk arbitrage situations include hostile takeovers, mergers, acquisitions, and liquidations (for a complete description of risk arbitrage strategies, see Chapter 7). Distressed securities situations include recapitalizations, bankruptcies, restructurings, and reorganizations (for a complete description of distressed securities strategies, see Chapter 8). Special situations include spin-offs, 13-D filings, and situations in which a company's asset mix is being significantly changed, such as the sale of major assets or a large share repurchase.

Event-driven specialists look for three elements in any investment situation. First, they seek a disparity between the current market value of an instrument and the value that they anticipate for it after the event is completed. Second, they look for a near-term event to act as a **CATALYST** that will change the market's perception of the company and therefore its valuation of the company's debt or equity instruments, and they assess how likely it is to become visible. Third, they estimate the amount of time that it will take the catalyst to become fully visible to investors and how long the market will take to correct the valuation disparity.

SIGNIFICANT CORPORATE EVENTS create profit opportunities because the outcome of the proposed changes is uncertain. Investment managers must ask: Will the event be completed? What will the result be if it does occur? How long will the process take? What effect will the event have on the prices of the securities of the involved companies? After a corporate event is announced, the price of the securities of the involved company reflects the market's uncertainty about whether the event will be completed. Event-driven specialists will make profits by correctly anticipating the outcome of these events.

INVESTMENT PROCESS

Because the overall volume and composition of corporate events vary over time and fluctuate with market cycles, event-driven specialists will shift the type of corporate event in which their portfolios are concentrated to take advantage of the best opportunities for risk-adjusted returns. In periods following a recession, when many good companies experience financial difficulties, distressed securities offer the best opportunities for returns. In periods characterized by excellent economic markets, when merger activity is high, there are more risk arbitrage opportunities that offer good returns. In periods when the market is relatively flat, event-driven specialists will concentrate on special situations because they offer the best returns in any conditions and the high systemic risk usually associated with them is offset by the flat market conditions.

For event-driven specialists, the investment process is triggered by the public announcement of an impending corporate event. The manager must be convinced that a significant corporate event will take place during a definable period of time. Rather than try to anticipate corporate events, a process that is extremely speculative, event-driven specialists analyze the possible outcomes of events once they are announced. Once a proposed event is announced, the market revalues the securities of the companies involved on the basis of how it perceives the proposed event and the possible outcomes. Event-driven specialists research situations by using industry contacts, the advice of legal and banking experts, information from the financial newswires and magazines, and previous experiences and expertise. They understand the complex legal, interpersonal, and strategic forces that may affect the event and the probabilities of different potential outcomes. If a careful evaluation of the event indicates favorable risk-reward criteria, the position is taken. Successful event-driven specialists can synthesize **FUNDAMENTAL VALUE ANALYSIS, EVENT ANALYSIS,** and **TIME HORIZON ANALYSIS.**

RISK CONTROL

Event-driven specialists try to predict the outcome of events or determine that the probability of the outcome is greater than the current prices of the involved instruments indicate. Because the manager can be wrong about any single case, the portfolio is diversified among a number of positions to reduce the impact of any single position that does not work out as anticipated. Maximum limits are set for the amount invested in any one event. As mentioned earlier, event-driven specialists also diversify across types of events (risk arbitrage, distressed securities, special situations), depending on market cycles. Leverage is used conservatively. They may hedge against market risk by purchasing index put options and short selling.

MANAGER EXAMPLE

Spin-offs have provided many opportunities for event-driven managers. Often spin-offs involve a large corporation that decides to spin off a subsidiary that may be a drag on the overall business or may not be seen as a "core" business. TMP Worldwide/Hudson Highland is one such example. TMP Worldwide decided to change its name to Monster Worldwide to reflect its refocus on its Internet recruiting business. Hudson Highland (HHGP) was the old-line, traditional headhunter business that no longer fit Monster's strategic vision.

Given the new strategic initiatives, Hudson Highland was to be spun off from TMP Worldwide. For every $13\frac{1}{3}$ shares of TMP Worldwide owned, holders would get 1 share of Hudson Highland. Hudson Highland was in the midst of a cyclical downturn, which translated into operating losses for this business. In addition, the company had been saddled with an excessive cost structure for employees and facilities that were built in the frenzy of the Internet peak as Monster inundated Hudson Highland with high fixed expenses at a time of seemingly endless growth. There was ample opportunity for costs to be rationalized as well as the likelihood that business conditions would improve as the economy improved. Therein lay the opportunity for the event-driven manager.

Often in spin-offs there is a technical trading element that can work to the event-driven manager's benefit. When the parent is a large-cap stock included in many indexes, often, as in this case, the spun-off entity would not be a constituent of such indexes, therefore, holders of the parent who seek to match the performance of an underlying index won't or can't hold on to the spun-off entity. As a result, they become forced sellers, regardless of price. And this dynamic is ideal for an event-driven manager in that it creates a structural mispricing. Hudson Highland was a relatively small company that was completely ignored by Wall Street research analysts and at a cyclical low, thereby making it the perfect spin-off for an event-driven manager.

The stock began trading at about $10 per share at the time of the spin and worked its way to the high teens after a short time; as of this writing it is trading in the high 20s.[1]

ADVANTAGES/DISADVANTAGES

Because event-driven strategies are positioned to take advantage of the valuation disparities produced by corporate events, they are less dependent on overall stock market gains than traditional equity investment approaches. Opportunities for high risk-adjusted returns may be identified even in a flat or declining market. Because their returns are determined in part by the volume of corporate events, event-driven specialists think that more opportunities will be available to them than to managers who specialize only in risk arbitrage or distressed securities and the events driving their positions will be more diversified. These advantages depend on the event-driven specialist's expertise in the various types of corporate events. Specialized knowledge of the whole range of corporate events is required because profits are determined not only by the number of corporate events but also by the manager's ability to identify and correctly anticipate their outcome.

PERFORMANCE

As shown in **FIGURE 9.1**, from January 1990 to December 2004, event-driven strategies registered an average annualized return of 14.49 percent, with an annualized standard deviation of 6.61. These returns were more than 50 percent higher than the S&P 500 index of blue-chip stocks for the same period, with a much lower standard deviation (6.61 compared with 14.64). Event-driven funds have registered only two negative years (1990 and 2002) in the past fifteen years. Furthermore, in the thirteen positive years, seven have produced returns higher than 20 percent, most recently in 2003 (25.33 percent). Because the strategy capitalizes on corporate events, the event-driven index's correlation statistic of 0.64 has showed stronger sensitivity to the movement of stock prices in general than many of the other hedge fund strategies since 1990.

FIGURE 9.2 shows the total strategy assets and net asset flows per year from 1990 to 2004 for event-driven strategies. The year-end asset total equals the previous year's asset size plus

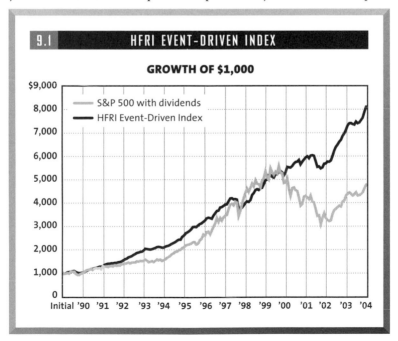

9.1   HFRI EVENT-DRIVEN INDEX

GROWTH OF $1,000

S&P 500 with dividends
HFRI Event-Driven Index

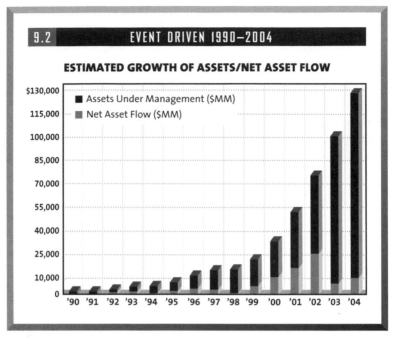

9.2   EVENT DRIVEN 1990–2004

ESTIMATED GROWTH OF ASSETS/NET ASSET FLOW

annual performance plus net asset flows. Since the end of 1999, approximately $70 billion in net inflows has helped increase the strategy's total assets under management to over $128 billion as of the end of 2004. Event-driven funds now manage over 13 percent of all industry assets, representing the second-highest total strategy assets in the industry (behind equity hedge).

FIGURE 9.3 shows the return distribution for event-driven strategies compared to the overall hedge fund industry, stocks, and bonds. Since 1990, almost half of the strategy's monthly performance falls in the 0 to 2 percent return range, while more than 26 percent of the monthly performance returns have registered between 2 and 4 percent, the second-highest percentage in that range of any hedge fund strategy.

FIGURE 9.4 shows the average upside and downside capture since 1990 for event-driven funds. The strategy's performance during down months is better than those of the overall hedge fund industry and the stock market. Although the strategy reflects negative performance during down months, its loss

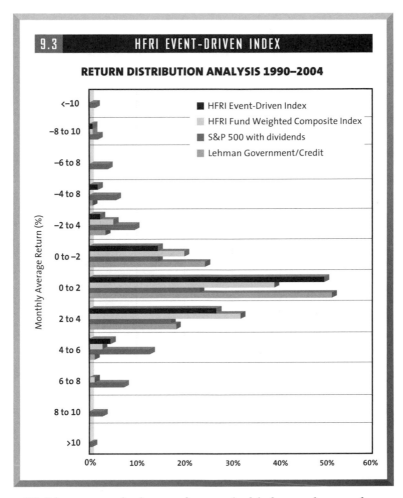

9.3 HFRI EVENT-DRIVEN INDEX

RETURN DISTRIBUTION ANALYSIS 1990–2004

Legend:
- HFRI Event-Driven Index
- HFRI Fund Weighted Composite Index
- S&P 500 with dividends
- Lehman Government/Credit

Y-axis (Monthly Average Return (%)): <-10, -8 to 10, -6 to 8, -4 to 8, -2 to 4, 0 to -2, 0 to 2, 2 to 4, 4 to 6, 6 to 8, 8 to 10, >10

X-axis: 0%, 10%, 20%, 30%, 40%, 50%, 60%

of 0.24 percent during such a period is better by nearly half than the total hedge fund industry, which loses 0.45 percent under the same circumstance.

SUMMARY POINTS

PROFIT OPPORTUNITY

◆ Event-driven strategists use specialized knowledge of all the significant events in the corporate life cycle and the flexibility to invest in the outcomes of a variety of corporate events to extract investment profits from the mispricings caused by uncertainty about the outcomes of significant corporate events.

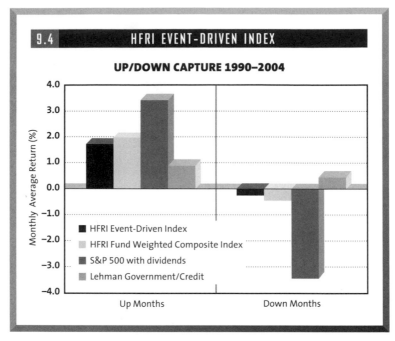

9.4   HFRI EVENT-DRIVEN INDEX

UP/DOWN CAPTURE 1990–2004

Legend:
- HFRI Event-Driven Index
- HFRI Fund Weighted Composite Index
- S&P 500 with dividends
- Lehman Government/Credit

Y-axis: Monthly Average Return (%)

X-axis: Up Months | Down Months

◆ Generally, these extraordinary corporate events fall into three categories: risk arbitrage opportunities, distressed securities situations, and special situations.

◆ Event-driven specialists invest in situations in which they expect a near-term event to act as a catalyst that will change the market's perception of the company and therefore its valuation of the company's debt or equity instruments.

SOURCE OF RETURN

◆ Significant corporate events create profit opportunities because the outcome of the proposed changes is uncertain.

◆ Profits are made by correctly anticipating the outcome of these events once they are announced and how that outcome will affect the valuation of the company's debt or equity instruments.

◆ Because event-driven strategies are positioned to take advantage of the valuation disparities created by corporate events, they are less dependent on overall stock market gains than traditional equity investment approaches.

INVESTMENT PROCESS

◆ Because the overall volume and composition of corporate events vary over time and fluctuate with market cycles, event-driven specialists will shift the majority weighting of their portfolios to take advantage of the different opportunities available during different parts of the business cycle.

◆ Successful event-driven specialists can synthesize fundamental value analysis, event analysis, and time horizon analysis.

◆ An event-driven specialist must have specialized knowledge of a broad range of corporate events because profits are determined not only by the number of corporate events, but also on the ability to identify and correctly anticipate their outcome.

KEY TERMS

Catalyst. A near-term event, such as a press release or a new product launch, that will heighten investor interest in or change the market's perception of a company.

Event analysis. The process by which an analyst assesses the probabilities of all the possible outcomes of a corporate event.

Fundamental value analysis. The process by which an analyst establishes a theoretical value of a company from an examination of its financial statements, operational history and forecasts, business climate, and the like.

Significant corporate events. Major public events, such as mergers, bankruptcies, and spin-offs, that have the potential to dramatically change a company's makeup and as a result the valuation of its debt and equity instruments.

Spread. The valuation disparity between two related financial instruments caused by uncertainty about the outcome of a corporate event.

Time horizon analysis. The examination of the time frame for completion of a corporate event (if the event is going to happen, then when will it occur?).

CHAPTER

10

Macro
INVESTING

MACRO STRATEGIES attempt to identify extreme price valuations in stock markets, fixed-income markets, interest rates, currencies, and commodities and make bets on the anticipated price movements in these markets, sometimes in a leveraged fashion. Trades may be designed as an outright directional bet on an asset class or geographical region (e.g., long Japanese equities), or they may be designed to take advantage of geographical imbalances within an asset class (e.g., German 10-years relative to U.S. 10-years). To identify extreme price valuations, managers generally employ a top-down, global approach that concentrates on forecasting how global macroeconomic and political events affect the valuations of financial instruments. These approaches may be either systematic or discretionary.

The strategy has a broad investment mandate, with the ability to hold positions in practically any market with any instrument. In general, managers try to identify opportunities with a definable downside and favorable risk-reward characteristics. Profits are made by correctly anticipating price movements in global markets and having the flexibility to use any suitable investment approach to take advantage of extreme price valuations. Managers may use a focused approach or diversify across approaches. They often pursue a number of base strategies to augment their selective large directional bets.

Perhaps it is because macro managers often receive the most attention in the press that a large portion of the investment community likes to see them as simply top-down analysts: **SPECULATORS** who try to make profits on currency, commodity, bond, and stock movements without researching specific companies and financial instruments. However, some macro managers argue that macro trends and conditions apply to micro investment approaches that are not normally considered "macro." They believe that specialist strategies such as risk arbitraging; investing in distressed securities, sectors, and emerging markets; and short selling are each successful in particular macro environments and not others. A large directional bet may be warranted when extraordinary sets of macro conditions create an extreme price disparity or a persistent trend that makes a particular investment approach very effective. In addition, many specialist strategies are difficult for managers in charge of huge amounts of assets. Macro managers are able to take advantage of the opportunities produced by extraordinary sets of macro conditions because they have the flexibility to move large amounts of capital into a variety of different investment positions in a timely fashion.

It may seem that macro strategies have nothing in common with the other hedge fund strategies, but that is because it is a general approach rather than a specialized approach. Although the differences are certainly obvious, the similarities are more important for the purposes of this book. Like the other hedge fund strategies, macro investing leverages a strategic advantage and the flexibility to move from opportunity to opportunity, without restriction, to extract investment returns from market inefficiencies that cannot always be accessed by traditional investment approaches that are more restricted. George Soros once said of his style of investing, "I don't play the game by a particular set of rules; I look for changes in the rules of the game."[1]

CORE STRATEGY

Macro investors look for the extraordinary sets of macro conditions that occur only occasionally and that make a particular investment approach very effective while those conditions persist. They enjoy a great deal of investment policy flexibility and will therefore invest on a leveraged base across multiple sectors, markets, instruments, and trading styles as the macro conditions dictate. They invest based on macroeconomic analysis and forecasts of changes in interest rates, currency markets, equity markets, and global political and economic policy. They often pursue other hedge fund strategies while waiting to take the large, opportunistic directional positions for which they are more famous. Generally, macro investors look for unusual price fluctuations. They refer to such extremes as **FAR-FROM-EQUILIBRIUM CONDITIONS**. In such situations, market participants' perceptions and the actual state of affairs are very far removed from one another and create a persistent price trend. The macro investor makes profits by identifying where in the economy the risk premium has swung farthest from equilibrium, investing in that situation, and recognizing when the extraordinary conditions that made that particular approach so profitable have deteriorated or have been counteracted by a new trend in the opposite direction. For the macro investor, timing is everything.

INVESTMENT PROCESS

Think of prices as falling on a bell curve. Macro investors argue that most price fluctuations in financial markets fall within one standard deviation of the mean. They consider this volatility to be the ordinary state of affairs, which does not offer particularly good investment opportunities. However, when price fluctuations of particular instruments or markets push out more than two standard deviations from the mean into the tails of the bell curve, an extreme condition occurs that may only appear once every two or three decades. As discussed in previous chapters, when market prices differ from the "real" value of an asset, there exists an **ARBITRAGE** opportunity. The macro investor makes profits by arbitraging such extreme price/value valuations back to normal levels. Some examples of far-from-equilibrium conditions that have occurred in recent years are the collapse of the tech industry in 2001 and 2002, the drop in the dollar beginning in 2002, junk bonds and emerging-market debt in the early 1990s, Eurodollars in 1994, and the Japanese yen during the late 1980s and again from 1995 to 1998.

Perhaps the most famous formulation of the macro theory of investing is George Soros's **BOOM-BUST SEQUENCE**. The sequence begins with an initial phase in which a prevailing macro trend becomes joined with a prevailing investor bias so that the two reinforce each other. If the trend can withstand external shocks such as a policy pronouncement and emerges strengthened, then it is in a period of acceleration. The moment of truth happens when market beliefs diverge from reality so much that their bias becomes recognized as a bias. This is followed by a twilight period, in which the trend is sustained by inertia but ceases to be reinforced by market participants and so flattens out. At some point (the **INFLEC-TION POINT**), this loss of faith causes a reversal in the trend, which had become dependent on an ever-stronger bias. The inflection point is usually marked or signaled by a major policy move, which then precipitates the crash, the point at which the market bias in the opposite direction of the original trend accelerates the return to normalcy. The art of macro investing lies in determining when a process has been stretched to its inflection point and when to become involved in its trend back to equilibrium.

MANAGER EXAMPLE

As with all investors, macro managers look to find situations with the optimum combination of risk, reward, and probability—ideally low risk and high return with high probability. Unlike many other strategies, however, their main edge is often not information collection, but their ability to exploit these asymmetric scenarios as a result of the broad scope of their mandate, and their ability to use leverage. One trade that many macro managers made was selling the dollar at various times since the middle of 2002. What made this trade difficult was that, to most observers, the dollar seemed overdue to fall once the stock market bubble burst in early 2000.

At that point, many economists and macro traders expected the dollar to fall because falling U.S. asset prices would deter critical foreign investment while the United States continued to have current account deficits in the hundreds of billions of dollars. However, the dollar defied conventional wisdom and continued to rally. As it turned out, despite the declines in U.S. assets values, foreign investors continued to reinvest the dollar surpluses and the dollar's value remained at or above the highs of the late 1990s.

There were chinks in the armor nonetheless. After the dramatic U.S. monetary easing through 2001, (including sharp moves post-9/11), the character of dollar flows changed. More and more purchases of U.S. dollars were coming from central banks that were less sensitive to investment returns than the private investors who came before them. Furthermore, the years of recycling of the U.S. current account deficits meant that private foreign holdings of U.S. assets (such as those of Asian and European pension funds) had ballooned. These foreign holdings generated a large asset/liability mismatch across currencies where foreign holders of U.S. assets had liabilities in their home currencies. Any rise in the perceived risk of U.S. assets or asset markets generally would leave the dollar vulnerable to repatriation of assets, or at the very least, slowing inflows.

These factors came together in the second and third quarters of 2002. First, the weight of the monetary ease began to be felt. The dollar began to fall initially and broke through many conventional momentum measures. This kind of technical confirmation of a macro investor's fundamental idea typically is a signal to become more aggressive in the trade because the technical indicators allow a manager to clearly define where he is right or wrong, allowing for tighter stop losses. At these points, the risk, reward, and probability of a major move is the most ideal.

In the months that followed, a confirming catalyst appeared in the form of U.S. corporate accounting scandals. As assets of all types were perceived to be more risky, negative dollar flows accelerated, and early positions entered on the initial price breakout began to pay multiples of the initial risk. Many macro managers will begin to reduce positions at these points of dynamic movement even though the fundamental confirmation of the trade has arrived. Macro position management again is focused on asymmetric risk and reward so when the move accelerates, the asymmetry is reduced. This opportunistic adjustment of positions, which is at the heart of macro trading, continues as the move unfolds over time.

MANAGER EXAMPLE

One of the key factors influencing Russia's creditworthiness was the collapse of most Asian economies in 1997. The impact on global demand was material and resulted in sharply lower oil prices in 1998, which hurt Russia's balance of payments position. Because Russia relies on oil and energy prices for the majority of the hard currency revenue it uses to service external debt, the collapse in oil and energy prices was significant and meant that Russians would have to reduce their spending or see their capacity to service debt meaningfully decline. But, when Russian export prices were declining, Russia was actually increasing its consumption of imports (i.e., spending), which was unsustainable.

Russia also had a fixed exchange rate at the time against the U.S. dollar. As oil prices plunged, it became clear that Russia would have to break its exchange rate peg. The exchange rate was becoming increasingly overvalued, thereby keeping exports (and hence its ability to generate hard currency revenue) depressed. This steadily worsening situation led us to short Russian debt and currency months prior to the actual crisis. Ultimately, the Russian government was forced to devalue the exchange rate and default on local currency debt and Soviet-era debt, bringing Russian hard currency debt prices to default-like levels.

In the aftermath of the devaluation/default, underlying conditions changed by nearly 180 degrees. Russian imports collapsed as the economy collapsed. Meanwhile, Russian exports increased materially as oil prices rose. This combination of events left Russia with an undervalued exchange rate and a nonexistent need for financing, as it defaulted on one segment of debt and its higher exports brought in increased levels of hard currency revenue. As a result of the much lower prices and the much-improved conditions, macro investors switched from bearish to bullish as the markets were selling off, seemingly because the market was focused on political chaos (i.e., willingness-to-pay issues). Since market sentiment lagged developments and our balance of payments process led them, macro investors profited from these moves. In fact, because of similar inefficiencies in pricing Russian debt and currency, macro investors were able to add value from Russia as a result of mispricings for five straight years, in up and down markets.[2]

ADVANTAGES/DISADVANTAGES

Macro investors are not confined by a market niche, enjoying the flexibility and objectivity to move from opportunity to opportunity and trend to trend. This is particularly important because macro investors' asset size per fund tends to be significantly large. Asset size potentially can hinder the execution of strategy, but macro investing makes asset size an advantage rather than a hindrance. Macro investing is often portrayed as risky directional betting or speculating. This view is reinforced by the large profits and losses that these funds generate when concentrated leveraged bets pay off—or fail.

PERFORMANCE

As shown in **FIGURE 10.1**, from January 1990 to December 2004, macro hedge funds recorded an average annualized return of 16.26 percent, with an annualized standard deviation of 8.45. These returns were more than 5 percent greater than the S&P 500 index of blue-chip stocks recorded for the same period, with significantly lower volatility. Since 1990, macro funds have returned positive performance in fourteen of the fifteen years. Seven of the years have produced returns greater than 15 percent: 1991–1993, 1995, 1997, 1999 and, most recently, 2003. Other than 1994, when they recorded a loss of 4.31 percent, macro funds have exhibited consistently high performance, with a 0.38 correlation to general stock market price changes since 1990. While total assets in the macro category have dropped from the largest to the fourth largest of all the strategies since 1998, the performance has carried the strategy with an annualized return of 9.21 percent during the six-year period.

FIGURE 10.2 shows the total strategy assets and net asset flows per year from 1990 to 2004 for macro. Each year-end asset total equals the previous year's asset size plus annual performance plus net asset flows. Since the end of 1997, the strategy has lost over $87 billion in net outflows, driving down the total asset size by 40 percent, to $107 billion as of the end of 2004.

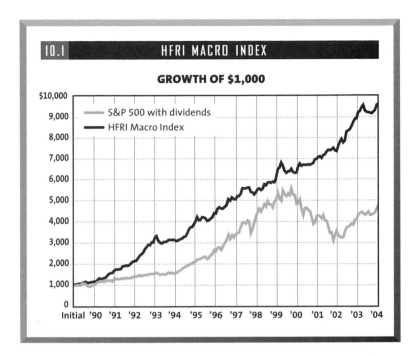

10.1 HFRI MACRO INDEX

GROWTH OF $1,000

S&P 500 with dividends
HFRI Macro Index

Initial '90 '91 '92 '93 '94 '95 '96 '97 '98 '99 '00 '01 '02 '03 '04

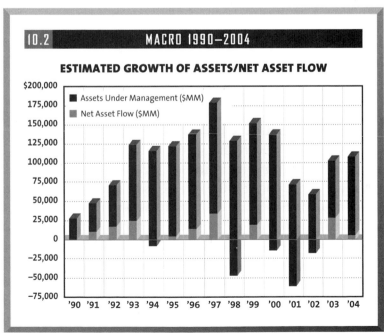

10.2 MACRO 1990–2004

ESTIMATED GROWTH OF ASSETS/NET ASSET FLOW

Assets Under Management ($MM)
Net Asset Flow ($MM)

'90 '91 '92 '93 '94 '95 '96 '97 '98 '99 '00 '01 '02 '03 '04

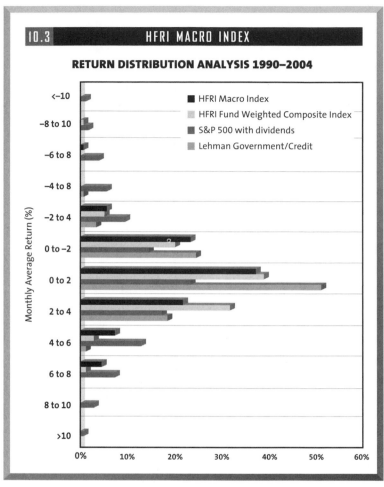

FIGURE 10.3 shows the return distribution for macro compared to the overall hedge fund industry, stocks, and bonds. Since 1990, just over a third of the strategy's monthly performance falls within the 0 to 2 percent return range. Unfortunately, on the flip side, almost a quarter of the overall returns have registered flat to –2 percent returns. And while the strategy has not returned a negative annual performance since 1994, macro funds have struggled to reach the mammoth performance returns of the early 1990s.

FIGURE 10.4 shows the average upside and downside capture since 1990 for macro funds. During positive-market months, the strategy has paced well with the overall hedge fund indus-

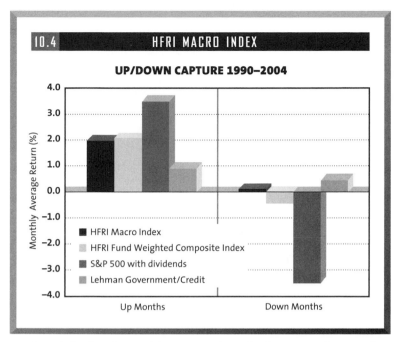

10.4 HFRI MACRO INDEX

UP/DOWN CAPTURE 1990–2004

Legend:
- HFRI Macro Index
- HFRI Fund Weighted Composite Index
- S&P 500 with dividends
- Lehman Government/Credit

Y-axis: Monthly Average Return (%)

X-axis categories: Up Months, Down Months

try, but it is the downside protection during negative-market months that has kept macro funds as an attractive investment, averaging a respectable 0.11 percent positive return in down months.

SUMMARY POINTS

PROFIT OPPORTUNITY

◆ Macro managers are able to take advantage of the extreme price valuations produced by extraordinary sets of macro conditions because they have the flexibility to move large amounts of capital into a variety of different investment positions in a timely fashion.

◆ Macro investors look for the extraordinary sets of macro conditions that occur only occasionally and that make a particular investment approach very effective while those conditions persist.

◆ Macro managers will often use leverage to express directional views.

SOURCE OF RETURN

◆ Macro investors make profits by identifying where in the economy the risk premium has swung farthest from equilibrium, investing in that situation, and recognizing when the extraordinary conditions that made that particular approach so profitable have deteriorated or been counteracted by a new trend in the opposite direction.

INVESTMENT PROCESS

◆ The art of macro investing is determining when a process has been stretched to its inflection point and when to become involved in its trend away from as well as back to normalcy.

◆ Macro investors enjoy the flexibility and objectivity to move from opportunity to opportunity and trend to trend.

KEY TERMS

Arbitrage. The simultaneous purchase and sale of a security or pair of similar securities to profit from a pricing discrepancy.

Boom-bust sequence. The process by which the value of an instrument or class of instruments is pushed to a valuation extreme, reverses itself, and crashes back to a more normal valuation.

Far-from-equilibrium condition. An unusual macro situation characterized by persistent price trends or extreme price valuations of particular financial instruments.

Inflection point. The point at which an extreme valuation reverses itself, usually marked or signaled by a major policy move.

Speculator. An investor who makes large directional bets on what financial markets will do next.

CHAPTER

11

Sector FUNDS

SECTOR STRATEGIES COMBINE core long holdings of equities with short sales of stock or sector indexes, confining their universe to a group of companies or a segment of the economy with similarities either in what is produced or who the market is. Managers combine fundamental financial analysis with industry expertise to identify the best profit opportunities in the sector. Net exposure of sector portfolios may range anywhere from net long to net short depending on market and sector-specific conditions. Managers generally increase net long exposure in bull markets for the sector and decrease net long exposure or may even be net short in bear markets for the sector. Generally, the short exposure is intended to generate an ongoing positive return in addition to acting as a hedge against a general sector decline. In a rising market for the sector, sector managers expect their long holdings to appreciate more than the sector and their short holdings to appreciate less than the sector. Similarly, in a declining market, they expect their short holdings to fall more rapidly than the sector falls and their long holdings to fall less rapidly than the sector. Profits are made when long positions appreciate and stocks sold short depreciate. Conversely, losses are incurred when long positions depreciate and/or the value of stocks sold short appreciates.

Sector funds can engage in one or more of the hedge fund strategies but limit their investment universe to a specific industry or other concentration. Although this strategy is categorized by the specific investment universe rather than investment activities and return source, most pursue equity hedge or event-driven approaches.

CORE STRATEGY

Investment managers who specialize in particular sectors or industries often invest in the sectors of the economy with long-term growth rates superior to the market in general, thus increasing their chances of identifying top-performing stocks. Many hold primarily long core positions in the companies that offer the best value in those industries. However, many sector hedge fund managers do not have such a bias toward their sector. They can profit in down markets by using their specialized knowledge, experience, and the flexibility to sell short the stocks of the worst companies, especially those also in the weakest sectors, and earn profit accordingly. In recent years, the most prominent and successful sector funds have been concentrated in the biomedical, health care, energy, information technology, media, and financial industries. Often, sector specialists are former or present participants in the industry in which they invest and can draw on industry expertise and industry contacts to which investors with a more general approach do not have access. In addition, they often count among their clients experts and current participants in the particular industry who are fluent in its processes and associated technologies. The sector fund formula is a simple one: combine fundamental financial analysis with industry expertise to create an informational advantage that allows the sector specialist to identify the best profit opportunities.

ONE MANAGER'S LOGIC OF SECTORS
Sector specialists usually look for at least two of the following three things in a sector: (1) high growth rates relative to the general market, (2) an industry in which the specialist holds a distinct informational advantage, and (3) the size and breadth to offer plentiful opportunities that are affected by a variety of factors.

Perhaps the most popular sector for hedge funds in recent times has been the energy sector. The current oil and gas situation has demand outstripping supply. Some managers believe that emerging markets demand may be underestimated and is at the very least not very well understood. Another manager has pointed out that U.S. gas reserves have recently been near all-time lows. Sixty-five percent of U.S. refined crude oil was imported by April of 2004, up from 28 percent in 1982.[1] Natural gas production was 12.8 percent lower in April of 2004 than a year earlier, and 20 percent lower than two years earlier.[2] Oil demand is forecasted by some sources to increase 33 percent from 2005 to 2020. Demand is on the rise at the same time the industry is coming off a long period of underinvestment. The total number of exploratory wells drilled in 2002 was less than in 1993. Thus, supply is tight in a capital-intensive industry where investment may take a number of years to yield results.

Today, sophisticated hedge funds can go both long and short, and pick from a variety of factors and companies in order to achieve significant returns. The trends detailed by managers will have an impact on different companies in different ways. The energy industry includes many subareas that will be affected in various ways, including oil, oil services, oil sands, oil transport, oil refining, gas power generation, gas transport, coal seam gas, coal bed methane, natural gas, gas pipelines, gas to liquids, coal, synthetics, and alternative energy.

INVESTMENT PROCESS

Many sector specialists try to identify **GROWTH STOCKS** with earnings and cash flow numbers that are selling at a significant discount to the company's intrinsic value. They also look for a **CATALYTIC EVENT**, or catalyst, to heighten investor interest in the company. A catalytic event could be, among other things, a new product launch, a regulatory approval, or a corporate restructuring. The logic is reversed when sector specialists are looking for stocks to sell short. In that case, they look for overvalued stocks and a catalytic event to expose the company's weaknesses. In addition, sector specialists remain aware of macroeconomic, monetary, and cyclical elements that affect the overall level of the equity market and the position of their particular sector relative to that market. Before making an investment, many sector specialists meet with company management to get to know the people behind the numbers and to understand their business model. To understand the company's position in the industry, they also meet with customers, suppliers, employees, and competitors.

An equity hedge style sector specialist's portfolio usually has two components: **CORE POSITIONS** and trading and hedging positions. Core positions are long-term positions that are rarely turned over and are a key source of investment returns.

The rest of the portfolio is composed of **TRADING POSITIONS**, short positions in overvalued companies, and **HEDGING** positions. These account for most of the portfolio turnover and allow sector hedge fund managers to make profits in both up and down markets. They may sell long positions when a company changes management or they cease to understand its business model. If they invest in a company because of a specific economic event, they will usually sell after that event has taken place. In sum, long positions will be reconsidered if there is a change in the original investment rationale.

MANAGER EXAMPLE

Energy infrastructure master limited partnerships (MLPs) are publicly traded limited partnerships that trade primarily on the NYSE. MLPs do not pay a corporate level tax, do pay out most of the available cash on an annual basis, and issue a Form K-1 versus a 1099. Due to their pass-through nature, depreciation, depletion, and other expenses are included within the K-1 and have the effect of reducing the taxability of distributions received from MLPs. As a result, most of an MLP's distributions would be treated as a return of capital or a reduction of cost basis for most investors. The downside is that the K-1 adds complexity to tax reporting, and MLPs have the ability to pass through unrelated business taxable income (UBTI), which can be a concern for many tax-exempt investors.

Kaneb Pipeline Partners, L.P. (KPP) is a publicly traded MLP that was formed in 1989. KPP owns two refined-products pipelines consisting of the 2,075 mile-long East Pipeline, which primarily services Kansas and Nebraska, and the West Pipeline, which services Wyoming and Montana into Colorado. Since 2000, KPP has completed three major pipeline and terminal acquisitions totaling $600 million, including an ammonia pipeline from Tessoro, a refined-products pipeline from Koch, and crude terminals in Nova Scotia, Canada, and Netherlands Antilles.

Organic growth on KPP's existing pipelines, the increases in cash flows expected from recent acquisitions, and a relatively high yield, have made KPP an attractive investment over the last several years. Annual distributions have increased over 20 percent during the last five years.

In September 2001, Kaneb Inc., a diversified company that owned the general partner of KPP, 5.1 million common units of KPP, and a refined products trading business, spun out these assets as a new company, Kaneb Services, LLC (KSL). The value of the KPP units owned by KSL represented more than $13.00 per share of KSL, which was trading for $11.69 at the time of the spin-out. In the opinion of Kayne Anderson Capital Advisors, the general partner interest was one of the more valuable assets of the company and was thus undervalued.

General partners of MLPs are interesting assets. The general partner of an MLP is incentivized to grow the distributions on the common units through the existence of incentive distribution rights. These rights offer the general partner the opportunity to participate in the increases in common unit distributions by receiving greater percentages of the incremental cash flows necessary to pay the higher distributions to common unit holders. For example, a general partner may receive 2 percent of the cash flows at a $2.00/unit distribution level, but may receive 25 percent or 50 percent of the incremental cash flows above $2.50/unit and $3.00/unit, respectively. In the case of KPP, the general partner's maximum incentive distribution was 30 percent, and it was quickly approaching that level at the time KSL was spun out.

Before the spin-out of KSL, Kayne Anderson Capital Advisors began modeling the valuations of KSL's three main assets relative to the public value of KPP, other MLPs, and other publicly traded general partners. The thesis was that KSL was inherently undervalued at the time, and that due to the incentive distribution received from KSL's general partner interest in KPP, it would experience significantly greater cash flow distribution growth, and therefore an investment in KSL would be more fruitful than would a direct investment in KPP. The latter has proven true, as KSL has grown its distributions (KSL is also formed as an MLP, and therefore, "distributions" is more appropriate than "dividends") at roughly double the rate of KPP.

Following the spin-out of KSL, Kayne Anderson Capital Advisors continued to model the relative value of KSL versus KPP, generally choosing to be long KSL, but at times long KSL and short KPP, and in some instances long both when Kayne Anderson Capital Advisors felt they were cheap versus other similar MLPs.

Acquisitions and, in particular, the related equity offering used to finance the acquisition would often have the effect of dampening the unit prices of KPP, but would also have the pro forma impact of increasing general partner cash flows. Therefore a common strategy around these times was to continue to own KSL and reduce exposure to KPP.

Most MLPs maintain investment-grade credit profiles. Acquisitions are typically financed 50 percent debt and 50 percent equity, a ratio that seems to please both Moody's and S&P. However, many MLPs initially finance acquisitions with shorter-term revolvers, preferring to announce a deal, let the markets determine the accretion of the acquisition, and then follow with an equity offering. This strategy may expose an MLP to a downgrade or placement on credit watch, as the MLP's credit ratios would temporarily deteriorate. Therefore, depending on circumstances, the advisor might choose to short the debt issued by KPP in anticipation of a credit downgrade, and also as a form of interest-rate hedge against the long positions in KSL and sometimes KPP. These debt shorts tended to be more opportunistic, impacted by the current yield and credit spread environment.

All good stories have to come to an end. On November 1, 2004, Valero Energy Partners, LP another publicly traded MLP, announced its intention to acquire KPP and KSL. The premiums to be paid over the prior day closing price by Valero for KPP and KSL are 21 percent and 38 percent, respectively. Since KSL's spin-out in September 2001, its unit price has appreciated approximately 270 percent, from $11.69 to $43.31, and it has paid distributions of nearly $6 per unit. During the same period of time, KPP's unit price has appreciated 101 percent from $30.57 to $61.50 (based on the currently anticipated exchange ratio between Valero and KPP at the closing of the merger), and it has paid distributions of nearly $10 per unit.[3]

RISK CONTROL

Sector specialists control risk by maintaining a balance between diversification and concentration in meaningful positions. If there are a variety of factors driving the sector that are independent of each other, the specialist will make investments that represent his understanding of the different factors so that different positions are not subject to the same fluctuations. Some sector specialists will also hedge their long positions with offsetting short positions or hedge the market by using index options. Another important risk consideration for sector specialists is investment time horizons. They try to align properly with the time horizons of companies in which they invest. If the manager invests in a company and the preferred investment horizon is shorter than that company's business plan warrants, the result is unintended volatility risks in the short term.

ADVANTAGES/DISADVANTAGES

Sector funds can be attractive investments because most sector fund candidate companies benefit from being in a fast-growing industry or sector. Top-performing companies can produce extremely high returns, and even mediocre ones may generate desirable returns. In addition, sector specialists usually bring a great deal of experience and expertise to the process of unlocking the best profit opportunities on both the long and short sides in a sector.

The sector portfolio allows investors to do their own diversification. If investors use sector funds as a component of a larger portfolio, they can decide how much to allocate to any given sector. More important, they can choose the manager for each sector who best matches their risk-reward requirements. Although generalists can be very successful, for many sectors a specialist may be better able to navigate the often complex businesses and available investment opportunities in that sector. Because they have a finite list of investment options, sector specialists have more time to examine industry details and build relationships with industry contacts and company management.

The limited focus of a sector fund can be seen as both an advantage and a disadvantage. A small sector provides relatively few investment options. In addition, because companies within a sector may be affected by related events, their investment returns may be highly correlated. If the entire sector takes a downturn, the sector specialist will often fall with it. The fortunes of a sector specialist often depend on technology life cycles and the caprices of product development. As a result, sector specialists must accept short-term portfolio volatility and sometimes find it difficult to sufficiently diversify their holdings. However, the limited universe of stocks in which they navigate means they can gain a more intimate knowledge of the industry. In larger sectors, managers can diversify across the many subsectors. The preponderance of subsectors makes it somewhat difficult to compare sector hedge fund managers in the traditional ways, so merely comparing the results of managers dealing in the same broad group of stocks is not always enough. A good comparison also takes into account the investment style of the managers and the use of leverage and hedging positions.

PERFORMANCE

As shown in **FIGURE 11.1**, from January 1990 through December 2004, the HFRI Sector (Total) Index recorded an average annualized return of 19.29 percent, the highest average annualized return of any of the hedge fund strategies over the same period. Furthermore, the annual standard deviation of 13.63 was 1 percent lower than that of the S&P 500 index. However, it is no more useful to evaluate all sector funds as a group than it is to combine the diverse hedge funds strategies. An overview of funds that are operating in some of the more prominent sectors provides a breakdown of the performance figures. From January 1992 through December 2004, hedge funds specializing in the financial

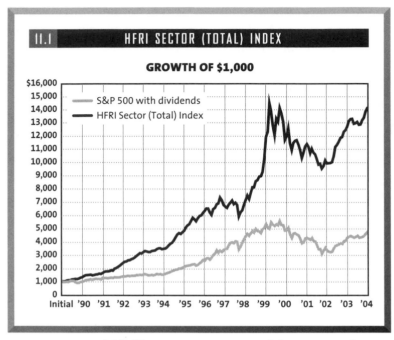

II.I   HFRI SECTOR (TOTAL) INDEX

GROWTH OF $1,000

Legend:
- S&P 500 with dividends
- HFRI Sector (Total) Index

sector averaged 19.60 percent returns, with an annual standard deviation of 11.52. After reporting back-to-back losing years in 1998 and 1999, they recorded an annualized return of 17.53 percent from 2000 to 2004. From January 1993 to December 2004, hedge funds specializing in health care and biotechnology averaged 17.66 percent returns, with an annual standard deviation of 22.67. This included a 20.45 percent loss in 2002 and 39.28 percent gain in 2003. From January 1991 to December 2004, hedge funds specializing in technology averaged 18.71 percent, with an annual standard deviation of 19.37. These returns included a 124.26 percent gain in the dot-com boom of 1999, but the funds lost an annual average of 14.89 percent the next three years before rebounding with a 25.41 percent gain in 2003. The figures for these different sectors expose some of the problems with defining the general principles of a sector strategy. Two points, mentioned earlier, must be emphasized: the logic changes from sector to sector, and these performance figures tell the story of sectors in only the most general way.

FIGURE 11.2 shows the total strategy assets and net asset flows per year from 1990 to 2004 for sector-specific funds. Driven mainly by the tech-sector explosion of the late 1990s and the stability of the financial sector during the early 2000s, the strategy's total asset size has boomed to over $42 billion as of the end of 2004.

FIGURE 11.3 on the following page shows the return distribution for sector compared to the overall hedge fund industry, stocks, and bonds. Sector funds represent one of only three hedge fund strategies that actually produced more monthly percentage gains between 2 and 4 percent than 0 and 2 percent since 1990.

FIGURE 11.4 shows the average upside and downside capture since 1990 for sector funds. Although the strategy outperforms the hedge fund industry as a whole during up months, sector funds tend to average a loss of 1.13 percent during down months, compared to the hedge fund industry's average 0.45 percent loss. In defense of sector-specific funds, they produce virtually the same positive performance as the stock market during up months, but suffer only a quarter of the loss during down months.

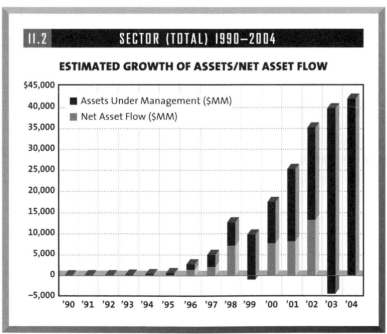

11.2 SECTOR (TOTAL) 1990–2004

ESTIMATED GROWTH OF ASSETS/NET ASSET FLOW

■ Assets Under Management ($MM)
■ Net Asset Flow ($MM)

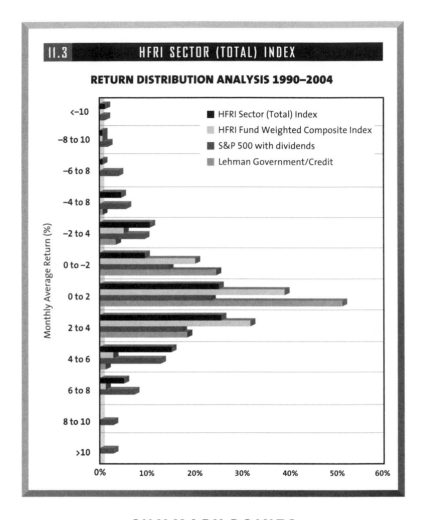

11.3   HFRI SECTOR (TOTAL) INDEX

RETURN DISTRIBUTION ANALYSIS 1990–2004

- HFRI Sector (Total) Index
- HFRI Fund Weighted Composite Index
- S&P 500 with dividends
- Lehman Government/Credit

SUMMARY POINTS

PROFIT OPPORTUNITY

◆ Sector specialists look for at least two of the following three things in a sector: high growth rates relative to the general market, an industry in which the specialist holds a distinct informational advantage, and the size and breadth to offer plentiful opportunities that are independently affected by a variety of factors.

◆ By investing in a sector that is outgrowing other sectors, managers can increase their chances of identifying top-performing stocks. Most companies benefit from being in a fast-growing industry. The top-performing companies can produce extremely

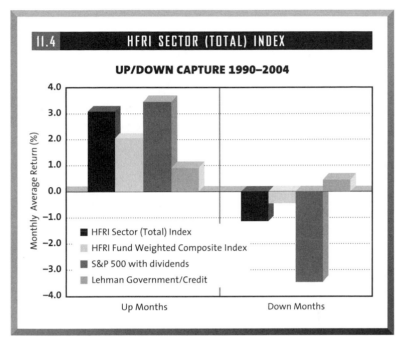

II.4 **HFRI SECTOR (TOTAL) INDEX**

UP/DOWN CAPTURE 1990–2004

Monthly Average Return (%)

- HFRI Sector (Total) Index
- HFRI Fund Weighted Composite Index
- S&P 500 with dividends
- Lehman Government/Credit

Up Months   Down Months

high returns, whereas even mediocre ones may generate desirable returns.

◆ Sector specialists may sell short to hedge or profit in down markets.

◆ The sector portfolio allows investors to handle their own diversification.

◆ A sector fund's limited focus can be seen as an advantage and a disadvantage. A small sector provides relatively few investment options, but the specialist gains an intimate knowledge of that universe of stocks.

SOURCE OF RETURN

◆ The sector fund formula is a simple one: combine fundamental financial analysis with industry expertise to create an informational advantage that allows the sector specialist to identify the best profit opportunities in the sector.

◆ An equity hedge style sector specialist's portfolio usually has two components: core positions and trading and hedging positions. Core positions are long-term positions that are rarely turned over and are a key source of investment returns. The rest of the portfolio will be made up of trading positions: short positions in overvalued companies and hedging positions that account for most of the portfolio's turnover and allow sector hedge fund managers to make profits in both up and down markets.

INVESTMENT PROCESS

◆ Sector specialists use earnings and cash flow numbers to identify stocks within their area of expertise that are selling at a significant discount to the company's intrinsic value.

◆ Sector specialists also look for a catalytic event that will heighten investor interest in the company, and thus reduce the current discount to intrinsic value.

KEY TERMS

Catalytic event. A near-term event, such as a new product launch, that heightens investor interest in a company.

Core positions. Long-term positions in growth stocks from which managers derive the majority of their profits.

Growth stock. A stock that an investor believes will appreciate because the company's output and earnings will grow.

Hedging. The taking of positions to offset changes in economic conditions falling outside the core investment idea, such as the purchase of index options to offset changes in the overall level of the equity market.

Sector. A group of companies or segment of the economy that is similar in either its product or its market, for example, health care, biotechnology, financial services, or information technologies.

Trading positions. Opportunistic positions designed to take advantage of short-term market mispricings and inefficiencies.

CHAPTER

12

Equity
HEDGE

E QUITY HEDGE, also known as long/short equity, combines core long holdings of equities with short sales of stock, stock indexes, or derivatives related to equity markets. Net exposure of equity hedge portfolios may range anywhere from net long to net short, depending on market conditions. Managers generally increase net long exposure in bull markets and decrease net long exposure (or may even be net short) in bear markets. Generally, the short exposure is intended to generate an ongoing positive return in addition to acting as a hedge against a general stock market decline. Stock index put options or exchange-traded funds are also often used as a hedge against market risk.

In a rising market, equity hedge managers expect their long holdings to appreciate more than the market and their short holdings to appreciate less than the market. Similarly, in a declining market, they expect their short holdings to fall more rapidly than the market falls and their long holdings to fall less rapidly than the market. Profits are made when long positions appreciate and stocks sold short depreciate. Conversely, losses are incurred when long positions depreciate and/or the value of stocks sold short appreciates. Equity hedge's source of return is similar to that of traditional stock-picking trading strategies on the upside, but it uses **SHORT SELLING** and **HEDGING** to attempt to outperform the market on the downside. Some equity hedge managers are value oriented, others are growth oriented, while a third category is opportunistic depending on market conditions.

Of all the hedge fund strategies, equity hedge strategies have the purest lineage. They are a direct descendent of A. W. Jones's original "hedge" fund. However, as was the case in the initial hedge fund rush of the late 1960s, during the bull market of the 1990s many practitioners forwent the short exposure that was characteristic of the original funds. Thus, the present incarnations of the strategy can be roughly divided into two groups: equity hedge and equity nonhedge. The equity hedge strategists who are true to the original formulation retain the old structure that combined a core leveraged long stock position with short exposure that protects against downside risk. Equity nonhedge strategists use a strategy similar to traditional long-only strategies but with the freedom to use varying amounts of **LEVERAGE**. Although most of them reserve the right to sell short, short sales are not an ongoing component of their investment portfolios, and many have not carried short positions at all. This chapter discusses equity nonhedge as a variation of the equity hedge strategy. At heart, these are both concentrated stock-picking strategies, one that hedges market risk by augmenting core long positions with short positions, and the other that forgoes that short exposure. The freedom to use leverage, take short positions, and hedge long positions is a strategic advantage that differentiates equity hedge strategists from traditional long-only equity investors.

CORE STRATEGY

Equity hedge strategists combine core long holdings with short sales of stock or stock index options. Investors sell stock short if they expect the price of the stock to decline. To sell a stock short, an investor borrows that stock and immediately sells it on the market with the intention of buying it back later at a lower price and returning it to the lender. If the price of the stock declines, then the investor makes profits on the difference between the selling price and the cost of the replacement stock. The cash proceeds from the sale are held in a money market account, earning interest. Short positions can be taken as specific sources of absolute profit or in conjunction with a long position to hedge out a specific risk common to both positions. Many equity hedge strategists maintain a basket of shorted stocks as a hedge against a drop in the overall market. To the degree that they match their long holdings with short positions, the matched portion of the portfolio may be called **WITHIN THE HEDGE**. In theory, the long positions will generate profits in a rising market, and short positions will generate profits in a declining one. Therefore, for the long and short positions within the hedge, the fund manager has eliminated any systemic risk associated with the market as a whole and shifted the emphasis to the ability to pick stocks.

In a rising market, equity hedge strategists expect their long holdings to appreciate more than the market and their short holdings to appreciate less than the market. Similarly, in a declining market, they expect their short positions to fall more rapidly than the market falls and their long holdings to fall less rapidly than the market. The idea is to take long positions in stocks that will outperform the market and sell short stocks that will underperform the market.

When investors borrow funds to increase the amount they have invested in a particular stock position, they are using **LEVERAGE**. Investors use leverage when they believe that the return from the stock position will exceed the cost of the borrowed funds. Investors who use leverage increase the risk of their investment; therefore, they usually use it only in extremely low-risk situations. Most equity hedge strategists use leverage. Leverage allows them to add new stocks to the portfolio without waiting to sell off something else first. Aggressive equity hedge managers will use leverage to move quickly to exploit investment opportunities. More conservative equity hedge managers will use leverage more sparingly, but the deployment of some amount of leverage is a characteristic of equity hedge funds in general.

Equity hedge specialists are aware that the prices of individual stocks can, and often do, move in response to factors unrelated to the direction of the overall market. Thus, if they pick their stocks well, it is entirely possible for equity hedge managers to make money on both long positions and short positions on the same day. Theoretically, they can make money in both up and down markets because they retain the flexibility to go both long and short. Equity hedge fund managers' source of return is similar to that of traditional stock pickers on the upside, but they use short selling and hedging to outperform the market on the downside. Although equity hedge portfolios may not outperform a traditional long-only stock portfolio in a bull market, over time they should outperform the stock market on a risk-adjusted basis because they will outperform the stock market in down and sideways markets.

INVESTMENT PROCESS

Equity hedge strategists will adjust their **NET MARKET EXPO-SURE** as market conditions warrant. In a bull market, they will try to be net long. In a bear market, they will try to have less market exposure, possibly going net short. A simplified version of the formula that they use to calculate market exposure is shown below:

$$\text{Market exposure} = \frac{\text{Long exposure} - \text{Short exposure}}{\text{Capital}}$$

For example, if a fund manager had $1,000,000 in capital to invest and borrowed a further $500,000, then if he took long positions worth $900,000 and short positions worth $600,000, the net market exposure would be 300,000/1,000,000, or 30 percent net long. Conservative fund managers will mitigate risk by keeping market exposure between 0 and 100 percent. More aggressive funds may magnify risk by exceeding 100 percent exposure or, alternatively, by maintaining a net short exposure. Some fund managers prefer to concentrate on stock picking and thus will pay little or no attention to macro trends. The aggregate market exposure of their portfolios will depend on whether they are finding better investment opportunities on the long or the short side. These managers take short positions primarily as opportunities to make investment returns, rather than merely to hedge against market decline. This is usually called a **TRADING POSITION** as opposed to a hedging position. Although almost all equity hedge managers vary the long/short relationship in their portfolios, it is important to take note of whether market exposure is a result of hedging or trading positions.

Equity hedge strategists generate investment ideas by reading newspapers and trade journals, talking to clients and partners, attending conferences and road shows, and keeping in constant contact with industry experts. They narrow their focus to the companies with the best fundamental outlook, the best dynamic within a group of related companies, and the best investment potential on the individual level. Managers evaluate both the business and the valuation of the business in the marketplace. Before allocating any capital to an idea, most equity hedge managers make site visits to assess the energy, ability, and commitment of the company's management and speak with competitors, suppliers, and customers to verify the company's position within its industry. They attempt to be early in identifying economic trends that will have a major impact on the market. As with any other investment strategy, investment ideas that are not yet widely known are the best ideas. In addition, they seek an identifiable catalyst that will focus the investment community's attention on the company, such as better-than-expected earnings or positive press releases. What does this mean for stock pickers? It means they must look hard at businesses to judge what it will take for them to succeed in the future, identify which companies have the most of it, and decide what price should be paid for the stock. In different industries, this could mean different things. It might be product development in one industry and marketing in another. In any case, equity hedge strategists evaluate companies and the valuations assigned to them. When the price and the manager's perception of business fundamentals align, there is an opportunity to take a position.

MANAGER EXAMPLE

Williams Companies has been one of Matador Capital Management's largest long positions since December 2002 and was one of the strongest performers in the portfolio during calendar years 2003 and 2004. When Matador Capital Management first entered the position, Williams was undergoing a major financial restructuring and was in the process of selling assets to improve its liquidity and avoid a potential bankruptcy filing. Matador Capital Management's view at the time was that the company had a high probability of successfully executing its restructuring plan and, once completed, it would be left with very attractive assets and businesses that the investment community was effectively ignoring. When looking at the various lines of business in which Williams participated, it was possible to parse the company into a few broad segments: exploration and production (E&P), midstream, pipelines, and merchant energy. Although Matador Capital Management had a high level of conviction in the work on Williams, there was concern about broader, possibly unforeseeable industry issues. In order to protect investors' capital against an unforeseeable industry event (much like the event that resulted in the opportunity in the first place—the demise of Enron), Matador Capital Management was compelled to identify businesses that correlated well with Williams's various lines of businesses from a macro perspective but that were fundamentally inferior. That search led to a variety of companies, such as Dyengy, Mirant, El Paso, and others, none of which was a perfect hedge against the entire Williams position, but each of which seemed inferior to one or two of Williams's underlying businesses (i.e., pipelines in the case of El Paso), providing an opportunity to profit on the short side, all things being equal, and to otherwise protect against a negative macro trend that might adversely impact the long holding. The end result: Williams has been a terrific performer on the long side of the portfolio for all the reasons originally contemplated and more, and various shorts have been profitable as well while providing protection against unforeseeable events. Approaching 2005, the Williams story evolved, and Matador Capital Management continued to be excited about the prospects for the company while actively hedging out the business risks in an effort to avoid that next "unforeseeable" macro industry event.[1]

MANAGER EXAMPLE

In mid-2003, Driehaus Capital Management began accumulating a long position in a wireless messaging company named Research in Motion, popular for its wireless email devices. It was a small company that was monitored closely since it came public in 1998. Research in Motion has several compelling competitive advantages, a superior technology with more than two hundred patents, IT-friendly support capabilities, and many carrier distribution relationships. For several years the stock did well, but the company's device remained an early adaptor or niche market product. Then in early 2003, it combined the two key wireless applications, voice and e-mail, into one easy-to-use, almost addictive smart phone, the Blackberry. Since that time, the Blackberry has become a mass market, must-have product for business users. At the same time, Research in Motion's subscribers, revenue, and earnings accelerated dramatically.

Subscribers increased from 534,000 in February 2003 to 1.07 million in February 2004 to more than 2 million in November 2004. Globally, the carrier's partners have grown from twenty-five in early 2004 to seventy in late 2004, and are expected to exceed one hundred carriers in 2005. Revenue has exploded from $594.7 million in 2004, to $1.3 billion estimated in 2005, to $2.2 billion estimated in 2006. Earnings have grown from $.32 in 2004, to an estimated $2.00 in 2005, and an estimated $2.90 in 2006. Quarter after quarter, the company has had strong positive earnings surprises, and large upward estimate revisions.

Research in Motion was identified as a scaleable, sustainable, recurring revenue business model with superior technology, attacking a huge, global open-ended market opportunity. Management has executed almost flawlessly as the stock has become a huge winner, up roughly nine times since Driehaus Capital Management's first purchase.[2]

RISK CONTROL

Equity hedge strategists expose themselves primarily to stock-picking risks. By doing fundamental, bottom-up research on the companies in which they invest, equity hedge managers try to avoid the disastrous state of affairs of having their long positions dropping while their short positions are rising. For those managers who carefully adjust their long and short exposures as the market dictates, there is the risk of getting caught too net long in a market decline or too net short in a market rally. Although the portion of an equity hedge port-folio that is within the hedge may approximate market neu-trality, at any given time managers can lose money on both their long and short positions. The portion of the portfolio that is not hedged is, of course, susceptible to all the various caprices of the market. The equity hedge manager will hedge as many of these risks as possible with specific hedging posi-tions. She may hedge against exposure to a specific industry by **PAIR TRADING**. When managers trade in pairs, they go long a stock in a particular industry and short a stock in the same industry, so that in the case of a systemic drop in the prices of the industry as a whole, the long and short positions offset each other. In addition, equity hedge managers will diversify their portfolios across industries and sectors to ensure that happenings in any one industry do not have too much effect on the portfolio as a whole.

Many equity hedge strategists use position limits to control the impact that any one position can have on the portfolio as a whole. If a position grows in market value and becomes a larger weighting in the portfolio, then they may trim it back. They will sell those stocks that reach their target valuations or those for which they lose conviction about the underlying growth qualities that originally prompted the position. When the price of a stock does not behave as expected, the manager reassesses the position. Generally, equity hedge managers are more tolerant of unexpected price moves in core holdings than in trading positions.

ADVANTAGES/DISADVANTAGES

As shown in **FIGURE 5.1**, the major advantage of an equity hedge strategy is its ability to hold both long and short positions. This allows the strategy to generate returns in both up and down markets. Proponents will argue that nobody knows exactly where the market is going next or why. Therefore, they will give up a certain amount of the upside to soften the blow of down markets. Equity hedge funds can generate returns that are similar to traditional long-only, stock-picking invest-ment vehicles but with less volatility and less market exposure

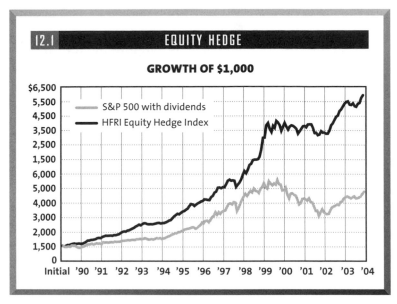

12.1   **EQUITY HEDGE**

GROWTH OF $1,000

S&P 500 with dividends
HFRI Equity Hedge Index

because of the short exposure. Equity hedge funds can generate returns that do not fluctuate as violently as traditional long-only funds. There is, of course, no guarantee that equity hedge managers will be able to achieve this. No matter how hedged, this strategy requires a manager who can pick stocks well and correctly manage the long/short mix.

Bull markets entice many equity hedge managers to forgo any short exposure in favor of leveraged long-only positions. Bear markets have historically punished those managers who do so. To succeed over time, equity hedge managers must retain the discipline to match market exposure to market conditions.

FIGURE 12.2 shows the total strategy assets and net asset flows per year from 1990 to 2004 for equity hedge. The year-end asset total equals the previous year's asset size plus annual performance plus net asset flows. Although performance of the strategy has been predictably solid over the years, the overall growth in asset size can be attributed to the more than $190 billion in net inflows since 1996. A key indication of the strategy's overall impact on the hedge fund industry is the near 30 percent market share equity hedge funds held at the end of 2004.

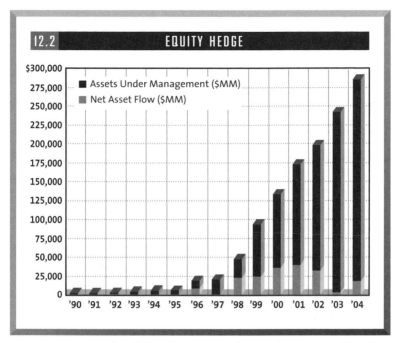

12.2   EQUITY HEDGE

■ Assets Under Management ($MM)
■ Net Asset Flow ($MM)

FIGURE 12.3 on the following page shows the return distribution for equity hedge compared to the overall hedge fund industry, stocks, and bonds. Note that although the majority of the strategy's monthly returns since 1990 have registered 0 to 2 percent returns, more than one-quarter of the months have produced returns between 2 and 4 percent. This compares favorably to the S&P 500 index, which has produced monthly returns between 2 and 4 percent only 17 percent of the time.

FIGURE 12.4 shows the average upside and downside capture since 1990 for equity hedge funds. Although the strategy outperformed the hedge fund industry as a whole during up months, equity hedge funds tend to average a loss of 0.56 percent during down months, compared to the hedge fund industry, which averages a 0.45 percent loss. And even though the strategy trails the stock market by less than 1 percent during up months, its average loss during down months is much better than the S&P 500, which averages almost 3 percent worse than equity hedge.

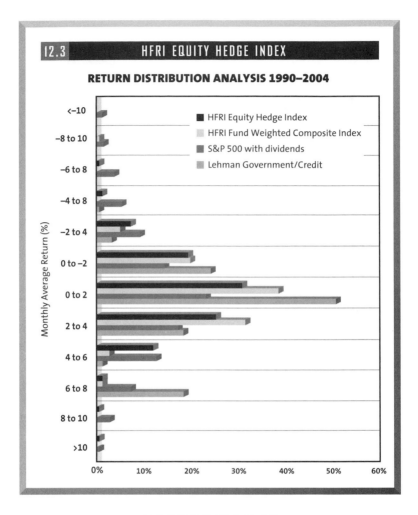

12.3   **HFRI EQUITY HEDGE INDEX**

RETURN DISTRIBUTION ANALYSIS 1990–2004

- HFRI Equity Hedge Index
- HFRI Fund Weighted Composite Index
- S&P 500 with dividends
- Lehman Government/Credit

Monthly Average Return (%): <-10, -8 to 10, -6 to 8, -4 to 8, -2 to 4, 0 to -2, 0 to 2, 2 to 4, 4 to 6, 6 to 8, 8 to 10, >10

0% 10% 20% 30% 40% 50% 60%

PERFORMANCE

As shown in **FIGURE 12.5**, from January 1990 to December 2004, equity hedge funds registered average annualized returns of 17.60 percent, with an annualized standard deviation of 8.93. For the same period, equity nonhedge funds registered average annualized returns of 16.37, with an annualized standard deviation of 14.29. Both groups had higher returns than the S&P 500 index of blue-chip stocks, and equity hedge funds achieved them with much less volatility. The downside protection characteristic of equity hedge funds made for slightly lower returns than equity nonhedge funds in the rising stock

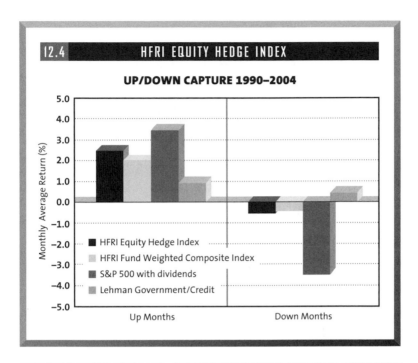

| 12.4 | HFRI EQUITY HEDGE INDEX |

UP/DOWN CAPTURE 1990–2004

- HFRI Equity Hedge Index
- HFRI Fund Weighted Composite Index
- S&P 500 with dividends
- Lehman Government/Credit

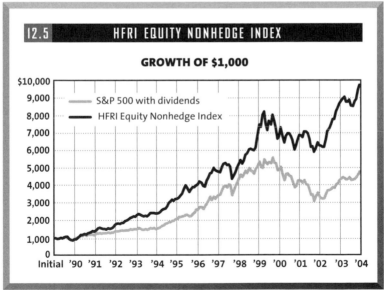

| 12.5 | HFRI EQUITY NONHEDGE INDEX |

GROWTH OF $1,000

- S&P 500 with dividends
- HFRI Equity Nonhedge Index

markets of 2003 and 2004 but more than made up for it in the falling market in 2000, gaining 9 percent while equity nonhedge funds lost 9 percent. Equity hedge fund returns are less sensitive to price changes in the overall stock market than are equity nonhedge returns, as evidenced by correlation statistics of 0.66 and 0.79, respectively.

SUMMARY POINTS

PROFIT OPPORTUNITY

◆ The flexibility to use leverage, take short positions, and hedge long positions is a strategic advantage that differentiates equity hedge strategists from traditional long-only equity investors.

◆ Equity hedge strategists combine core long holdings with short sales of stock or stock index options. They maintain a basket of shorted stocks as a hedge against a drop in the overall market.

◆ By having equal amounts of long and short positions within the hedge, the fund manager has eliminated any systemic risk associated with the market as a whole and shifted the emphasis to her ability to pick stocks.

SOURCE OF RETURN

◆ Aggressive equity hedge managers will use leverage to move quickly to exploit investment opportunities. More conservative equity hedge managers will use leverage sparingly, but the deployment of some amount of leverage is a characteristic of equity hedge funds in general.

◆ Theoretically, equity hedge specialists can make money in both up and down markets because they retain the flexibility to go both long and short.

◆ Although equity hedge portfolios may not outperform a traditional long-only stock portfolio in a bull market, over time they should outperform the stock market on a risk-adjusted basis because they should outperform in down and sideways markets.

INVESTMENT PROCESS

◆ Equity hedge strategists will adjust their net market exposure as market conditions dictate. In a bull market, they will try to be net long. In a bear market, they will try to have less market exposure.

◆ Equity hedge strategists evaluate companies and the valuations assigned to them. When price and the manager's perception of business fundamentals align, there is an opportunity to take a position.

◆ Although the portion of an equity hedge portfolio within the hedge may approximate market neutrality, at any given time managers can lose money on both their long and short positions. The portion of the portfolio that is not hedged is, of course, susceptible to all the various caprices of the market.

KEY TERMS

Hedging. The taking of positions to offset changes in economic conditions falling outside the core investment idea, such as purchasing a long position and a short position in a similar stock to offset the effect any changes in the overall level of the equity market will have on the long position.

Leverage. The practice of borrowing to add to an investment position when one believes that the return from the stock position will exceed the cost of the borrowed funds.

Net market exposure. The percentage of the portfolio exposed to market fluctuations because long positions are not matched by equal dollar amounts of short positions. In general terms,

$$\text{Market exposure} = \frac{\text{Long exposure} - \text{Short exposure}}{\text{Capital}}$$

Pair trading. A long position in one company "paired" with a short position in a very similar company in the same industry.

Short selling. Borrowing a stock on collateral and immediately selling it on the market with the intention of buying it back later at a lower price.

Trading position. Opportunistic position designed to take advantage of short-term market mispricings and inefficiencies rather than hedge against market decline.

Within the hedge. Phrase used to describe that portion of an equity hedge portfolio in which long positions are matched by equal amounts of short positions.

CHAPTER

13

Emerging
MARKETS

EMERGING MARKETS STRATEGIES involve primarily long investments in the securities of companies in countries with developing, or emerging, financial markets. Managers make particular use of specialized knowledge and an on-the-ground presence in markets where financial information is often scarce. Such knowledge and presence creates an informational edge that allows them to take advantage of mispricings caused by emerging markets inefficiencies. **GLOBAL INVESTORS** make profits by mining these markets for undervalued assets and purchasing them before the market corrects itself. Because of the less developed and less liquid nature of these markets, emerging markets securities are generally more volatile than securities traded in developed markets. Managers can be differentiated by country exposures and types of instruments utilized.

EMERGING MARKETS can be a difficult investment arena because they often present illiquidity, limited market infrastructure, few investment options, likelihood of political turmoil, and barriers to information access. As a result, investors expose themselves to far greater risks than when they invest in more developed markets. However, the same factors that create risks can also produce very attractive investment opportunities. Because they are primarily long-only, emerging markets strategies are widely shared by mutual fund managers and hedge fund managers.

CORE STRATEGY

There are different types of emerging markets, but all of them share certain investment features. The majority of these features are the direct result of **MARKET INEFFICIENCIES**. Market inefficiencies result when information on companies is unavailable, hard to come by, or wrong, and therefore assets often remain undervalued. Emerging markets specialists who can mine these markets for undervalued assets and purchase them before the market corrects itself may be rewarded with large investment returns.

Emerging markets are distinguished from both traditional agricultural economies and highly developed economies.

They are not simply making the historical transition from an agricultural to an industrialized economy. Rather, most emerging markets are developed to some extent, but their economy is being restructured on the free market model. The emerging market that was "created" in Russia in the 1990s is a perfect example. Many of these countries are learning to function by using the market model rather than some form of bureaucratic control. These markets are changing rapidly at both the macroeconomic level and the company level. They are not entirely trusted by free market investors and are usually trying to change investor sentiment through political and economic reforms. However, the reforms may not be uniformly applied or accepted.

Most emerging markets do not have sophisticated **SECURITIES MARKET INFRASTRUCTURE**, though many have vastly improved since the early 1990s. Securities market infrastructure includes accounting standards, the availability of trading and financial information, and sophistication of available financial instruments. Ideally, investors can obtain information about company decisions and actions and results the company has produced. Because this information is not easily available in emerging markets, specialists who are willing to generate their own research can find assets that the market has undervalued due to misperceived or limited information.

The dynamics of emerging markets can be hard to understand. Because these markets are highly volatile, participants often misjudge what they perceive to be economic decline and corruption. For example, Asia experienced a major shock to its economies and markets from 1997 to 1998. Some investors ignored Asia's problems prior to the difficulties, and some ignored its rebound potential after the crash. The Asian markets were slow to recover on a macroeconomic level, but that recovery presented excellent investment opportunities for diligent, value-oriented money managers who were not scared off by the macro trends. One approach that emerging markets specialists use to take advantage of such situations is to invest early in markets undergoing political and economic transformations. Often, the assets they select have excellent return potential, not only because they are strong companies, but also because the available information has been distorted by former political systems, a lack of technology, or underdeveloped capital market structures.

Some emerging markets specialists confine their analysis to country level dynamics using sovereign debt or equity indexes as a proxy for the fortunes of the country. Other emerging markets specialists concentrate on analyzing company fundamentals to identify investments that will allow them to extract the most value from inefficient emerging markets. They anticipate taking advantage of the lack of information flow that keeps all but a few enterprises out of the spotlight and many of them trading at a fraction of their intrinsic value. They must develop a mechanism for uncovering information, because by the time ideas become available to the broader marketplace, much of the potential for returns is gone. To uncover ideas, they not only read newspapers, periodicals, trade journals, and online sources but also travel through the countries to meet with local managers and government administrators and keep in constant communication with a network of brokers and contacts in the various markets to discuss political, economic, and market events and specific investment opportunities. The most important component of emerging markets research is an on-the-ground presence in the market, especially on-site visits before committing capital.

Emerging markets fund managers can invest globally, regionally (e.g., in Latin America), or in a single country (e.g., Russia). Other participants include those who allocate capital on a selective global basis, shifting their focus based on the changing attractiveness of different markets and asset classes. Some of them treat emerging markets as one potential asset class along with developed markets and fixed-income investments. They allocate capital to emerging markets when they believe that this asset class offers attractive potential returns compared with investment opportunities in other asset classes. Similarly, regional managers allocate among countries within their region where they perceive the greatest opportunities to invest, and single-country managers invest in the best choices within a single country.

INVESTMENT PROCESS

Emerging markets specialists try to capitalize on their ability to gather information in markets in which information does not yet flow as freely as in developed markets. To take advantage of this inefficiency, they engage in fundamental bottom-up research to identify undervalued stocks.

First, they develop early relationships with local brokers, industry participants, and government officials; identify recently or soon-to-be privatized companies; and look at financial reports of companies to understand the variability of their returns and their use of capital. Then they look at the business of the company and assess customers, competitors, and industry trends to determine what to expect in the future. Next, they try to quantify these various issues to determine whether the company is really creating value or simply growing by issuing equity and debt. Finally, after determining growth prospects, the appropriate rates to discount possible risks, and expected currency rates, they invest only if the stock appears to be undervalued to ensure a good margin of safety.

Emerging markets specialists use rigorous fundamental analysis to estimate the value of financial assets as they believe the market will reflect that estimated asset value in the long run. Thus, they make investments when they believe the market has misvalued a security and sell or reassess when the investment approaches their valuation targets. On the downside, they usually sell if a security declines more than a set stop-loss amount, declines for unexpected reasons, or a material factor changes their valuation. Emerging markets specialists buy securities when one or several of the following criteria are met: they are undervalued on an earnings and/or net asset basis, they have projected high growth in earnings and sales, they are dominant in a product or industry, management is progressive toward shareholder rights, they have good prospects for increased liquidity, or their financials are improving toward international accounting standards.

They sell securities when they are overvalued relative to their industry, market, or other companies in the fund; the market poses an unacceptable risk; or the fundamentals of the market, industry, or company deteriorate. They will give emerging markets positions more latitude than they would give a position in a developed market because emerging markets are prone to erratic behavior. Overall, emerging markets specialists try to grow the number of attractive positions in their portfolios while opportunistically paring out those that have become fully valued.

Emerging markets specialists may have biases toward particular industries. They look for businesses that they understand and management teams that are honest, dedicated to their work, and oriented toward a free market model. They seek diversity and invest across sectors they find promising and undervalued.

Many emerging markets have a limited financial infrastructure in place that doesn't allow money managers to short sell and hedge, but those that do charge high premiums. Some managers also hedge by shorting American Depositary Receipts (ADRs). An ADR is a U.S. exchange-traded security representing ownership in a foreign company. Hedging can help eliminate short-term volatility but may reduce the performance of a portfolio in the long run. In addition, factors other than fundamental value may temporarily move prices in emerging markets. Consequently, to short sell and hedge effectively emerging markets specialists must take into account liquidity flows, unexpected political developments, and changes in emerging markets risk premiums.

Money managers use leverage, when it is available, only when they think they can segment the risk of a particular investment and leverage the attractive risk. Flawed assessment of risk combined with leverage can be disastrous, as was witnessed in the erosion of hedge funds with leveraged investments in Russia during the collapse of its markets in the summer of 1998. Generally speaking, most emerging markets specialists do not use leverage because it would magnify the already highly volatile nature of these markets.

RISK CONTROL

Emerging markets are often thought of as inherently volatile and risky. An event can create correlations between asset positions that usually would not exist in more developed markets. Stock prices in emerging markets can become depressed for reasons other than the underlying company losing real value. Emerging markets specialists attempt to control these risks by diversifying the exposure in their portfolio across companies, industries, or markets; attempting to purchase assets at low valuation levels to provide a margin for error; segmenting risk by building a portfolio with different kinds of risk; and hedging long exposures where possible and appropriate. They try to buy assets with prices that will not all move together in response to market forces, and they are careful to make sure that long and short positions do not represent the same investment idea. Why? Because this uniformity would magnify risk rather than reduce it. Not only can a portfolio with diverse positions reap the rewards of long-term return potential, it can also withstand unexpected short-term pricing risks or risks peculiar to an individual market. To restrict maximum exposure to any one country or company, some emerging markets specialists use macroeconomic weighting models. In general, they keep enough positions in their fund to get the benefits of diversification, but few enough so that each position is meaningful to the fund's return. Although traditional investors manage risk by looking at volatility and how assets have correlated historically, that approach will often ignore new relationships developing between different assets. Consequently, in addition to traditional measures, some emerging markets specialists use their own forecasts and intuition to estimate future volatility and correlation between assets.

The inherent volatility in emerging markets is the price of having exposure to undervalued, high-growth investment opportunities. Because the emerging markets strategy is generally a long-run strategy, emerging markets specialists see the numerous steep declines that punctuate the general long-term ascent of these economies as great opportunities to buy cheap assets. In the long term, an emerging market usually becomes less volatile as it develops a larger private sector and domestic capital becomes a larger portion of market capitalization.

MANAGER EXAMPLE

In 1997, CODAD, a Colombian construction company, was rebuilding runway number one and building runway number two at the Eldorado airport in Bogotá. It issued a $165 million project finance bond in 1999, CODAD 10.19 percent of 5/31/11. It received a BBB rating by S&P in part due to a guarantee from a backing by AeroCivil, the Columbian equivalent of the Federal Aviation Authority in the United States. It was an emerging markets security with a BBB rating, so a number of rules-based investors purchased this issue. Because CODAD was no longer going to access the capital markets, over the next year or so it simply stopped sending financials to S&P and was removed from that rating system, while continuing "profitable" operations and continuing to pay its 10.19 percent coupon. Becoming a nonrated security forced the rules-based investors to liquidate their holdings.

Throughout this time, the fund's managers were aware of CODAD but had not made an investment. When managers received a call from a current block holder, the bonds were offered at 0.70; they declined to purchase the bonds but decided to update their research in order to value the securities. During the research they placed value in the fact that the bonds were partially backed by AeroCivil, and ultimately uncovered a healthy financial situation. They also realized S&P had dropped them due to a lack of reporting and not due to financial concerns. Under the terms of the bond's indenture this was a technical default without CODAD having actually missed any coupon payments. With these limited risks they believed the bonds were worth between 0.50 and 0.60. Thus, they went back to the seller and bid 0.50. After a number of negotiations, they purchased the bonds for 0.50 and began the process of contacting the company officials about reporting financials to S&P. When reporting was resumed, the bonds were promptly rated BB and ultimately sold to a rules-based investor for 0.77, booking a 54 percent profit over a nine-month time frame while receiving a 10.19 percent coupon.[1]

ADVANTAGES/DISADVANTAGES

Emerging markets can be difficult investments because of the paucity of information, poor accounting, lack of proper legal systems, unsophisticated local investors, political and economic turmoil, and companies with dishonest and unqualified managers. As a result, nonspecialists expose themselves to far greater risks when they invest in emerging markets than when they invest in more developed markets. However, emerging markets specialists find these markets appealing because of the profit possibilities that these same difficulties create. What some would call difficulties, emerging markets specialists call opportunities. A market that is volatile and unpredictable in the short run because information about companies is hard to come by and distortions run rampant is also a market full of mispricings; this creates significant openings for investors willing to do the extra work to uncover hidden situations. The structural changes in these markets create inefficiencies that are eventually driven out, yielding outstanding returns to those who invest in the early stages.

PERFORMANCE

As shown in FIGURE 13.1, from January 1990 to December 2004, emerging markets funds recorded average annualized returns of 15.37, with an annualized standard deviation of 14.93. These returns were nearly 4.5 percent higher than the S&P 500 index of blue-chip stocks for the same period, at virtually the same level of volatility. Although the strategy lost 33 percent in 1998, it rebounded strongly in 1999 with a 56 percent return. The three years that followed produced a total net return that was basically flat, but the strategy returned to its high-performance roots in 2003 and 2004, producing 39.36 and 18.8 percent, respectively. These figures underscore the

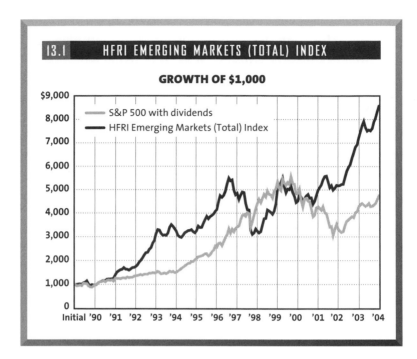

13.1   HFRI EMERGING MARKETS (TOTAL) INDEX

GROWTH OF $1,000

- S&P 500 with dividends
- HFRI Emerging Markets (Total) Index

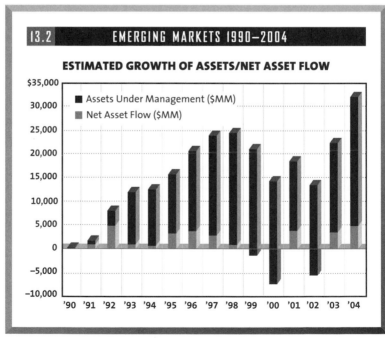

13.2   EMERGING MARKETS 1990–2004

ESTIMATED GROWTH OF ASSETS/NET ASSET FLOW

- Assets Under Management ($MM)
- Net Asset Flow ($MM)

point that investment in emerging markets comes with great risk, but more often than not, produces great reward.

FIGURE 13.2 shows the total strategy assets and net asset flows per year from 1990 to 2004 for emerging markets. The year-end asset total equals the previous year's asset size plus annual performance plus net asset flows. The continued imbalance of inflows and outflows from emerging markets illustrates the volatile nature of the strategy's investments. However, interest peaked in 2004 with inflows following the exceptional performance of 2003, when the strategy returned 39 percent.

FIGURE 13.3 on the following page shows the return distribution for emerging markets compared to the overall hedge fund industry, stocks, and bonds. Although the stock market has produced its majority of monthly returns in the 0 to 2 percent range, emerging markets has actually registered more of its returns in the 2 to 4 percent range. In addition, the strategy has produced flat-to-positive performance in over 68 percent of the months since January 1990, whereas the S&P 500 index has produced the same performance in less than 64 percent of the months over the same time span.

FIGURE 13.4 shows the average upside and downside capture since 1990 for emerging markets funds. Although the strategy outperforms the hedge fund industry as a whole during up months, it averages a loss of 1.24 percent during down months, as compared to the hedge fund industry, which averages a 0.45 percent loss. However, the strategy trails the stock market by less than 1 percent during up months, and its average loss during down months is almost a third less than that of the S&P 500.

SUMMARY POINTS

PROFIT OPPORTUNITY

◆ Emerging markets specialists use specialized knowledge and an on-the-ground presence in markets in which financial information is often scarce to create an informational advantage that helps uncover mispricings caused by emerging markets inefficiencies.

◆ Most emerging markets are developed to some extent, but their economies are being restructured on the free market model.

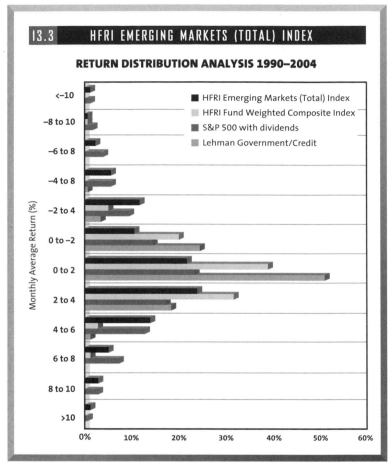

13.3   HFRI EMERGING MARKETS (TOTAL) INDEX

RETURN DISTRIBUTION ANALYSIS 1990–2004

Legend:
- HFRI Emerging Markets (Total) Index
- HFRI Fund Weighted Composite Index
- S&P 500 with dividends
- Lehman Government/Credit

Y-axis (Monthly Average Return (%)): <−10, −8 to 10, −6 to 8, −4 to 8, −2 to 4, 0 to −2, 0 to 2, 2 to 4, 4 to 6, 6 to 8, 8 to 10, >10

X-axis: 0%, 10%, 20%, 30%, 40%, 50%, 60%

◆ Because these markets are highly volatile, the participants often mistakenly perceive economic decline and corruption.

◆ Markets that are volatile and unpredictable in the short run, because information about companies is hard to come by and often distorted, are also markets full of mispricings that provide investment opportunities.

SOURCE OF RETURN

◆ Because emerging markets do not have sophisticated securities market infrastructure, specialists who are willing to generate their own information by doing their own research in the country can find assets that the market has undervalued due to a lack of, or poorly understood, information.

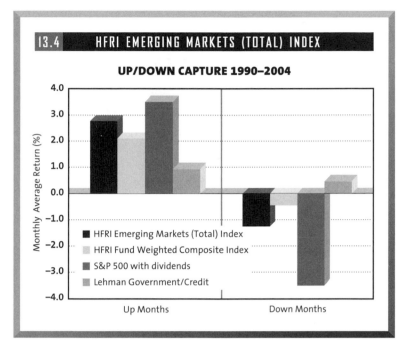

13.4 HFRI EMERGING MARKETS (TOTAL) INDEX

UP/DOWN CAPTURE 1990–2004

Monthly Average Return (%)

- ■ HFRI Emerging Markets (Total) Index
- ▨ HFRI Fund Weighted Composite Index
- ■ S&P 500 with dividends
- ▨ Lehman Government/Credit

Up Months   Down Months

◆ Emerging markets specialists can capture superior returns in the long run by venturing carefully into areas of the market in which information can be obtained but is not readily available. They must develop a mechanism for uncovering information, because by the time ideas become available in the marketplace, much of the potential for returns is gone.

◆ The inherent volatility in emerging markets is the price of having exposure to undervalued, high-growth investment opportunities.

◆ The structural changes in these markets create inefficiencies that are eventually driven out, yielding outstanding returns to those who invested in the early stages.

INVESTMENT PROCESS

◆ Emerging markets specialists concentrate on analyzing company fundamentals to extract the most value from inefficient emerging markets.

◆ The most important component of emerging markets research is an on-the-ground presence in the market.

◆ Often, the costs outweigh the benefits of short selling and hedging in emerging markets, but as these financial markets get more sophisticated and transaction costs drop, short selling and hedging will become more prevalent.

KEY TERMS

Emerging market. A market that is changing rapidly at the macro-economic and company level, usually because it is restructuring on the free market model.

Global investors. Investors who consider emerging markets to be one potential asset class, along with developed markets and fixed-income securities, and allocate capital to emerging markets when they believe that they offer attractive potential returns compared with other asset classes.

Market inefficiencies. Pricing disparities caused by a lack of information about a market or company or by a distortion of the information that is available.

Securities market infrastructure. The means of making investments and tracking financial information, including accounting standards, availability of trading and financial information, and sophistication of available financial instruments.

CHAPTER

14

Short
SELLING

MANAGERS WHO USE short selling strategies seek to profit from a decline in the value of stocks. The strategy involves selling a security the investor does not own in order to take advantage of a price decline the investor anticipates. Managers borrow the securities from a third party in order to deliver them to the purchaser. Managers eventually repurchase the securities on the open market in order to return them to the third-party lender. If the manager can repurchase the stock at a lower price than for what it was sold, a profit is made. In addition, managers earn interest on the cash proceeds from the short sale of stock. If the price of the stock rises, the manager incurs a loss. This strategy is seldom used as a stand-alone investment. Because of its negative correlation to the stock market it tends to produce outsize returns in negative environments, and can serve as disaster insurance in a multimanager allocation. Some managers may take on some long exposure but remain net short, or short biased. Short bias strategies are much less volatile than pure short selling exposure, but they do not provide as much upside in severely negative equity markets.

Many hedge fund strategies short sell as a component of strategy, usually as a hedging device or as a trading technique used to take advantage of short-term pricing inefficiencies. However, certain managers will construct short-only portfolios to take advantage of the fact that short selling can provide both fixed income and trading profits.

CORE STRATEGY

Short selling specialists borrow stock owned by a long investor and sell it on the market with the intention of buying it back later at a lower price after the market corrects itself. By selling the stock short, the short seller creates a restricted cash asset (the proceeds from the sale) and a liability (she must return the borrowed shares at some future date). Technically, a short sale does not require an investment, but it does require **COLLATERAL**, usually cash or relatively liquid U.S. Treasury securities. The short seller must pay any dividends paid out on the borrowed stock, so it can be costly to sell short stocks with a high yield. The proceeds from the short sale are then held as a restricted credit by the brokerage firm that holds the account and the short seller earns interest on it (the **SHORT INTEREST REBATE**). The amount of restricted credit is adjusted daily as the portfolio is **MARKED TO THE MARKET** (revalued at current market prices). As the market value of the shorted stock declines (becomes profitable), the restricted cash (the collateral) is released to become free cash, which earns a higher rate of return. If the value of the shorted stock increases (becomes unprofitable), the short seller must add to the restricted credit, either by selling other investments or by borrowing funds.

INVESTMENT PROCESS

The best way to demonstrate a short seller's source of returns is to contrast a short sale with a comparable long investment. The examples in **FIGURE 14.1** on the following two pages show that theoretically a short-only portfolio of stocks that pay small or no dividends can outperform a long portfolio in certain market environments because of the added income from the interest on the collateral and the short rebate. Despite this advantage, short selling as a stand-alone strategy became very rare in the 1990s.

ADVANTAGES/DISADVANTAGES

The bull market of the 1990s had nearly driven short selling as a stand-alone investment strategy into extinction. Besides the fact that it is hard to find overvalued stocks to profitably sell short when the whole market is charging, short selling can suffer from a number of other disadvantages that relate to market conditions. The potential losses on a long position are finite, whereas the potential losses on a short sale are infinite. Furthermore, the potential gain on a short sale is limited. If an investor shorts a stock at $50, the price of that stock can decline only to 0, a maximum of 100 percent gain. On the downside, that stock can increase in value infinitely. So if it appreciates to $150, the short seller can lose 200 percent. Because gains are limited and losses are theoretically unlimited, short sellers often have their entire net worth at stake.

In the past, many short sellers made profits by shorting overhyped stocks that had received attention out of line with the intrinsic value of the company. However, in the 1990s, these overvalued stocks were carried upward by the general momentum of the market. Overvalued stocks do not tend to collapse without a **CATALYTIC EVENT**, and those were few and

14.1   INVESTMENT PROCESS SCENARIOS 1–4

SCENARIO 1

A long investor with $100,000 in capital to invest purchases 20,000 shares of stock A, a non-dividend-paying common stock, at $5 per share, and over the course of one year the price of the stock increases by $1, to $6 per share.

Beginning investment (20,000 shares of stock A @ $5)	$100,000
Ending investment (20,000 shares of stock A @ $6)	$120,000
Gain	$20,000
As a percentage of investment	20%

SCENARIO 2

A short seller with $100,000 in 1-year U.S. Treasury securities with a 6 percent yield uses this capital as collateral to borrow 20,000 shares of stock B at $5 per share, and over the course of one year the price of the stock declines $1, to $4 per share.

Beginning positions:

Long: Collateral of $100,000 of 1-year 6% U.S. Treasury securities
Short: 20,000 shares of stock B at $5 per share

Returns:

Gain on short sale of stock B	$20,000
Interest on U.S. Treasury securities at 6%	$6,000
Interest rebate on proceeds from short sale of stock B assuming an interest rate of 5%	$4,490
Earnings on cash freed by short gain	$614
Total gain	$31,104
As a percentage of equity	31.1%

far between in the 1990s. It does not matter if stocks are over-valued if there is nothing to bring this overvaluation to the market's attention. Short sellers also receive little help from Wall Street analysts who are reluctant to issue sell recommendations though sell recommendations have become less unusual since the bursting of the technology stock bubble in 2000.

On the upside, short selling strategies provide a yield regardless of capital gains or losses, a high level of liquid-

SCENARIO 3

A long investor with $100,000 in capital to invest purchases 20,000 shares of stock A, a non-dividend-paying common stock, at $5 per share, and over the course of one year the price of the stock decreases by $1, to $4 per share.

Beginning investment (20,000 shares of stock A @ $5)	$100,000
Ending investment (20,000 shares of stock A @ $4)	$80,000
Loss	($20,000)
As a percentage of investment	20%

SCENARIO 4

A short seller with $100,000 in 1-year U.S. Treasury securities with a 6 percent yield uses this capital as collateral to borrow 20,000 shares of stock B at $5 per share, and over the course of one year the price of the stock appreciates $1, to $6 per share.

Beginning positions:

Long: Collateral of $100,000 of 1-year 6% U.S. Treasury securities
Short: 20,000 shares of stock B at $5 per share
Returns:

Loss on short sale of stock B	($20,000)
Interest on U.S. Treasury securities at 6%	$6,000
Interest rebate on proceeds from short sale of stock B assuming an interest rate of 5%	$5,510
Margin interest paid on short loss	($824)
Total loss	($9,314)
As a percentage of equity	9.3%

ity, and can produce high investment returns in bear markets. Short selling as an investment strategy proved unsustainable for all but a few investment managers in the 1990s
bull market. This is not surprising considering we were in
the midst of the longest period in history without a major
market correction. However, short selling has garnered
more interest as a strategy since the bursting of the technology bubble in 2000.

PERFORMANCE

As shown in **FIGURE 14.2**, from January 1990 to December 2004,
short selling registered average annualized returns of 1.28
percent, with an annualized standard deviation of 21.51. As
would be expected, these funds registered substantial returns
in the retractions of 2000 and 2002 (34.63 and 29.17 percent,
respectively) and a modest 8.99 percent return in 2001. However, they registered significant losses in 1999 and 2003, losing
24.40 and 21.78 percent, respectively. These types of continu-
ous swings from positive to negative returns raise the general
level of volatility for the strategy. The short seller fund's cor-

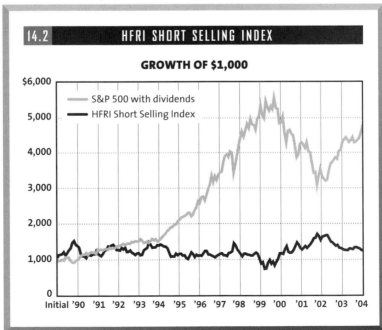

14.2   HFRI SHORT SELLING INDEX

GROWTH OF $1,000

S&P 500 with dividends
HFRI Short Selling Index

Initial '90 '91 '92 '93 '94 '95 '96 '97 '98 '99 '00 '01 '02 '03 '04

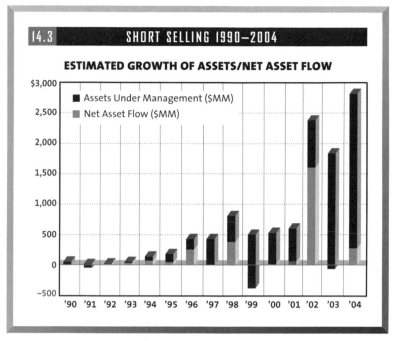

14.3 SHORT SELLING 1990–2004

ESTIMATED GROWTH OF ASSETS/NET ASSET FLOW

■ Assets Under Management ($MM)
■ Net Asset Flow ($MM)

relation statistic of –0.70 reveals a high degree of sensitivity to general changes in stock prices; their beta statistic of –1.03, which measures the magnitude of correlation, shows that their returns move inversely to the prices of stocks.

FIGURE 14.3 shows the total strategy assets and net asset flows per year from 1990 to 2004 for short selling. The year-end asset total equals the previous year's asset size plus annual performance plus net asset flows. As one would expect, the biggest impact year in short selling was 2002, when more than $1.6 billion in net inflows helped increase the total strategy assets almost four-fold, from $0.603 to $2.380 billion.

FIGURE 14.4 shows the return distribution for short selling compared to the overall hedge fund industry, stocks, and bonds. Despite strong performance from 2000 to 2002, short selling is the only strategy to have produced the majority of its performance in a negative column, with 16.7 percent of all months since 1990 registering 0 to –2 percent returns.

FIGURE 14.5 shows the average upside and downside capture since 1990 for short selling funds. As would be expected, the

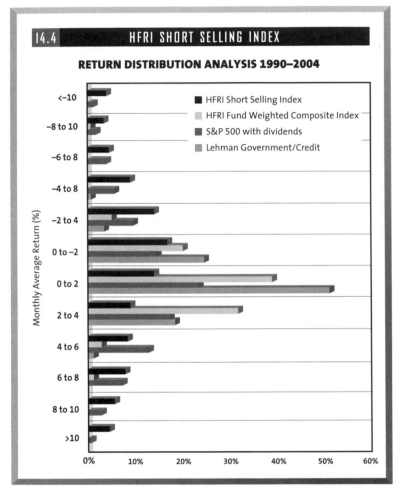

14.4   HFRI SHORT SELLING INDEX

RETURN DISTRIBUTION ANALYSIS 1990–2004

strategy outperforms every other hedge fund strategy, the stock market, and the bond market during down periods, generating an average return of 5.39 percent. During positive market months, short selling funds average a loss of 2.58 percent.

SUMMARY POINTS

PROFIT OPPORTUNITY

◆ Certain managers will construct short-only portfolios to take advantage of the theory that short selling can outperform a long strategy because it provides both fixed income and trading profits.

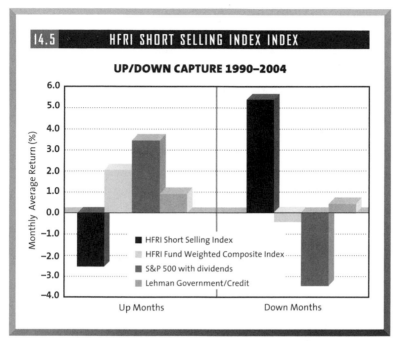

I4.5   HFRI SHORT SELLING INDEX INDEX

UP/DOWN CAPTURE 1990–2004

- HFRI Short Selling Index
- HFRI Fund Weighted Composite Index
- S&P 500 with dividends
- Lehman Government/Credit

Up Months   Down Months

(y-axis: Monthly Average Return (%), scale from −4.0 to 6.0)

◆ On the upside, short selling strategies provide a yield regardless of capital gains or losses, as well as a very high level of liquidity, and can produce high investment returns in bear markets.

SOURCE OF RETURN

◆ Short selling specialists borrow overvalued stock owned by a long investor and sell it on the market with the intention of buying it back later at a lower price after the market corrects itself.

◆ Theoretically, a short-only portfolio of stocks that pay small or no dividends will outperform a long portfolio because of the added income from the interest on the collateral and the short rebate.

INVESTMENT PROCESS

◆ Short sellers seek to identify companies with flawed business models, accounting irregularities, or poor management.

◆ Fundamental research is the primary method for identifying short selling candidates.

KEY TERMS

Catalytic event. A near-term event that will change the market's perception of a particular stock.

Collateral. Cash or very liquid securities that are held as a deposit on borrowed stock.

Mark to market. To determine the price one can get today for currently owned securities.

Short interest rebate. The interest earned on the cash proceeds from a short sale of stock.

MAKING AN
Investment

CHAPTER 15

Investing in
HEDGE
FUNDS

LIKE MOST investment decisions, investing in hedge funds is a rational process that begins with an investment goal and results in making one or more investment selections. The process is designed to improve the chances of achieving a set of investment objectives. It is important to follow a methodology in constructing a portfolio of hedge funds: to create a framework within which to select investments and to evaluate and monitor the portfolio's risk and performance. Such a framework provides an efficient information feedback loop that allows the adjustment, refinement, and successful management of a multiple fund or manager investment portfolio.

To properly analyze hedge fund strategies, combine them to construct portfolios, and monitor such investments, an investor must have access to the underlying investment portfolio. Without this information only a one-sided evaluation can be conducted, ignoring the actual risk exposures of the strategy. Blind investments should be avoided.

The following is a suggested framework for selecting hedge funds and alternative investment strategies and combining them in a portfolio. Although it is intended for investors who want to construct a multiple-manager portfolio, the concepts can be applied to the selection of a single manager or hedge fund as well. There are three basic steps in making an allocation to hedge funds:

1 Planning the investment. This is the stage in which investors decide what they wish to achieve and how they will achieve those goals. It includes (a) defining the investment objective(s) and (b) establishing investment parameters for individual hedge funds, for strategies, and for the portfolio as a whole.

2 Choosing a structure and the appropriate strategies. The second step is to research and then select the investment structure(s) that will be used in the program to access hedge fund strategies that best satisfy the investment goals. To determine the appropriate structure(s) and strategies, investors must apply the objectives and parameters established in the planning stage to the available structure and strategy options. The two components are (a) selection of the optimal structure(s) and (b) selection of suitable strategies.

3 Selecting hedge funds or managers. The third step is the manager search, in which individual hedge funds and/or investment managers that satisfy the structure, strategy, and other parameter requirements established in steps 1 and 2 are evaluated for investment. The individual hedge funds or hedge fund managers are researched, and the funds that best fit the parameters and fulfill the objectives are selected for the portfolio.

STEP ONE

PLANNING THE INVESTMENT

Although alternative investment strategies are dissimilar in some ways to more traditional investments, the fundamentals of prudent investing still apply. Decisions to invest in these strategies must be based on realistic goals and expectations. To establish realistic goals, investors must have an understanding of the available return characteristics of the main hedge fund strategies. The first fourteen chapters of this book present an overview of a variety of investment approaches and methods of investing that will help investors understand hedge fund opportunities and formulate realistic goals.

As discussed, a hedge fund can be housed in any of a number of investment structures. Managers use one or more of a variety of alternative investment strategies that provide a diverse range of investment exposures and risk-reward characteristics. Although these strategies are diverse and involve more complex approaches than traditional investments, they are all understandable and definable. The investment process therefore involves considering what the best hedge fund structure(s) for the investment will be and the risks and benefits of accessing the different strategies through that structure.

The planning process is critical to making a hedge fund investment. The investor must form a framework for structuring and managing a multiple-manager hedge fund investment program. The first step is to clearly define what he expects to achieve by investing in hedge funds; then the investor can establish investment parameters that guide how those objectives are to be met.

DEFINING PORTFOLIO OBJECTIVES

The first step that an investor should take is to define the objectives of the portfolio. The objectives make explicit what the investor expects to achieve from the hedge fund investment. These usually include return and risk measures over the time frame of the investment, such as target return, consistency, volatility, maximum loss, and correlation to stocks or bonds. Other objectives might address leverage (both borrowing and derived), liquidity of the investment, and region and country exposures. Structural issues pertaining to custody of the assets and fund transparency are also important considerations when establishing objectives. Although almost all investors share achieving investment returns (either absolute or relative to some benchmark) as a main objective, investors may have one or more objectives of differing priorities, ranging from pursuing risk-adjusted return to accessing specific types of financial instruments or investment strategies. **FIGURE 15.1** illustrates an example of a possible set of portfolio objectives.

Investors may modify portfolio objectives throughout the planning process, particularly if they are learning about the industry and the various opportunities that it presents.

15.1 A HYPOTHETICAL SET OF PORTFOLIO OBJECTIVES	
Return per Annum	15%
Leverage	Nonborrowing
Volatility	Less than 5%
Maximum Loss	Less than 10%
Correlation	Less than 0.30
Transparency	Daily

ESTABLISHING INVESTMENT PARAMETERS

Whereas portfolio objectives make explicit what investors wish to achieve through a hedge fund investment, investment parameters help to control how those portfolio objectives are accomplished. They include the rules and guidelines that determine how an investment portfolio is constructed and operated. Parameters are the constraints, requirements, inclusions, and exclusions imposed on the investor's selection of hedge fund structures and strategies and the operation of the investment program. These can be self-imposed by investors or required by regulatory bodies.

Investment parameters can be applied on three levels:

1 to the overall portfolio;
2 to each strategy;
3 to each individual manager or fund.

FIGURE 15.2, below, represents the investment parameter hierarchy.

Working up from the bottom of the pyramid, the investment parameters imposed on the selection of managers for a particular strategy in combination are designed to achieve the overall strategy parameters. Similarly, the parameters established for the strategies in combination allow for the portfolio parameters to be met.

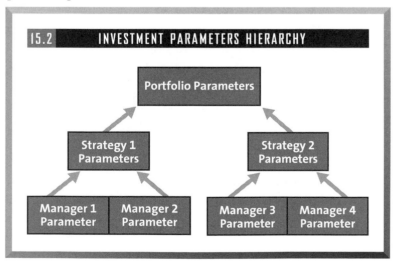

15.2   INVESTMENT PARAMETERS HIERARCHY

Investment parameters may also refine or elaborate portfolio objectives. For example, a portfolio objective of using exchange-listed equities only will have an investment parameter that limits the hedge funds that will be considered to those investing in such securities. Thus, investors should consider five useful categories when establishing investment parameters:

1 Regulatory restrictions. Constraints placed on investment activities by governmental agencies regulating securities, commodities, taxation, banking, insurance, and retirement assets must be incorporated into the investment parameters, according to the type of investors involved.

2 Investment policy limitations. Self-imposed restrictions are based on the investor's interpretation of investment guidelines or on prudent investment standards.

3 Risk-control considerations. Specific constraints for risk-related issues and market exposures include the use of leverage, volatility of returns, and correlation of returns to other investments in the portfolio.

4 Performance controls. Appropriate target ranges are set for returns.

5 Portfolio composition methodology. Guidelines are constructed for allocating assets, diversifying holdings, and rebalancing the portfolio on an ongoing basis.

Investment parameters may be established for individual fund managers based on the types of instruments in which they invest and trade, the length of their track record, the amount of assets they have under management, their greatest losing period or maximum drawdown, the liquidity of the fund, the minimum investment required, historic risk measures, and actual risk probabilities. Certain trading strategies or financial instruments might be required to be included in or excluded from the portfolio (e.g., equity strategies only, but no illiquid securities). Portfolio-level parameters could also require that the funds be invested only in U.S. securities or in specific industry sectors or, alternatively, that the portfolio be globally diversified. Considerations include instruments and markets, investment methods, leverage, asset size, liquidity, and performance (absolute or relative, target and floor).

"Stress testing" the portfolio is a valuable analytical tool; basically, it is an evaluation of the portfolio's performance under a series of "what if" scenarios. These scenarios address the objectives and parameters set in the planning stage. If noncorrelation to stock and bond markets is an objective, each manager and the combination of managers must be evaluated. What if the stock market drops 30 percent? What if interest rates are increased by 50 basis points? To perform a completely accurate stress test requires knowledge of the investments in each manager's portfolio so that overall market exposures can be accurately determined. Assumptions about how the instruments will behave under the various scenarios may be based on historic or other methods of estimation. By considering the impact of various market scenarios, investors can develop performance expectations for each hedge fund in the portfolio under different conditions, anticipate the expected correlation of the returns from the different funds, and therefore better forecast the overall performance of the portfolio. In the final portfolio, this forecast should correspond to the original objectives.

PLANNING TIPS

The investment parameters for individual fund managers may differ considerably from those of the portfolio as a whole. For example, the volatility of returns allowable for any particular hedge fund in the portfolio might be greater than the return volatility objectives of the total portfolio because of the offsetting nature of the volatility of noncorrelated strategies (see Figure 15.2). By diversifying the portfolio across these various funds, the portfolio manager reduces the return volatility of the portfolio as a whole.

MINIMIZING AND NEUTRALIZING RISK

Risk at the manager, strategy, and portfolio levels should be addressed in the investment parameters. One of the main reasons for establishing investment parameters is to manage

or avoid existing and potential investment risks. Investment
risk can take many forms, including:

◆ the general condition of markets in which one trades
◆ creditworthiness
◆ exposure to potential fraud
◆ manager incompetence
◆ misrepresentation of investment activities
◆ form of investment vehicle
◆ government regulations
◆ the underlying instruments used by the fund
◆ industry concentration
◆ the investment strategy selected.

Obviously, certain risks are specific to certain positions and
funds, and others apply to the portfolio as a whole. How the
risks of any particular fund relate to the risk associated with
the portfolio as a whole must be evaluated, and the two sets
of risk must be balanced relative to the benefits provided. At
that point the investor should decide whether to avoid, neutralize, minimize, or accept each risk. Risks can be avoided or
minimized by:

◆ strategy selection
◆ selecting managers with superior risk controls
◆ establishing investment guidelines that contain the risks
  (for example, limiting the exposure to any single issuer)
◆ combining strategies that are complementary (such as,
  when a market condition that is risky for one approach is
  favorable for the other)
◆ incorporating a risk-monitoring program.

If an investor allocates assets to a strategy or a manager with
full knowledge of the risk but without taking any precautions
for it, then the risk becomes an accepted part of the investment. An investor who invests in a nontransparent fund has
accepted the risk that anything could happen.

Often full attention is devoted to obvious risks and too little
attention to less likely ones. Proper probabilities are assigned
to risk scenarios that are highly likely but probabilities of zero

are assigned to tail scenarios with lower, but not zero, probabilities of occurring. All investment strategies have flaws that can produce substantial losses of capital, and, as remote as any risk may seem, it should be recognized and addressed accordingly.

DIVERSIFICATION

By diversifying portfolios across strategies and financial instruments, the overall portfolio risk is reduced by limiting the effect that any one exposure can have on the portfolio as a whole. A primary goal of fund diversification is to include funds in the portfolio that will perform well in different market environments. This is accomplished by combining a variety of strategies. Funds that use the same strategies will often perform similarly to one another. For example, a portfolio of ten fixed-income arbitrage hedge funds will not reduce risk significantly when each allocation represents a similar investment idea. A portfolio with few limiting parameters allows for broad diversification across strategies and instruments. Keep in mind that parameters that attempt to screen out risk may also narrow the universe of acceptable strategies or hedge funds. With fewer acceptable funds to choose from, the final portfolio may be less diversified. In this case, the investor has effectively traded one kind of risk for another. If the investment parameters limit the scope of the portfolio, diversification should be focused on the eligible approaches and number of acceptable strategies.

NUMBER OF FUNDS

The optimal number of hedge funds to include in a portfolio is the subject of some debate. Expert opinions recommend from five to fifty. Of course, the number of funds included is often determined by the amount of investment capital and the desired form of investment. Because larger and more established hedge funds have higher minimum investment requirements, fewer of these funds can be included in a portfolio compared with funds that require lower minimum investments. If separate accounts are used, the minimum investment amount per manager will usually be significantly larger than those required for investing in comingled funds.

STRUCTURE AND STRATEGY SELECTION

The selection process applies the investment parameters to the construction of the portfolio. It begins with the identification of acceptable investment structures. Once an appropriate structure is chosen, the next step is to select strategies.

SELECTING STRUCTURES

Choose an investment structure based on its ability to satisfy the investment parameters and objectives. Hedge fund structures and investment vehicles are covered in detail in Chapter 2, but some critical points are worth reviewing here.

A threshold question is whether the investment will be made in existing fund structures, transparent or not transparent, or in separate managed accounts. If control and custody over the assets to be invested are required, the investment must be made through a separate account or transparent fund, as investing in a typical hedge fund gives up custody and all control over the investment activities. Transparency refers to investors' ability to "see through" a manager's portfolio to the underlying investments (transparency is covered in more detail in Chapter 16).

SELECTING STRATEGIES

A large portion of this book (Chapters 3 to 14) is devoted to a discussion of the various hedge fund strategies. They represent a broad range of risk and return characteristics. Even within strategy classifications, there is distinct variation. Strategies should be selected based on a reasonable expectation that they will:

1 achieve performance objectives
2 satisfy parameter requirements
3 operate under the selected hedge fund structure.

MANAGER/FUND SEARCH AND SELECTION

MANAGER SEARCH PROCEDURE

Although the large number and diversity of hedge funds that must be analyzed may seem daunting, identifying the structure and strategies that are acceptable focuses the choice of possible funds and managers. Parameters—such as amount of assets under management, experience of the fund manager, performance, and instruments traded—reduce the field of candidates further, resulting in a short list that can be analyzed more thoroughly. A closer inspection of the managers—even those who describe their strategies similarly—will reveal variations and nuances in style and specialization. Managers who practice similar strategies do not necessarily have the same talent for doing so. However, comparing managers' performance numbers can be problematic because a particular manager's performance numbers may, on closer inspection, be revealed to be an amalgam of inconsistent investment approaches implemented over time. Investment managers' promotional materials and disclosure documents can be helpful, but in many cases these are written in such broad terms that their usefulness is limited. The need for transparency for prudent investing begins at this stage. By reconciling the performance record to the underlying exposures held as a consideration of the market conditions at the time allows a much more complete understanding of a manger's investment activities and the associated benefits and risks.

Once a list of the manager's funds is selected, a more detailed evaluation is conducted. The purpose of hedge fund evaluation is to develop a sense of what kind of future performance can reasonably be expected. Funds are selected for the portfolio based on how each fund is expected to perform on an absolute basis and how each is expected to perform in relation to the other hedge funds in the portfolio. Performance expectations are both general and specific and should correspond to the level of ongoing monitoring and evaluation that investors intend to conduct.

The evaluation process involves the collection and evaluation of all available material, past and present, to arrive at a set of future expectations for the fund. Quantitative and qualitative investment criteria used for this purpose are described below. They are also used as the basis for ongoing portfolio monitoring and performance evaluation (ongoing risk and performance monitoring is covered in Chapter 16). These criteria help the investor and the portfolio manager develop a set of reasonable expectations about future performance of the funds on which to construct the portfolio.

◆ **Quantitative analysis.** Quantitative analysis is the statistical evaluation of the past performance and investment activity of hedge funds and separate accounts. This process involves gathering and analyzing such data using various measures of risk, reward, and risk-reward relationships. Analysis of risk and performance statistics also allows investors to compare one investment with another or with peer groups and benchmarks.

By itself, quantitative analysis of the performance data is a perfect evaluation of the past results but an unreliable predictor of future performance. As long as all conditions were the same during the period of evaluation and will continue to stay exactly the same in the future, a statistical study of the past is very helpful in predicting the future. However, conditions change, and past performance, although an important input, can by itself be highly misleading and is just one of a number of factors that help indicate expected future performance.

In addition, because many hedge funds have been established only recently, the performance data for these managers often only reflect a particular economic climate. Relying entirely on statistical analysis often results in poor investment decisions, but it is a common practice because it is the easiest analysis to perform.

◆ **Qualitative analysis.** Qualitative analysis looks behind the performance numbers at how they were achieved, who the firm's principle individuals are, and what the make up of their business is. Qualitative analysis is critical in evaluating a fund manager's historic performance. If a fund manager's past performance is to be of any use in predicting future performance, then there must be continuity. Thorough qualitative evaluations take into account past and current market conditions, the latent risks and benefits of the strategy, the consistency of the fund manager's investment operation over time, and the strengths and weaknesses of the individuals making investment decisions.

The investor should look for continuity first in the fund manager's approach and application of a chosen strategy and second in the nature of the markets to which the manager applied the strategy. For example, the track record of a fund manager that reflects specialized arbitrage trades will not be useful for forecasting future performance if the market in question becomes more efficient, wiping out arbitrage opportunities, or becomes more volatile, creating excessive risk for leveraged strategies.

Similarly, the track record of a systematic manager would provide little insight into future performance if the manager changed disciplines and began investing on a discretionary basis. In addition, a fund manager's past performance does not indicate how the manager will cope with a different market environment or whether the manager's strategy can generate similar returns with an increase or decrease in assets under management.

◆ **Summary.** Because an investment in a hedge fund is an investment in an entrepreneurial business operation, investors should seek to answer the question: What business is the manager really in? The various areas of the business that should be reviewed include operations, personnel backgrounds, investment methodology, and performance record.

BUSINESS OPERATIONS

In reviewing the operation of the business, assess the various aspects of the business's internal functions, including management, trading, research, operations, compliance, and client service. Outside professionals—such as the firm's accountant, auditor, attorney, prime broker, bank, administrator, and custodian—should be evaluated as well. In addition, the information systems on which a firm relies—including trading, back office, and research systems—should be considered. Also address contingency plans for backing up the information systems and the existence of an alternative operating location to maintain continuity of portfolio management in the event of a crisis.

PERSONNEL BACKGROUNDS

Before investing in a hedge fund, there are questions that should be answered, including: What is the regulatory history of key personnel? Have any of them led any "past lives" as investment managers, requiring further investigation? Where is their money invested? What do references and background checks reveal about them? Registrations with the Securities and Exchange Commission, Commodities Futures Trading Commission, National Association of Securities Dealers, and National Futures Association are important information sources. Check with such agencies to learn more about the manager's regulatory history. The answers to these background questions give an investor a clearer idea of who the fund manager is and help indicate what actions can be expected in the future.

INVESTMENT METHODOLOGY

Even managers who use similar strategies may implement those strategies in different ways. Therefore, it is important to learn as much as possible about a manager's investment methodology. Many of these considerations are discussed in the Core Strategy and Investment Process sections of the strategy chapters in this book. Each manager should be able to describe all material aspects of her investment activities including: the fund's sources of expected return; use of leverage; liquidity; diversification; position concentrations; portfolio turnover; methods for evaluating securities; research sources; investment universe; use of derivatives and short selling; hedging practices; significant risks; and risk-control procedures. Determine the factors that influence decisions to put positions on and take them off and how the actual trading is accomplished as well as whether the fund's investment methodology has changed over time. The most consistent funds usually have well-refined and tested investment methodologies. On top of these basics, investors should find out who makes the fund's investment decisions, and what the contingency plan is to safeguard the portfolio if a key individual becomes incapacitated. In sum, it is important to examine the process that a fund goes through to arrive at its final investment decisions as well as how, mechanically, the investments are made.

PERFORMANCE RECORD

The first thing that most investors will look at is a fund's performance record. However, prudent investors should not take that record at face value. They will examine how the performance record reflects past and current market conditions. They will note that managers with longer track records tend to be more established and to have dealt with a wider variety of market situations. On the other hand, each year managers with long, stable track records run into difficulties and post significant losses.

Investors should also determine how any strategy changes made by a fund are reflected in its performance record. In addition, investors should look at how a fund's assets under management have changed over time. For example, as assets have grown, how has the manager handled increased size? Does the fund use a niche strategy that cannot efficiently invest the larger asset base? In sum, investors should question a fund's performance record rather than accept it at face value.

The selection of hedge funds and managers is the final step in the structuring process. The number selected and the basis for their inclusion in a diversified portfolio will be based on parameters established at the planning stage. The risk and performance expectations material to each hedge fund manager's selection also form the basis for ongoing monitoring after the investment is made.

SUMMARY

◆ Investments in hedge funds should follow a well-defined and structured process that provides an efficient information feedback loop that allows the adjustment, refinement, and successful management of a multiple-manager or fund investment portfolio.

◆ Prudent investing requires portfolio transparency to:
  1 Understand the investment merits and risk exposures of the investment strategy
  2 Select managers and funds
  3 Monitor the day-to-day risk exposures.

◆ The steps in making a hedge fund allocation include:
  1 Planning the investment
    a Defining the portfolio objectives
    b Establishing investment parameters
  2 Choosing a structure and selecting strategies that satisfy the objectives and parameters established in the planning stage
  3 Selecting hedge fund managers who
    a Have a reasonable expectation of achieving performance objectives
    b Satisfy parameter requirements
    c Will operate under the selected hedge fund structure.

CHAPTER

16

After the
INITIAL
ALLOCATION

ONGOING DUE DILIGENCE

Due diligence is an intelligence-gathering process in which all the information available about a fund or manager is collected, verified if possible, and analyzed. The purpose is to determine the nature and potential benefits and risks associated with the fund's investment strategy and the structure used to access that strategy and to develop expectations about future investment activities and performance. These conclusions and expectations allow the investor to determine whether the fund is a suitable investment. However, the work does not end when an investment selection is made; due diligence is an ongoing process.

Due diligence produces information about how assets can be expected to be managed in the future. It identifies the risks associated with the managers and strategies. Steps are taken to eliminate, neutralize, or contain those risks. A variety of important factors are identified and representations are made during the due diligence process prior to investment. They form the foundation upon which future investment activity and performance expectations are based. Funds or managers are in turn selected with reliance on these expectations. If the factors change, the basis for the future expectations, and thus the investment selection, no longer exists. Therefore, the ongoing due diligence process involves keeping up with the qualitative aspects of the manager or hedge fund as well as the quantifiable aspects of the investment portfolio. How investors monitor the risk and performance of any particular allocation is partly dependent on the type, quality, and timeliness of information available based on the degree of portfolio transparency.

QUALITATIVE RISK CONTROL:
HISTORIC PROBLEM AREAS

Ongoing qualitative due diligence involves periodically reviewing the various factors (often, but not always, stated as parameters), outside of investment activities and performance, that were material to selecting a manager or fund. If these have changed, the rationale for being in the investment may no longer exist. The following are some of the areas in which problems have occurred with hedge funds. As they are often repeated, it is advisable to consider them on an ongoing basis.

◆ **Assets exceed strategy capacity.** Many of the hedge fund strategies profit from inefficiencies in niches of limited size. However, the high returns often attract more investor money than can be invested in the manner in which the original returns were generated. This may lead to more risky behavior by the manager to maintain return levels, such as an expansion into areas in which the manager has limited experience, or the increased use of leverage or more risky investments.

◆ **Market inefficiency no longer exists.** Certain strategies capitalize on new market inefficiencies. Success attracts new investment capital and more competitors to the area. As more capital flows in, the inefficiency becomes reduced, resulting in lower returns or other changes that increase risk.

◆ **End of the trend.** Many investment strategies are following and dependent on a market environment trend, such as declining interest rates. A slowdown, end, or reversal of the trend will usually adversely affect the strategy's performance.

◆ **Latent problems.** Disguised risks and exposure weaknesses may exist in a portfolio. They include concentrations that are susceptible to changes in market conditions that are not a source of return. For example, a strategy that invests in financially weak companies may have a substantial bankruptcy risk. A slight increase in the number of defaults may result in significant losses for such a strategy.

◆ **Leverage.** Leveraging both magnifies the risk of the strategy and creates risk by giving the lender power over the disposition of the investment portfolio. This may occur in the form of increased margin requirements or adverse market shifts, forcing a partial or complete liquidation of the portfolio.

◆ **Change in strategy.** Shifting course certainly undercuts the meaningfulness of past performance, and if the investment has already been made, the basis for investing might no longer exist. It is often a symptom of some of the other issues discussed in this section.

◆ **Exceeding stated risk parameters.** This development often indicates a problem with the strategy or manager capacity.

◆ **Character/ego.** Personality flaws can blind or cloud the thinking of a manager, resulting in a conscious deviation from prudent money-management activities.

◆ **Key personnel.** Reliance on historical performance records and investment activities may no longer be valid if the person or persons responsible for them leaves the firm.

◆ **Fraud.** Direct fraud is not common, and questionable managers can sometimes be weeded out through proper due diligence. However, fraud can only be prevented through closed system transparency where custody and control of the assets, and their valuations, are separated from the investment and trading activities. If investing in a non-transparent manner, be on the lookout for more subtle misrepresentation and material omissions, as these are often indications of deeper problems.

TRANSPARENCY

Transparency is the ability to look through a hedge fund to its underlying investment portfolio. Transparency is essential in determining whether the fund complies with and adheres to the fund's stated investment and risk parameters and other representations made to the investor.

Investors want to be assured that they are getting the exposure and type of investment that they believe the manager sold them. This is particularly important to those with fiduciary responsibilities for investing others' assets. In reality, many managers tend to promote a more specific investment strategy than their funds actually pursue. Most investors are aware that blind faith creates a foolhardy investment strategy. Without transparency, they can determine actual risk exposure and risk-reward prospects only from secondary sources. As discussed in Chapter 15, prudent investing requires an investigation of the specifics of a fund manager's investment strategy, past performance, and the risk controls used to achieve the fund's returns. Based on this information, the investor constructs a set of future expectations for performance and risk parameters to which the manager must adhere. Parameters include use of leverage, types of instruments used, exposure to asset classes and sectors, number of positions, position size, amount of hedging, and frequency of trades. For each strategy, the investor should develop general parameters, and for each manager within that strategy there should be additional, more refined, parameters. Transparency ensures that the fund or the manager can be monitored for parameter compliance.

With transparency, the risk exposures of a hedge fund investment as well as a multiple fund or manager allocation can be monitored continuously by screening the portfolio on a daily basis for compliance with the parameters established during the initial due diligence process. This approach allows the investor to ensure conformity to investment guidelines. If a parameter is breached, the violation is detected, allowing it to be addressed immediately.

The portfolio is analyzed in three ways:

1 exposures,
2 relationships, and
3 time series.

An exposure is a snapshot view of the portfolio's contents. Exposures are analyzed to determine portfolio position concentrations, how many are long positions and how many are short, and how much leverage is being used. The second level analyzed is the relationship between the instruments: not just how much of the portfolio is long and how much short, but the relationship between the longs and the shorts. Are they matched pairs? Are they iterative constructions? Are the short positions hedges against the long? Against the market? Time series analysis examines time-dependent variables such as duration, time horizons of particular positions, and cyclical features. An example of this would be the average length of time a position is held in a risk arbitrage portfolio.

Investors use risk monitoring to confirm that each fund manager complies with the established risk parameters on a daily basis. For investors whose portfolios are allocated to more than a style manager, risk monitoring can be used to oversee the preset risk exposure of the multiple-manager composite. It allows investors to monitor whether their portfolio is diversified and risk exposure reduced, as would be expected when investment strategies are combined.

Technologies that allow for cost-effective risk management are now available, and these can be provided to investors who are afforded transparency by the managers with whom they invest. These include independent trade reconciliation, third-party pricing of the investment holdings, daily oversight of exposure limits, and active adherence to style management.

ILLUSTRATION OF RISK MONITORING IN PRACTICE

Ongoing risk monitoring can be divided into two main areas: tactical risk monitoring and strategic risk monitoring. Tactical risk monitoring focuses on daily measures designed to ensure independent verification of positions, valuations, and exposures. Strategic risk monitoring is the periodic review of macro level factors such as performance and total portfolio risk.

The following is a step-by-step illustration of how the risk-monitoring process works. The basis for this example is the methodologies and systems developed by and used at HFR Asset Management.

DAILY TACTICAL RISK MONITORING

Once allocations are made, the portfolio is monitored daily for risk, performance, and administrative purposes. Risk monitoring involves three processes: portfolio valuation, compliance analysis, and reporting.

PORTFOLIO VALUATION

Third-party verification of positions is the key first step in the risk management process. For each investment manager who is represented in the portfolio, the previous day's transactions, portfolio holdings, and account activities are downloaded directly from the prime broker, counterparty, or custodian with which each investment manager books trades and maintains an account. Any cash movements are verified and matched to the corresponding trade. Capital structure changes such as stock splits, distributions for reorganizations, and so forth are booked appropriately and verified with brokers. Independent pricing is absolutely necessary. Broker pricing is often inaccurate or incomplete. In many cases, the portfolio is priced by the manager. Obviously, there has to be an independent review. Prices should be confirmed for every instrument in the portfolio by using information provided by an independent pricing data source. Closing exchange rates should be obtained to convert any securities priced in non–dollar-denominated assets for purposes of risk analysis and portfolio valuation.

In the event that a current market price is not available for a particular security, the risk monitor should obtain market pricing information from third-party sources such as market makers, brokers, and dealers. Theoretically priced instruments such as collateralized mortgage obligations, swaps, and repurchase agreements are valued by using an industry standard model. Accrued interest can be calculated using standard calculation methods developed by the Securities Industry Association.

After the portfolio is priced, the performance for that portfolio is evaluated. Any significant up or down movement at the portfolio level is then investigated and documented. Performance across a group of managers with similar strategies is evaluated for outliers.

At the conclusion of the last trade day of each month, a final confirmation and validation of market price, quantity, and market value of each investment in the account is conducted. In addition, fees and fee accruals for each account are confirmed with each fund manager.

COMPLIANCE ANALYSIS

When the portfolio valuation process is complete, each investment manager is assessed for compliance with the risk parameters that were established for the portfolio. Every risk parameter is checked against the account's actual exposure. Compliance with each parameter is documented daily in a guideline summary report. This report identifies each risk parameter and indicates whether the parameter was violated. Every investment parameter violation will undergo an analysis on a daily basis to determine its severity. Levels of violation severity are classified to designate which violations require further investigation and/or action and specify the course of corrective action to be taken. Each violation is assigned a severity level based on previously determined risk parameters. If the violation adversely affects the risk and/or performance of the account, then the violation will be assigned a higher severity level. For a multiple hedge fund portfolio, the following severity levels might be established:

Level One
◆ **Definition.** Any non–risk-increasing violation, or any instance in which a parameter is within 5 percent of being met and not otherwise determined to be a material violation or to materially increase risk (i.e., underinvestment).

◆ **Action.** The violation is documented, and the violating investment manager is placed on a watch list. If the violation represents a nonmaterial increase in risk rather than a non–risk-increasing violation, the manager will be notified and the violation will be investigated within two business days. Other level one violations will be addressed with the investment managers within a reasonable period of time if these violations persist.

Level Two
◆ **Definition.** Parameter violation of 5 to 10 percent that increases risk.

◆ **Action.** The violation is documented, and the investment manager is contacted to investigate the violation within one business day.

Level Three
◆ **Definition.** Parameter violation exceeding 10 percent, or any account activity not specifically permitted in the guidelines, or any material increase in risk.

◆ **Action.** Both the investment manager and the prime broker are notified immediately to investigate violations. Corrective action may include, but is not limited to, liquidation, position offset, and reallocation of the noncompliant investment manager's assets and removal of the investment manager from the portfolio. The client is notified within five business days of the violation and of the resultant corrective action.

Each parameter violation is ranked according to severity levels custom-designed for the portfolio. All violations are listed on the daily guideline summary report, and the appropriate level is indicated

Three levels of review are required for all guideline exceptions. A portfolio risk analyst investigates each violation and provides comment and a recommended severity level. A senior risk team leader confirms each violation and severity ranking. Finally, a member of senior management reviews the complete guideline report on a daily basis.

REPORTING PROCEDURES

In order for the daily risk management process to serve its purpose, effective reporting must be available. The following reports are typical:

1 Daily guideline summary report. This daily report lists each risk parameter for each investment manager, specifies the account's activity in relation to the parameter, and indicates whether the parameter was violated. The report also shows the ranking for each violated parameter.

2 Daily valuation summary. This daily report provides the accurate value of the account, by both investment manager and overall portfolio. Manager summaries itemize each manager's holdings by value of long, short, and cash positions. If valuations change for a particular account in subsequent days, a corrected report reflecting these changes is provided.

3 Monthly and quarterly performance reports. Performance reports detail each investment manager's performance as well as the overall performance of the portfolio.

4 Customized reports. These reports are tailored to address parameters specific to a particular client or portfolio.

STRATEGIC RISK MONITORING

Whereas tactical risk monitoring focuses on a daily, quantitative process; strategic risk monitoring is concerned with a more subjective evaluation of the manager on a periodic basis. Every manager on the platform is contacted at least monthly. Confirmation of due diligence data is completed, and any significant changes discussed for clarity. The manager's style is confirmed, and any changes in asset types, allocation levels, or risk posture are clearly understood. Specific attention should be paid to key personnel changes, persistent poor investment performance, or large growth (or decline) in a manager's assets under management.

In addition, risk modeling tools are employed to evaluate total portfolio risk under a variety of market scenarios. Position-level transparency allows for the inclusion of all assets in quantitative modeling tools that predict the reaction of each security to market shocks. These reports provide a perspective on macro-level risks for the portfolio using measures such as value at risk. Changes in responses to market scenarios and absolute predicted risk levels over time are investigated with the manager.

Regular, monthly qualitative evaluations for each manager are prepared, and any managers who are of concern are placed on a watch list for special attention and follow-up.

SUMMARY POINTS

◆ Due diligence is an ongoing process.
◆ Factors and representations from the due diligence process form the basis for investment activity and performance expectations.
◆ Managers and funds are selected based on these expectations.
◆ If the factors change or the representations are not met, the expectations may change and, in turn, the basis for the investment with the fund or manager may no longer exist.
◆ Therefore, qualitative factors should be reviewed periodically and investment activities and portfolio exposures should be monitored on a daily basis for compliance with the risk parameters.

.

APPENDICES

APPENDIX A

CALCULATION METHODOLOGY

The relevance of any performance index is its ability to gauge objectively market movement so that it may be used as a benchmark for various investment styles. In particular, when using an index such as the S&P 500 index or the Dow Jones Industrial Average, it is important to understand the construction of these indexes. It would seem inappropriate to use the S&P 500 as a benchmark for an investment firm that concentrates on small-cap equities, just as it would be inappropriate to use the Dow as a benchmark for a firm that invests in corporate debt. I believe that it is inaccurate to compare hedge fund performance with only passive indexes such as the S&P 500.

All statistics included in this book were compiled by Hedge Fund Research, Inc. (HFR). HFR has created an index of hedge fund performance categorized by investment strategy. The HFR Performance Indices (HFRI) are equal-weighted indices based on more than 2,200 hedge funds and fund of funds, categorized by 37 investment strategies (which include specific subindices for prominent emerging markets, fixed-income categories, sectors, and fund of funds) and including a final composite index. These indices retain performance of liquidated funds over the life span of the funds, eliminating survivor bias. The strategies covered in this book were chosen because they represent the majority of this universe of funds in terms of both quantity and assets under management.

Each strategy is reweighted every month based on the number of funds that have provided their monthly performance. For example, if ten market neutral funds reported their performance for January, each fund's performance would be given a one-tenth weight for January. If fourteen funds report in February, each of these funds would then be given a one-fourteenth weight for February. The statistics provided in this book are based on the monthly performance of the respective indices. Each statistic was calculated over the period spanning January 1990 to December 2004.

APPENDIX B

RESOURCES FOR INVESTORS

Burlington Hall Asset Management (La Porte)   908-813-0077
43-A Newburgh Road, Suite 200   www.laportesoft.com
Hackettstown, NJ   07840

Database and Analysis Software   901-888-7500
Strategic Financial Solutions, LLC (Pertrac)   www.pertrac.com
2611 South Mendenhall, Suite 200
Memphis, TN   38115

Hedge Fund Investments
HFR Asset Management   312-327-0430
10 South Riverside Plaza, Suite 1450   www.hfr.com
Chicago, IL   60606

Wells Fargo Alternative Asset Management   415-222-4000
420 Montgomery Street, 5th Floor
San Francisco, CA   94104

Zephyr Associates, Inc. (StyleADVISOR)   775-588-0654
P.O. Box 12368   www.styleadvisor.com
Zephyr Cove, NV   89448

ASSOCIATIONS

Alternative Investment Management   44-20-7659-9920
  Association (AIMA)   www.aima.org
Meadows House, 20-22 Queen Street
London W1J 5PR
United Kingdom

Managed Funds Association
2025 M Street NW, Suite 800
Washington, DC 20036

202-367-1140
www.mfainfo.org

APPENDIX C

FUND	YEAR	JAN	FEB	MAR
Convertible Arbitrage Index	1990	(1.47)	(0.92)	1.26
Convertible Arbitrage Index	1991	0.44	1.61	1.39
Convertible Arbitrage Index	1992	2.12	0.94	0.99
Convertible Arbitrage Index	1993	0.93	0.86	2.19
Convertible Arbitrage Index	1994	0.66	0.24	(2.11)
Convertible Arbitrage Index	1995	0.55	0.98	1.83
Convertible Arbitrage Index	1996	1.82	1.06	1.17
Convertible Arbitrage Index	1997	1.01	1.11	0.59
Convertible Arbitrage Index	1998	1.91	1.52	1.58
Convertible Arbitrage Index	1999	2.11	0.25	1.53
Convertible Arbitrage Index	2000	1.91	2.21	1.75
Convertible Arbitrage Index	2001	2.73	1.70	1.68
Convertible Arbitrage Index	2002	1.38	0.19	0.46
Convertible Arbitrage Index	2003	2.50	1.29	0.73
Convertible Arbitrage Index	2004	1.01	0.18	0.68
Distressed Securities Index	1990	(0.24)	2.79	3.08
Distressed Securities Index	1991	2.00	4.14	6.84
Distressed Securities Index	1992	7.06	5.45	2.32
Distressed Securities Index	1993	4.50	2.54	3.14
Distressed Securities Index	1994	3.82	(0.30)	(0.93)
Distressed Securities Index	1995	1.08	2.08	1.56
Distressed Securities Index	1996	2.22	1.43	2.18
Distressed Securities Index	1997	1.88	1.84	0.22
Distressed Securities Index	1998	1.10	2.35	2.17
Distressed Securities Index	1999	1.40	(0.27)	2.20
Distressed Securities Index	2000	0.70	3.98	0.67
Distressed Securities Index	2001	2.79	1.30	(0.62)
Distressed Securities Index	2002	2.04	(0.39)	0.49
Distressed Securities Index	2003	2.63	0.89	1.04
Distressed Securities Index	2004	3.47	0.89	0.44
Emerging Markets (Total)	1990	(0.84)	2.06	0.63
Emerging Markets (Total)	1991	2.43	8.19	4.16
Emerging Markets (Total)	1992	8.06	3.26	2.77
Emerging Markets (Total)	1993	3.69	6.29	4.07
Emerging Markets (Total)	1994	5.32	(0.56)	(4.38)

APR	MAY	JUN	JUL	AUG	SEP	OCT	NOV	DEC	ANNUAL
1.48	1.75	1.72	1.15	(0.18)	(0.47)	(1.56)	(0.05)	(0.49)	2.16
1.49	0.94	0.98	1.57	2.09	1.31	1.22	1.66	1.63	17.60
0.80	1.70	0.71	1.85	1.65	1.46	1.24	0.70	1.09	16.35
1.50	1.24	1.04	1.41	1.40	1.03	1.29	0.60	0.77	15.22
(2.79)	0.03	0.15	1.55	0.80	0.12	(0.09)	(0.79)	(1.48)	(3.73)
1.90	1.88	2.32	2.13	0.96	1.55	1.25	1.58	1.33	19.85
1.88	1.73	0.44	(0.37)	1.40	1.23	1.27	1.40	0.66	14.56
0.68	1.40	1.71	1.61	1.14	1.11	1.19	0.09	0.41	12.72
1.35	0.40	0.22	0.49	(3.19)	(1.07)	(0.48)	3.33	1.60	7.77
2.66	1.40	1.09	1.05	0.42	0.66	0.33	0.99	1.08	14.41
1.78	1.34	1.66	0.68	1.42	1.21	0.42	(0.71)	(0.01)	14.50
1.57	0.71	0.13	0.76	1.26	0.64	0.93	0.62	(0.08)	13.37
0.87	0.53	0.22	(1.28)	0.35	1.59	1.00	2.02	1.42	9.05
1.36	1.14	(0.57)	(0.70)	(0.69)	1.41	1.40	0.81	0.88	9.93
0.25	(1.19)	(1.04)	0.46	0.27	(0.25)	(0.48)	0.86	0.45	1.18
0.65	0.82	3.65	2.02	(1.90)	(3.58)	(2.86)	1.00	1.12	6.44
5.33	1.36	1.72	3.18	1.37	1.91	2.02	0.39	0.83	35.66
0.32	1.13	(0.01)	0.27	0.89	0.93	0.12	1.66	2.84	25.24
1.63	2.23	2.71	2.99	2.52	0.70	1.97	0.87	2.76	32.54
(0.15)	0.38	(0.45)	1.13	1.20	0.40	0.42	(1.71)	0.07	3.84
1.83	1.24	2.06	2.31	1.34	2.09	(0.09)	1.14	1.53	19.73
3.06	2.07	1.35	0.21	1.73	1.82	0.95	0.88	1.15	20.77
0.07	1.74	1.89	2.11	1.08	2.84	(0.20)	0.69	0.30	15.40
1.55	0.28	0.13	(0.40)	(8.50)	(3.57)	(0.75)	1.70	0.15	(4.23)
5.06	1.91	1.93	0.68	0.37	(1.00)	(0.15)	1.14	2.62	16.94
(1.43)	(0.78)	2.31	0.26	1.29	(0.44)	(0.85)	(2.49)	(0.31)	2.78
0.18	2.75	3.09	0.79	0.68	(0.37)	0.84	1.27	(0.08)	13.28
1.13	0.79	(1.09)	(2.07)	0.31	(0.73)	(0.38)	2.30	2.88	5.28
4.00	3.32	2.82	0.92	1.58	2.71	2.69	1.42	2.23	29.56
0.96	(0.07)	2.16	0.06	0.81	1.06	1.60	3.30	2.95	19.03
(1.87)	6.57	1.88	5.88	(12.07)	(6.71)	4.82	(2.19)	0.03	(3.35)
1.94	2.51	(1.17)	5.43	0.79	(0.03)	0.37	1.89	12.27	45.40
1.39	4.13	(3.74)	(0.47)	(2.01)	3.41	3.28	0.31	2.12	24.35
5.02	5.58	4.59	0.86	5.63	2.57	7.84	3.95	9.99	79.22
(2.36)	0.45	(0.55)	3.17	7.87	3.21	(2.09)	(2.81)	(3.17)	3.38

FUND	YEAR	JAN	FEB	MAR
Emerging Markets (Total)	1994	5.32	(0.56)	(4.38)
Emerging Markets (Total)	1995	(5.50)	(2.17)	(0.71)
Emerging Markets (Total)	1996	5.69	(1.62)	0.09
Emerging Markets (Total)	1997	7.83	5.92	(1.48)
Emerging Markets (Total)	1998	(5.43)	3.96	2.94
Emerging Markets (Total)	1999	(2.32)	1.54	8.86
Emerging Markets (Total)	2000	0.20	4.80	3.38
Emerging Markets (Total)	2001	6.61	(2.71)	(3.07)
Emerging Markets (Total)	2002	2.25	2.15	4.07
Emerging Markets (Total)	2003	0.16	0.87	0.16
Emerging Markets (Total)	2004	3.51	3.62	2.23
Emerging Markets: Asia Index	1990	(0.84)	2.06	0.63
Emerging Markets: Asia Index	1991	2.93	9.08	3.59
Emerging Markets: Asia Index	1992	4.66	3.28	1.05
Emerging Markets: Asia Index	1993	3.23	6.09	4.40
Emerging Markets: Asia Index	1994	0.00	(0.58)	(6.40)
Emerging Markets: Asia Index	1995	(6.03)	1.26	0.66
Emerging Markets: Asia Index	1996	4.49	(0.54)	(0.85)
Emerging Markets: Asia Index	1997	3.41	3.40	(1.81)
Emerging Markets: Asia Index	1998	(4.05)	5.97	0.14
Emerging Markets: Asia Index	1999	(0.58)	(0.86)	6.16
Emerging Markets: Asia Index	2000	0.46	0.89	(0.22)
Emerging Markets: Asia Index	2001	5.21	(1.95)	(5.81)
Emerging Markets: Asia Index	2002	3.54	1.52	3.99
Emerging Markets: Asia Index	2003	1.51	(0.04)	(1.75)
Emerging Markets: Asia Index	2004	3.33	2.63	0.83
Emerging Markets: Eastern Europe/CIS Index	1994			
Emerging Markets: Eastern Europe/CIS Index	1995	(8.08)	(8.38)	5.68
Emergng Markets: Eastern Europe/CIS Index	1996	0.47	(4.88)	0.89
Emerging Markets: Eastern Europe/CIS Index	1997	21.39	14.05	(3.57)
Emerging Markets: Eastern Europe/CIS Index	1998	(11.54)	3.17	3.93
Emerging Markets: Eastern Europe/CIS Index	1999	(3.74)	8.74	7.72
Emerging Markets: Eastern Europe/CIS Index	2000	1.85	6.22	14.33
Emerging Markets: Eastern Europe/CIS Index	2001	10.12	(2.18)	1.53
Emerging Markets: Eastern Europe/CIS Index	2002	6.49	1.88	8.66
Emerging Markets: Eastern Europe/CIS Index	2003	(0.65)	4.65	(1.71)
Emerging Markets: Eastern Europe/CIS Index	2004	6.28	8.41	4.43
Emerging Markets: Global Index	1992	5.53	2.68	2.36
Emerging Markets: Global Index	1993	5.10	7.00	2.19
Emerging Markets: Global Index	1994	8.32	(0.85)	(3.37)
Emerging Markets: Global Index	1995	(3.45)	(2.42)	(1.81)
Emerging Markets: Global Index	1996	6.99	(1.69)	1.05

APR	MAY	JUN	JUL	AUG	SEP	OCT	NOV	DEC	ANNUAL
(2.36)	0.45	(0.55)	3.17	7.87	3.21	(2.09)	(2.81)	(3.17)	3.38
2.81	3.69	1.24	1.58	0.25	1.07	(2.66)	(1.47)	2.96	0.69
5.04	4.27	3.88	(2.65)	2.42	1.38	1.48	2.85	1.78	27.14
1.59	3.80	6.41	4.64	(2.08)	0.61	(7.96)	(3.92)	1.27	16.57
(0.55)	(9.32)	(6.01)	(0.30)	(21.02)	(4.98)	2.16	5.14	(2.76)	(32.96)
7.45	0.47	9.34	(0.99)	(1.45)	(1.89)	3.13	7.90	14.80	55.86
(6.59)	(5.05)	3.11	(0.38)	3.17	(5.53)	(3.28)	(5.50)	1.35	(10.71)
1.56	2.62	1.34	(3.22)	0.18	(5.60)	2.81	5.42	4.77	10.36
2.66	0.34	(4.18)	(4.97)	1.75	(3.55)	1.62	2.29	(0.30)	3.70
5.70	4.55	2.81	1.83	4.62	3.56	3.69	1.52	4.38	39.36
(3.26)	(2.01)	0.59	(0.43)	1.35	3.66	2.07	3.51	2.86	18.86
(1.87)	6.57	1.88	5.88	(12.07)	(6.71)	4.82	(2.19)	0.03	(3.35)
1.37	2.77	(1.95)	4.02	(2.49)	0.31	0.14	3.94	3.49	30.20
1.22	7.09	(0.42)	(3.25)	(3.43)	2.72	5.30	1.99	(1.11)	20.17
7.81	4.19	(1.30)	1.56	4.68	1.65	13.30	3.09	12.57	80.11
0.75	0.58	(1.85)	1.61	3.23	0.85	(0.89)	(3.93)	(1.76)	(8.42)
(0.81)	2.87	(0.39)	1.82	(0.79)	0.31	(1.36)	(2.79)	3.18	(2.40)
2.76	(0.44)	0.08	(5.41)	0.26	0.29	(0.57)	2.99	0.52	3.29
1.44	3.82	4.36	2.60	(2.78)	(4.43)	(6.96)	(2.66)	(1.88)	(2.25)
(1.75)	(5.52)	(5.74)	(2.11)	(6.63)	(0.66)	3.22	4.56	0.88	(11.93)
10.23	2.29	12.37	0.26	0.69	(1.29)	2.16	6.73	11.30	60.33
(6.81)	(5.88)	3.18	(3.76)	0.88	(6.42)	(3.72)	(3.38)	(0.88)	(23.33)
1.86	2.28	0.15	(2.80)	(0.64)	(6.84)	2.15	4.44	1.89	(0.85)
2.85	2.95	(2.48)	(3.53)	(1.50)	(4.72)	(1.24)	2.62	(0.76)	2.76
2.75	6.25	3.66	6.18	6.05	3.22	5.46	1.00	4.95	46.58
(3.29)	(2.29)	(0.85)	(1.53)	(0.27)	2.95	0.56	5.93	2.48	10.57
	(2.86)	12.16	13.64	32.77	2.42	(9.79)	(10.55)	(7.99)	25.00
(7.62)	14.97	15.92	0.63	(2.95)	(2.23)	(6.98)	(2.96)	6.52	0.60
15.17	19.71	18.38	(3.15)	9.15	(3.27)	9.36	2.77	1.28	83.16
1.77	4.84	11.55	12.29	1.87	2.56	(7.85)	(12.77)	6.46	59.52
(0.61)	(17.09)	(10.18)	(2.78)	(38.59)	(14.83)	4.09	2.54	(5.35)	(63.94)
4.76	5.08	17.95	0.48	(6.89)	(10.37)	4.96	9.34	30.12	83.32
(3.16)	(7.49)	(3.34)	6.30	9.58	(7.84)	(1.54)	(11.41)	1.29	1.59
4.57	6.81	3.61	(2.75)	2.31	(6.28)	5.31	6.72	7.77	42.94
8.20	1.65	(4.66)	(5.57)	1.46	(0.52)	4.19	3.08	(0.03)	26.48
6.86	6.16	3.30	(0.18)	5.41	5.04	1.01	1.64	4.30	41.70
(6.06)	(2.70)	1.35	(2.01)	2.53	6.67	4.93	1.07	4.99	33.02
0.94	0.92	1.36	(1.03)	(2.95)	4.36	9.82	3.64	0.16	30.87
6.06	6.80	6.82	2.52	4.16	2.00	6.61	4.76	10.61	87.10
(3.06)	0.88	(0.32)	3.06	7.96	4.79	(2.35)	(2.39)	(4.25)	7.65
5.69	3.35	1.43	1.65	0.71	2.23	(1.77)	(0.16)	3.64	9.02
6.06	3.56	3.30	(0.53)	2.83	3.12	1.04	3.57	1.94	35.69

FUND	YEAR	JAN	FEB	MAR
Emerging Markets: Global Index	1997	7.77	4.92	(1.58)
Emerging Markets: Global Index	1998	(4.37)	3.38	2.84
Emerging Markets: Global Index	1999	(0.43)	(0.21)	4.86
Emerging Markets: Global Index	2000	0.41	6.30	2.61
Emerging Markets: Global Index	2001	6.44	(2.33)	(1.51)
Emerging Markets: Global Index	2002	1.64	2.01	2.99
Emerging Markets: Global Index	2003	0.17	1.04	(0.29)
Emerging Markets: Global Index	2004	2.31	2.48	1.40
Emerging Markets: Latin America Index	1991	(0.56)	2.86	7.57
Emerging Markets: Latin America Index	1992	15.06	3.66	5.65
Emerging Markets: Latin America Index	1993	3.39	6.11	4.88
Emerging Markets: Latin America Index	1994	12.19	(0.21)	(1.30)
Emerging Markets: Latin America Index	1995	(6.29)	(6.54)	(4.48)
Emerging Markets: Latin America Index	1996	8.07	(1.77)	0.04
Emerging Markets: Latin America Index	1997	5.50	5.54	0.61
Emerging Markets: Latin America Index	1998	(3.16)	3.26	5.39
Emerging Markets: Latin America Index	1999	(5.56)	1.59	19.24
Emerging Markets: Latin America Index	2000	(1.98)	6.14	3.54
Emerging Markets: Latin America Index	2001	5.31	(4.69)	(5.65)
Emerging Markets: Latin America Index	2002	(2.68)	3.55	1.07
Emerging Markets: Latin America Index	2003	(0.64)	(4.29)	6.11
Emerging Markets: Latin America Index	2004	1.91	(1.17)	2.75
Equity Hedge Index	1990	(3.34)	2.85	5.67
Equity Hedge Index	1991	4.90	5.20	7.22
Equity Hedge Index	1992	2.49	2.90	(0.28)
Equity Hedge Index	1993	2.09	(0.57)	3.26
Equity Hedge Index	1994	2.35	(0.40)	(2.08)
Equity Hedge Index	1995	0.30	1.68	2.09
HFRI Equity Hedge Index	1996	1.06	2.82	1.90
Equity Hedge Index	1997	2.78	(0.24)	(0.73)
Equity Hedge Index	1998	(0.16)	4.09	4.54
Equity Hedge Index	1999	4.98	(2.41)	4.05
Equity Hedge Index	2000	0.25	10.00	1.73
Equity Hedge Index	2001	2.88	(2.56)	(2.30)
Equity Hedge Index	2002	0.22	(0.89)	2.03
Equity Hedge Index	2003	(0.01)	(0.78)	(0.07)
Equity Hedge Index	2004	1.95	1.11	0.36
Equity Market Neutral Index	1990	1.23	1.23	0.82
Equity Market Neutral Index	1991	2.51	0.04	2.70
Equity Market Neutral Index	1992	0.36	0.96	0.58
Equity Market Neutral Index	1993	1.91	1.06	1.67
Equity Market Neutral Index	1994	0.78	0.58	0.44

APR	MAY	JUN	JUL	AUG	SEP	OCT	NOV	DEC	ANNUAL
1.16	2.52	5.89	5.94	(0.16)	2.70	(6.18)	(4.96)	1.25	19.85
0.67	(8.05)	(4.97)	0.54	(27.46)	(5.66)	0.81	4.35	(1.73)	(36.39)
6.80	(0.98)	6.29	(0.45)	(1.30)	(1.44)	2.81	7.73	11.50	40.06
(6.71)	(4.71)	2.86	(0.73)	2.54	(4.75)	(3.08)	(4.66)	0.99	(9.39)
0.35	1.89	1.41	(2.39)	0.58	(3.62)	2.16	4.04	4.44	11.51
1.47	(0.03)	(3.66)	(2.82)	0.01	(1.65)	(0.50)	2.21	(1.45)	(0.03)
4.68	4.13	2.81	1.37	3.83	2.28	3.14	1.15	4.26	32.43
(1.35)	(1.59)	0.22	0.19	1.17	2.69	1.89	3.37	2.26	15.95
5.34	0.91	0.80	9.52	9.14	(1.26)	(0.01)	(2.24)	28.56	74.86
2.03	1.34	(13.38)	4.84	1.03	3.70	(4.09)	(4.71)	8.80	23.26
0.53	7.26	13.95	(1.71)	8.81	4.85	1.14	4.70	4.18	74.89
(8.20)	(0.04)	1.22	6.19	15.75	6.27	(2.69)	0.26	(3.64)	26.03
8.91	2.33	(0.48)	0.89	2.72	2.61	(4.64)	(0.34)	0.70	(5.57)
3.11	4.45	2.68	(0.16)	1.23	3.23	0.69	1.79	3.34	29.78
2.25	5.15	6.32	1.57	(5.75)	2.82	(11.12)	0.04	2.30	14.65
(0.92)	(7.99)	(4.01)	3.53	(15.63)	(2.37)	1.46	9.34	(7.34)	(19.16)
8.34	(3.99)	4.32	(5.59)	(0.44)	3.39	3.72	8.82	14.79	56.30
(8.23)	(2.73)	8.90	(0.11)	3.00	(4.08)	(4.26)	(5.92)	5.53	(1.77)
0.50	0.48	0.59	(6.78)	(2.40)	(8.12)	2.12	8.59	5.77	(5.68)
(1.56)	(3.99)	(6.92)	(10.53)	9.38	(9.87)	6.31	0.94	2.66	(12.94)
10.39	1.51	0.83	(0.43)	3.59	5.02	6.97	3.28	4.07	42.01
(4.72)	(1.95)	2.42	1.85	2.68	3.12	0.43	3.39	2.47	13.61
(0.87)	5.92	2.52	2.00	(1.88)	1.65	0.77	(2.29)	1.02	14.43
0.47	3.20	0.59	1.41	2.17	4.30	1.16	(1.08)	5.02	40.15
0.27	0.85	(0.92)	2.76	(0.85)	2.51	2.03	4.51	3.38	21.32
1.30	2.72	3.01	2.12	3.84	2.52	3.11	(1.93)	3.59	27.94
(0.37)	0.41	(0.41)	0.91	1.27	1.32	0.40	(1.48)	0.74	2.61
2.64	1.22	4.73	4.46	2.93	2.90	(1.44)	3.43	2.56	31.04
5.34	3.70	(0.73)	(2.87)	2.63	2.18	1.56	1.66	0.83	21.75
(0.27)	5.04	1.97	5.05	1.35	5.69	0.39	(0.93)	1.42	23.41
1.39	(1.27)	0.50	(0.67)	(7.65)	3.16	2.47	3.84	5.39	15.98
5.25	1.22	3.80	0.61	0.04	0.35	2.33	6.76	10.88	44.22
(4.19)	(2.44)	4.85	(1.58)	5.35	(1.08)	(2.01)	(4.30)	3.16	9.09
2.27	0.90	(0.32)	(1.06)	(1.22)	(3.73)	1.85	1.97	1.99	0.40
0.17	0.00	(2.63)	(3.93)	0.28	(1.96)	0.56	2.67	(1.14)	(4.71)
2.43	4.08	1.52	2.41	2.38	0.78	3.12	1.14	1.93	20.54
(2.08)	(0.19)	1.07	(1.88)	(0.37)	1.99	0.45	3.29	1.71	7.51
0.73	0.50	1.37	0.77	1.80	1.81	1.37	0.83	2.01	15.45
(0.01)	(0.02)	0.56	2.50	0.28	1.92	0.97	1.17	2.07	15.65
(0.03)	0.11	0.62	1.24	(0.35)	1.17	1.04	1.18	1.54	8.73
(0.14)	0.58	2.37	0.63	0.91	2.44	(0.10)	(1.45)	0.77	11.11
0.92	(0.95)	0.58	0.37	(0.35)	0.02	(0.12)	(0.45)	0.82	2.65

FUND	YEAR	JAN	FEB	MAR
Equity Market Neutral Index	1995	0.22	1.42	1.77
Equity Market Neutral Index	1996	2.18	0.95	0.86
Equity Market Neutral Index	1997	1.20	0.12	0.43
Equity Market Neutral Index	1998	0.54	0.76	1.26
Equity Market Neutral Index	1999	0.15	(1.33)	(0.76)
Equity Market Neutral Index	2000	(1.19)	2.26	0.48
Equity Market Neutral Index	2001	(1.57)	2.07	1.77
Equity Market Neutral Index	2002	0.76	(0.22)	0.06
Equity Market Neutral Index	2003	0.30	(0.18)	(0.05)
Equity Market Neutral Index	2004	1.07	0.57	0.41
Equity Non-Hedge Index	1990	(5.07)	1.66	4.50
Equity Non-Hedge Index	1991	4.91	9.31	9.58
Equity Non-Hedge Index	1992	5.44	2.30	(2.05)
Equity Non-Hedge Index	1993	2.30	(1.49)	3.77
Equity Non-Hedge Index	1994	3.17	(1.22)	(3.07)
Equity Non-Hedge Index	1995	0.33	3.24	3.34
Equity Non-Hedge Index	1996	2.12	3.36	2.79
Equity Non-Hedge Index	1997	3.39	(1.08)	(5.04)
Equity Non-Hedge Index	1998	(0.88)	5.69	3.98
Equity Non-Hedge Index	1999	3.65	(3.84)	2.87
Equity Non-Hedge Index	2000	(1.56)	9.41	2.36
Equity Non-Hedge Index	2001	8.00	(7.41)	(5.05)
Equity Non-Hedge Index	2002	(0.35)	(1.54)	4.76
Equity Non-Hedge Index	2003	(0.43)	(1.43)	0.38
Equity Non-Hedge Index	2004	2.38	1.46	0.79
Event-Driven Index	1990	(5.69)	1.69	4.92
Event-Driven Index	1991	1.00	4.42	3.37
Event-Driven Index	1992	4.21	2.13	1.59
Event-Driven Index	1993	3.07	1.63	3.85
Event-Driven Index	1994	3.51	(0.49)	(0.55)
Event-Driven Index	1995	2.04	1.27	0.69
Event-Driven Index	1996	3.89	1.45	1.88
Event-Driven Index	1997	2.84	0.93	(0.53)
Event-Driven Index	1998	0.25	3.36	2.93
Event-Driven Index	1999	1.65	(0.48)	2.06
Event-Driven Index	2000	0.74	3.76	0.03
Event-Driven Index	2001	4.59	(0.38)	(0.25)
Event-Driven Index	2002	0.79	(1.37)	1.91
Event-Driven Index	2003	1.31	(0.10)	0.95
Event-Driven Index	2004	2.80	1.20	0.06
Fixed Income (Total)	1990	(0.03)	0.42	1.11

APR	MAY	JUN	JUL	AUG	SEP	OCT	NOV	DEC	ANNUAL
1.86	0.60	0.92	2.23	0.98	1.85	1.58	0.78	1.03	16.33
0.35	1.39	1.37	1.62	0.78	0.66	2.10	0.16	0.95	14.20
0.96	1.49	1.54	2.17	0.21	2.18	1.36	0.53	0.67	13.62
0.66	0.48	1.69	(0.27)	(1.67)	0.81	(0.61)	0.85	3.59	8.30
(0.65)	0.17	2.02	1.91	0.70	0.85	0.44	1.05	2.39	7.09
2.64	0.27	1.50	(0.04)	3.06	0.94	0.23	1.03	2.58	14.56
0.06	0.28	0.36	0.45	1.73	1.31	0.01	(0.36)	0.46	6.71
0.99	0.03	0.05	(0.27)	0.53	(0.25)	(0.29)	(0.91)	0.51	0.98
0.36	0.35	0.40	(0.44)	0.13	0.60	1.06	0.20	(0.29)	2.44
(1.15)	0.35	0.38	0.18	(0.23)	0.79	(0.00)	1.29	0.56	4.27
(3.09)	7.43	1.99	(0.76)	(10.66)	(6.13)	(2.20)	4.16	2.25	(7.17)
0.28	4.56	(2.52)	4.83	3.84	2.23	3.85	(2.32)	8.33	57.07
(2.31)	1.19	(2.90)	3.67	(1.65)	2.59	4.81	6.93	3.28	22.78
(0.26)	5.23	1.44	2.21	4.38	1.97	3.65	(2.22)	3.80	27.42
(0.41)	0.71	(0.95)	2.50	4.81	0.22	0.90	(2.43)	1.04	5.10
2.46	1.89	4.83	6.52	3.11	3.02	(2.35)	2.64	1.47	34.80
7.50	5.40	(2.62)	(6.79)	3.88	3.97	(0.51)	2.96	1.68	25.52
(0.54)	8.98	3.19	5.56	0.86	6.36	(2.67)	(1.47)	(0.34)	17.56
1.43	(2.77)	1.02	(2.87)	(13.34)	3.44	3.98	6.64	4.80	9.80
6.36	1.10	4.77	0.53	(1.16)	(0.62)	2.66	9.37	10.74	41.82
(8.36)	(4.83)	7.17	(2.74)	7.35	(4.31)	(5.15)	(8.43)	1.73	(9.04)
5.71	2.32	0.04	(2.36)	(3.08)	(8.65)	4.46	5.27	3.78	1.36
(0.18)	(1.04)	(4.43)	(7.17)	0.27	(4.90)	3.28	5.63	(2.35)	(8.50)
6.59	7.18	2.73	3.23	3.53	0.19	5.74	2.52	2.49	37.53
(3.03)	(0.13)	1.41	(3.73)	(0.47)	3.36	1.60	5.67	3.12	12.74
1.16	1.93	1.37	1.14	(4.53)	(2.78)	(1.60)	0.80	1.63	(0.47)
3.06	2.85	0.24	2.33	1.26	1.48	2.34	0.52	1.69	27.42
0.33	1.01	0.11	1.22	0.24	1.36	0.96	1.71	3.12	19.46
1.21	1.88	2.99	2.10	2.79	0.87	1.68	0.16	2.95	28.22
(0.70)	0.94	1.12	1.56	1.81	0.41	(0.40)	(1.27)	0.00	6.00
2.11	1.84	1.48	1.98	2.14	1.85	0.09	5.01	2.19	25.11
2.62	3.53	0.43	(0.50)	2.42	1.97	0.97	2.03	1.78	24.84
(0.83)	4.36	2.65	2.72	0.52	3.59	0.45	1.36	1.49	21.23
0.31	(1.19)	0.31	(0.57)	(8.90)	(0.62)	1.25	2.43	2.73	1.70
5.13	2.00	2.93	0.81	(0.78)	1.62	0.42	3.38	3.39	24.33
(1.48)	(0.77)	2.92	0.15	2.01	0.63	(1.32)	(2.32)	2.39	6.74
1.23	1.94	1.11	0.30	1.29	(3.26)	2.07	1.59	1.51	12.18
0.28	(0.33)	(3.82)	(4.35)	0.37	(1.49)	0.70	2.92	0.26	(4.30)
3.15	4.15	2.46	1.46	1.95	1.27	2.51	1.63	2.12	25.33
(0.56)	(0.31)	1.76	(0.93)	0.49	1.37	1.28	3.44	2.91	14.24
1.16	1.70	0.93	1.00	(1.86)	(0.94)	0.07	1.70	1.10	6.48

FUND	YEAR	JAN	FEB	MAR
Fixed Income (Total)	1991	5.34	4.01	2.15
Fixed Income (Total)	1992	2.94	1.88	1.63
Fixed Income (Total)	1993	0.75	1.61	1.23
Fixed Income (Total)	1994	1.85	1.07	(0.23)
Fixed Income (Total)	1995	0.36	1.27	1.38
Fixed Income (Total)	1996	1.55	0.96	1.13
Fixed Income (Total)	1997	1.31	1.34	(0.13)
Fixed Income (Total)	1998	0.73	1.36	1.60
Fixed Income (Total)	1999	1.67	0.34	1.17
Fixed Income (Total)	2000	0.01	1.35	(0.66)
Fixed Income (Total)	2001	3.28	0.01	0.33
Fixed Income (Total)	2002	0.92	0.41	1.42
Fixed Income (Total)	2003	1.14	1.00	0.25
Fixed Income (Total)	2004	1.11	0.90	0.23
Fixed Income: Arbitrage Index	1990	2.25	2.10	(0.21)
Fixed Income: Arbitrage Index	1991	4.00	2.42	1.52
Fixed Income: Arbitrage Index	1992	4.70	2.53	2.53
Fixed Income: Arbitrage Index	1993	0.25	0.89	1.47
Fixed Income: Arbitrage Index	1994	2.32	1.63	0.93
Fixed Income: Arbitrage Index	1995	0.64	0.34	1.79
Fixed Income: Arbitrage Index	1996	0.95	0.69	0.58
Fixed Income: Arbitrage Index	1997	1.43	1.17	0.54
Fixed Income: Arbitrage Index	1998	0.39	1.28	1.34
Fixed Income: Arbitrage Index	1999	1.17	1.09	1.31
Fixed Income: Arbitrage Index	2000	(0.67)	1.31	(1.35)
Fixed Income: Arbitrage Index	2001	2.17	0.41	(0.44)
Fixed Income: Arbitrage Index	2002	0.99	0.47	0.17
Fixed Income: Arbitrage Index	2003	0.70	0.83	0.57
Fixed Income: Arbitrage Index	2004	0.79	1.04	(0.19)
Fixed Income: Convertible Bonds Index	1993	0.59	0.21	3.80
Fixed Income: Convertible Bonds Index	1994	4.11	0.03	(2.97)
Fixed Income: Convertible Bonds Index	1995	(2.09)	0.81	1.34
Fixed Income: Convertible Bonds Index	1996	3.39	0.77	2.55
Fixed Income: Convertible Bonds Index	1997	3.61	1.43	(1.37)
Fixed Income: Convertible Bonds Index	1998	0.58	5.19	5.02
Fixed Income: Convertible Bonds Index	1999	4.28	(1.44)	1.12
Fixed Income: Convertible Bonds Index	2000	1.89	5.16	2.36
Fixed Income: Convertible Bonds Index	2001	14.42	(7.25)	(5.04)
Fixed Income: Convertible Bonds Index	2002	(2.54)	(1.41)	5.18
Fixed Income: Convertible Bonds Index	2003	2.34	(0.39)	(0.52)
Fixed Income: Convertible Bonds Index	2004	1.66	0.80	0.57
Fixed Income: Diversified Index	1995	1.42	2.43	0.96

APR	MAY	JUN	JUL	AUG	SEP	OCT	NOV	DEC	ANNUAL
1.48	1.20	1.04	2.71	1.77	0.84	2.28	0.13	1.66	27.45
0.82	1.95	0.71	1.17	1.03	0.33	1.28	1.74	1.61	18.46
1.02	1.14	1.40	1.54	1.73	0.73	1.51	1.15	1.71	16.67
0.01	0.62	0.76	0.88	0.77	0.38	0.61	0.25	0.36	7.56
1.40	0.86	0.33	1.93	1.14	0.10	0.69	0.99	1.34	12.43
1.64	1.19	0.80	0.57	1.20	1.50	1.35	0.99	1.03	14.83
0.67	1.42	1.80	1.92	0.41	1.60	(0.24)	0.26	0.93	11.86
0.41	0.21	(0.66)	0.43	(3.13)	(1.86)	(3.27)	1.19	1.09	(2.04)
2.35	0.08	0.59	(0.19)	(0.25)	0.43	0.09	2.30	1.93	10.98
(0.54)	(0.81)	1.02	0.37	2.14	0.45	(0.82)	(0.27)	1.18	3.42
1.08	0.69	0.08	0.24	1.29	(0.85)	1.59	1.14	1.08	10.36
1.13	0.96	0.50	0.00	0.82	(1.72)	(0.41)	1.17	1.14	6.48
1.27	1.65	0.71	(0.31)	0.57	1.29	0.71	0.96	1.75	11.53
0.17	(0.11)	0.67	0.51	0.65	0.75	1.04	1.32	1.00	8.54
2.23	0.32	0.15	0.68	0.03	0.49	1.22	0.55	0.57	10.84
1.88	2.34	1.39	1.96	(0.82)	(2.58)	(0.03)	(1.17)	1.46	12.89
2.26	0.62	(0.45)	(0.08)	0.84	(0.79)	3.33	2.18	2.62	22.11
1.45	1.94	0.37	1.99	1.50	0.70	0.96	2.12	1.87	16.64
0.98	0.75	1.32	0.36	0.71	0.88	0.65	0.76	0.06	11.94
0.64	(0.54)	(1.18)	2.49	0.92	(1.89)	1.58	(0.01)	1.22	6.08
1.39	1.15	1.35	1.30	0.63	0.52	1.18	(0.37)	1.94	11.89
0.98	0.34	0.67	0.58	0.40	0.51	(0.37)	(0.14)	0.71	7.02
1.03	0.19	(1.31)	1.69	(1.18)	(6.45)	(6.09)	(1.42)	0.15	(10.29)
0.11	(0.03)	1.32	0.65	(0.34)	0.25	0.25	1.07	0.31	7.38
0.51	3.04	0.25	(1.02)	1.83	0.46	(0.50)	0.60	0.30	4.78
1.12	0.62	(0.48)	0.16	1.13	(1.54)	0.98	0.13	0.50	4.81
0.90	0.66	0.93	1.51	0.89	0.68	(0.09)	(0.05)	1.39	8.78
0.29	1.89	0.54	(0.33)	0.65	1.16	0.66	0.99	1.05	9.35
0.38	0.38	0.52	0.45	0.38	0.47	0.48	0.51	0.45	5.81
0.11	0.97	0.91	3.52	2.83	1.13	3.54	(0.02)	3.92	23.60
(1.12)	0.31	(0.21)	1.96	2.43	(2.01)	(0.75)	(2.22)	0.05	(0.62)
3.04	2.20	3.01	3.68	3.67	0.46	(1.90)	2.39	1.26	19.17
2.63	1.41	(1.41)	(3.44)	2.43	3.05	0.81	3.63	1.29	18.24
(0.28)	4.49	3.61	3.82	0.31	3.65	(3.44)	(1.02)	1.87	17.60
1.28	(1.35)	(1.84)	(1.61)	(11.51)	1.15	3.70	5.08	2.83	7.53
7.56	(0.78)	0.70	2.36	1.11	(0.04)	0.16	8.94	8.61	36.94
(3.32)	(3.96)	2.57	(0.04)	7.47	(1.55)	(4.62)	(10.55)	(5.75)	(11.17)
7.04	0.05	(0.41)	(2.73)	(2.20)	(5.96)	1.52	3.53	2.22	3.30
2.04	2.05	(9.30)	(9.59)	(0.44)	(5.27)	(0.51)	9.05	(1.57)	(13.07)
3.04	4.01	0.65	(0.27)	0.52	1.17	2.92	0.40	2.51	17.53
(0.84)	(1.37)	0.95	(1.73)	0.71	1.28	0.52	2.79	2.70	8.24
0.92	1.93	0.17	1.27	0.62	0.38	0.94	0.57	0.59	12.88

FUND	YEAR	JAN	FEB	MAR
Fixed Income: Diversified Index	1996	1.11	1.20	0.17
Fixed Income: Diversified Index	1997	(0.09)	0.78	(1.05)
Fixed Income: Diversified Index	1998	0.86	0.35	1.25
Fixed Income: Diversified Index	1999	0.88	(0.56)	1.14
Fixed Income: Diversified Index	2000	0.23	0.81	(0.13)
Fixed Income: Diversified Index	2001	0.71	1.13	2.64
Fixed Income: Diversified Index	2002	(0.19)	(0.05)	1.03
Fixed Income: Diversified Index	2003	1.06	1.76	(0.45)
Fixed Income: Diversified Index	2004	0.77	0.64	0.31
Fixed Income: High Yield Index	1990	(4.30)	(1.20)	1.80
Fixed Income: High Yield Index	1991	2.83	9.54	5.42
Fixed Income: High Yield Index	1992	3.20	2.44	3.90
Fixed Income: High Yield Index	1993	3.35	2.65	2.19
Fixed Income: High Yield Index	1994	2.77	(0.19)	(1.89)
Fixed Income: High Yield Index	1995	0.88	2.55	1.20
Fixed Income: High Yield Index	1996	1.99	1.47	0.61
Fixed Income: High Yield Index	1997	1.09	1.80	(1.36)
Fixed Income: High Yield Index	1998	1.21	1.09	1.20
Fixed Income: High Yield Index	1999	1.19	0.40	1.05
Fixed Income: High Yield Index	2000	0.08	0.60	(0.68)
Fixed Income: High Yield Index	2001	2.59	1.12	(0.38)
Fixed Income: High Yield Index	2002	1.17	0.33	1.88
Fixed Income: High Yield Index	2003	1.30	1.29	1.06
Fixed Income: High Yield Index	2004	1.86	0.41	0.43
Fixed Income: Mortgage-Backed Index	1993	0.88	1.33	0.76
Fixed Income: Mortgage-Backed Index	1994	1.18	1.18	1.00
Fixed Income: Mortgage-Backed Index	1995	0.84	1.35	1.40
Fixed Income: Mortgage-Backed Index	1996	1.36	1.03	1.37
Fixed Income: Mortgage-Backed Index	1997	1.07	1.56	1.22
Fixed Income: Mortgage-Backed Index	1998	0.81	1.02	0.69
Fixed Income: Mortgage-Backed Index	1999	1.63	1.23	1.68
Fixed Income: Mortgage-Backed Index	2000	(1.41)	0.21	(3.35)
Fixed Income: Mortgage-Backed Index	2001	2.37	1.21	1.04
Fixed Income: Mortgage-Backed Index	2002	3.27	1.58	1.50
Fixed Income: Mortgage-Backed Index	2003	1.25	0.76	0.27
Fixed Income: Mortgage-Backed Index	2004	1.32	1.36	0.62
Fund of Funds Composite Index	1990	0.07	1.34	2.07
Fund of Funds Composite Index	1991	0.39	(0.03)	3.52
Fund of Funds Composite Index	1992	1.32	1.16	0.80
Fund of Funds Composite Index	1993	0.87	2.20	1.51
Fund of Funds Composite Index	1994	1.26	(2.27)	(2.31)
Fund of Funds Composite Index	1995	(1.26)	(0.09)	1.43

APR	MAY	JUN	JUL	AUG	SEP	OCT	NOV	DEC	ANNUAL
0.73	0.63	0.88	1.04	0.98	0.96	1.11	1.08	0.73	11.15
(0.82)	(0.11)	1.49	3.47	(1.26)	1.75	(0.01)	0.69	0.88	5.77
(0.20)	1.01	0.52	0.50	(0.86)	1.42	(1.13)	1.16	0.65	5.63
1.94	(0.24)	(0.37)	(1.44)	(0.83)	0.62	(0.47)	1.03	1.11	2.79
(0.01)	(1.57)	1.03	0.97	2.55	0.98	(0.12)	2.91	5.39	13.65
(1.22)	0.32	0.04	0.21	2.12	0.14	2.50	(0.81)	0.90	8.95
0.07	0.83	2.08	0.76	1.85	0.23	(1.50)	0.61	2.82	8.81
1.99	2.67	(0.06)	(0.53)	0.03	1.86	(0.12)	0.40	2.77	11.91
(0.48)	(0.73)	0.32	0.54	0.49	0.60	1.08	1.61	0.96	6.24
(0.43)	1.99	1.81	2.83	(5.87)	(6.09)	(6.17)	2.25	1.27	(12.11)
3.22	0.32	2.42	3.46	1.90	1.72	3.72	0.24	1.01	41.83
(0.96)	3.85	(0.66)	1.00	0.98	1.55	(0.80)	1.12	1.66	18.53
0.69	1.68	2.49	1.34	0.79	0.44	2.32	1.18	1.53	22.67
(0.87)	0.46	(0.05)	0.01	(0.21)	1.04	0.60	(0.68)	0.54	1.47
1.99	2.00	0.80	1.89	0.32	0.94	0.26	0.61	0.82	15.20
1.72	1.43	0.61	0.52	1.75	2.29	0.63	1.37	0.77	16.24
1.07	2.37	1.79	2.12	0.78	2.50	(0.19)	(0.82)	0.79	12.52
1.02	0.02	(0.20)	0.39	(7.16)	(3.29)	(2.45)	2.98	0.19	(5.28)
2.05	0.15	2.13	0.29	(0.44)	(1.06)	(0.35)	0.91	0.84	7.35
0.28	(0.79)	0.76	0.81	(0.28)	(0.18)	(1.83)	(1.68)	(0.12)	(3.03)
(0.34)	0.64	(0.67)	0.52	1.60	(3.43)	1.05	2.10	0.58	5.37
1.74	0.26	0.75	(1.26)	(0.30)	(0.97)	(0.07)	1.49	0.68	5.80
2.62	1.31	2.71	1.43	1.08	1.95	1.69	1.33	1.70	21.30
0.21	(0.65)	1.00	0.52	1.00	0.98	1.60	1.54	1.09	10.43
0.72	0.97	1.45	0.68	1.98	1.41	0.98	0.69	1.82	14.55
0.32	0.74	1.16	1.47	1.10	0.59	0.69	0.89	0.72	11.61
1.08	0.79	1.27	1.10	1.14	2.00	1.20	1.42	1.85	16.57
1.13	1.35	1.51	1.45	1.33	1.58	1.91	1.37	0.49	17.08
1.58	1.69	2.29	1.37	1.34	1.33	0.98	0.62	1.03	17.31
(0.42)	0.19	(1.36)	0.17	(1.17)	(2.15)	(9.24)	0.59	1.76	(9.18)
1.86	0.22	(0.12)	(0.69)	0.49	2.03	1.29	1.15	0.01	11.28
(1.08)	(0.96)	0.80	0.57	0.72	1.25	1.01	1.29	(0.32)	(1.37)
2.15	1.60	1.33	1.34	1.40	1.34	1.22	2.64	1.73	21.17
1.91	1.54	1.25	1.41	0.62	(5.12)	0.14	(0.11)	0.54	8.62
0.56	0.39	0.55	(0.99)	0.65	0.53	0.71	1.19	1.68	7.79
0.65	0.44	0.95	1.02	0.92	1.04	1.53	1.68	1.44	13.74
0.89	0.47	2.21	3.07	1.63	2.84	1.64	0.00	0.09	17.53
(0.83)	0.77	1.18	0.51	1.31	1.76	0.61	0.05	4.50	14.50
0.12	0.28	0.44	0.82	0.47	2.49	1.70	0.30	1.81	12.33
2.30	2.07	2.75	2.43	1.79	0.33	2.26	0.40	4.76	26.32
(1.11)	0.42	0.77	0.17	1.29	0.78	(0.95)	(1.01)	(0.49)	(3.48)
1.48	0.90	0.57	1.74	2.28	0.75	(0.53)	1.15	2.22	11.10

FUND	YEAR	JAN	FEB	MAR
Fund of Funds Composite Index	1996	2.73	(0.62)	0.99
Fund of Funds Composite Index	1997	3.55	1.68	(0.82)
Fund of Funds Composite Index	1998	(0.96)	1.90	4.01
Fund of Funds Composite Index	1999	1.41	(0.22)	2.08
Fund of Funds Composite Index	2000	1.54	5.21	0.23
Fund of Funds Composite Index	2001	1.93	(0.74)	(0.44)
Fund of Funds Composite Index	2002	0.45	(0.26)	0.78
Fund of Funds Composite Index	2003	0.84	0.34	(0.03)
Fund of Funds Composite Index	2004	1.59	1.10	0.45
Fund Weighted Composite Index	1990	(2.11)	1.54	3.21
Fund Weighted Composite Index	1991	2.59	4.02	4.95
Fund Weighted Composite Index	1992	3.84	2.14	0.59
Fund Weighted Composite Index	1993	2.32	1.34	3.06
Fund Weighted Composite Index	1994	2.50	(0.55)	(1.51)
Fund Weighted Composite Index	1995	(0.22)	1.31	1.65
Fund Weighted Composite Index	1996	2.89	1.23	1.46
Fund Weighted Composite Index	1997	3.17	1.03	(1.64)
Fund Weighted Composite Index	1998	(0.71)	3.27	3.00
Fund Weighted Composite Index	1999	2.24	(1.32)	3.14
Fund Weighted Composite Index	2000	0.64	6.16	0.93
Fund Weighted Composite Index	2001	3.39	(2.21)	(1.59)
Fund Weighted Composite Index	2002	0.45	(0.70)	1.91
Fund Weighted Composite Index	2003	0.65	0.02	0.14
Fund Weighted Composite Index	2004	1.98	1.19	0.51
Macro Index	1990	(1.23)	0.48	3.54
Macro Index	1991	(0.25)	6.31	6.85
Macro Index	1992	2.80	0.34	0.32
Macro Index	1993	0.91	5.17	5.54
Macro Index	1994	2.11	(6.40)	(3.43)
Macro Index	1995	(0.87)	1.45	1.40
Macro Index	1996	5.28	(3.77)	0.37
Macro Index	1997	5.14	1.59	(1.24)
Macro Index	1998	0.20	1.90	5.05
Macro Index	1999	0.81	(1.24)	1.07
Macro Index	2000	1.14	3.67	(2.27)
Macro Index	2001	2.15	(1.71)	0.83
Macro Index	2002	0.41	(1.21)	2.11
Macro Index	2003	2.52	1.91	(2.23)
Macro Index	2004	0.65	2.00	1.12
Market Timing Index	1990	2.03	(0.51)	2.98
Market Timing Index	1991	1.81	4.14	1.89
Market Timing Index	1992	0.93	(0.12)	(0.35)

APR	MAY	JUN	JUL	AUG	SEP	OCT	NOV	DEC	ANNUAL
3.09	1.54	0.38	(1.87)	1.53	1.25	1.59	2.34	0.68	14.39
0.37	1.82	2.50	4.64	(0.32)	2.78	(1.44)	(0.51)	1.05	16.20
0.91	(0.93)	(0.55)	(0.21)	(7.47)	(2.55)	(1.96)	1.44	1.60	(5.11)
3.26	0.84	2.84	0.73	0.11	(0.12)	1.27	4.91	6.85	26.47
(3.37)	(1.58)	2.82	(0.22)	2.00	(1.16)	(1.01)	(1.54)	1.38	4.07
0.69	0.90	(0.06)	(0.43)	0.18	(1.58)	0.93	0.36	1.07	2.80
0.64	0.44	(0.88)	(1.34)	0.33	(0.45)	(0.20)	0.84	0.68	1.02
1.22	2.08	0.67	0.23	0.83	1.18	1.53	0.62	1.55	11.61
(0.88)	(0.87)	0.24	(0.58)	(0.01)	0.89	0.78	2.52	1.40	6.76
(0.04)	3.05	2.10	1.50	(3.45)	(1.96)	(0.04)	0.75	1.35	5.81
1.34	1.98	0.41	2.62	2.06	2.32	1.83	0.27	3.95	32.19
0.30	1.84	(0.41)	2.08	(0.27)	1.94	2.11	2.80	2.53	21.22
1.49	2.60	2.62	2.09	2.93	1.58	3.18	0.15	3.91	30.88
(0.59)	0.68	0.27	1.35	2.46	0.89	(0.03)	(1.27)	(0.08)	4.10
2.10	1.70	2.48	3.20	2.20	1.96	(0.65)	1.89	2.08	21.50
3.96	3.05	0.18	(2.08)	2.28	2.07	0.98	2.08	1.33	21.10
(0.11)	4.38	2.70	3.87	0.34	3.72	(1.53)	(0.93)	0.88	16.79
0.96	(2.08)	(0.13)	(0.79)	(8.70)	0.69	1.22	3.71	2.79	2.62
4.50	0.72	3.63	0.52	(0.01)	0.16	1.60	5.06	7.65	31.29
(2.85)	(1.96)	3.68	(0.60)	3.81	(1.24)	(1.79)	(3.49)	2.07	4.98
1.95	1.19	0.29	(0.83)	(0.41)	(2.83)	2.01	2.07	1.71	4.62
0.28	0.04	(1.94)	(2.86)	0.53	(1.54)	0.59	2.12	(0.21)	(1.45)
2.64	3.58	1.35	1.30	1.83	1.16	2.45	1.06	1.87	19.55
(1.48)	(0.31)	0.75	(0.96)	0.12	1.65	0.83	2.81	1.65	8.99
(0.74)	3.98	1.65	3.83	(3.78)	(0.98)	2.60	1.14	1.71	12.56
(1.68)	0.01	2.62	2.43	6.70	5.96	2.33	0.75	7.44	46.66
1.12	6.99	0.87	1.71	(1.06)	2.28	4.66	3.13	1.37	27.17
2.69	2.99	7.15	3.71	3.71	(0.66)	4.80	(0.01)	7.88	53.31
(1.20)	2.25	0.15	0.71	2.60	(0.12)	(0.11)	0.39	(0.98)	(4.30)
0.78	2.54	0.47	3.93	5.59	3.22	0.41	3.63	3.63	29.32
3.11	(0.08)	(1.06)	(3.04)	0.73	2.01	1.58	4.72	(0.49)	9.32
(0.22)	1.83	1.82	5.90	(1.25)	3.05	(1.60)	(0.25)	2.93	18.82
(0.13)	0.08	0.57	0.23	(3.70)	(0.50)	(1.83)	1.98	2.44	6.19
3.86	(0.90)	2.16	0.46	(0.55)	1.08	(0.75)	3.83	6.82	17.62
(3.68)	(1.54)	1.24	0.05	1.73	(2.19)	(0.73)	0.25	4.61	1.97
(0.12)	(0.10)	0.43	(0.30)	0.57	0.63	2.71	0.14	1.51	6.87
0.39	1.87	1.20	(0.34)	0.63	0.93	(1.65)	(0.46)	3.41	7.44
1.23	5.67	0.53	0.73	1.86	2.26	1.73	0.19	3.38	21.42
(2.84)	(0.70)	(0.11)	(0.33)	(0.23)	0.84	0.84	2.85	0.29	4.34
(0.89)	3.15	1.82	0.97	0.56	(2.25)	(0.41)	2.29	3.18	13.52
0.46	1.91	(1.29)	3.02	3.08	(0.25)	2.38	(1.40)	5.49	23.15
(0.63)	1.79	(0.49)	1.78	(1.89)	(0.32)	1.78	3.19	1.93	7.74

FUND	YEAR	JAN	FEB	MAR
Market Timing Index	1993	1.16	1.38	3.45
Market Timing Index	1994	1.87	(0.70)	(1.18)
Market Timing Index	1995	(0.54)	1.11	1.09
Market Timing Index	1996	3.26	1.28	0.04
Market Timing Index	1997	1.84	(0.76)	(2.04)
Market Timing Index	1998	(0.73)	2.63	2.19
Market Timing Index	1999	4.91	(2.99)	4.28
Market Timing Index	2000	1.55	5.96	2.09
Market Timing Index	2001	0.33	(3.28)	(2.04)
Market Timing Index	2002	(1.33)	0.29	1.86
Market Timing Index	2003	(0.85)	(0.28)	(0.06)
Market Timing Index	2004	0.95	0.38	0.15
Merger Arbitrage Index	1990	(6.46)	1.71	2.90
Merger Arbitrage Index	1991	0.01	1.59	2.30
Merger Arbitrage Index	1992	1.96	0.96	1.34
Merger Arbitrage Index	1993	2.12	1.64	0.49
Merger Arbitrage Index	1994	1.50	(0.41)	1.37
Merger Arbitrage Index	1995	0.86	1.45	1.49
Merger Arbitrage Index	1996	1.57	1.29	1.51
Merger Arbitrage Index	1997	1.04	0.39	1.05
Merger Arbitrage Index	1998	0.96	1.89	1.05
Merger Arbitrage Index	1999	0.71	0.25	1.05
Merger Arbitrage Index	2000	1.63	1.88	0.82
Merger Arbitrage Index	2001	1.10	0.44	(0.75)
Merger Arbitrage Index	2002	0.86	(0.36)	0.56
Merger Arbitrage Index	2003	0.15	(0.01)	(0.10)
Merger Arbitrage Index	2004	1.02	0.59	0.07
Regulation D Index	1996	4.62	4.59	3.86
Regulation D Index	1997	2.75	1.97	1.70
Regulation D Index	1998	1.35	2.77	1.68
Regulation D Index	1999	2.55	1.21	2.05
Regulation D Index	2000	7.74	6.03	2.79
Regulation D Index	2001	(0.25)	(1.67)	(1.97)
Regulation D Index	2002	0.25	(1.84)	1.78
Regulation D Index	2003	7.32	(1.20)	(0.78)
Regulation D Index	2004	2.78	2.36	(0.21)
Relative Value Arbitrage Index	1990	0.84	1.67	1.90
Relative Value Arbitrage Index	1991	2.59	3.10	2.66
Relative Value Arbitrage Index	1992	5.72	2.60	(0.79)
Relative Value Arbitrage Index	1993	2.33	0.90	3.68
Relative Value Arbitrage Index	1994	2.48	0.44	0.33
Relative Value Arbitrage Index	1995	1.28	1.09	0.63

APR	MAY	JUN	JUL	AUG	SEP	OCT	NOV	DEC	ANNUAL
2.64	4.27	0.79	1.79	1.01	0.56	2.86	(1.60)	3.69	24.18
(0.20)	(0.60)	(1.41)	1.35	3.26	0.58	1.25	(1.64)	0.98	3.49
1.09	2.56	1.35	2.65	(0.01)	1.04	(0.58)	1.38	0.82	12.58
2.78	1.40	(0.64)	(1.62)	1.09	3.34	0.79	2.45	(1.31)	13.47
(0.20)	4.06	2.27	4.34	(0.51)	3.81	(1.28)	(0.05)	1.58	13.57
2.19	(1.42)	3.39	(0.01)	0.66	(0.39)	5.45	5.39	3.31	24.82
4.16	(2.80)	4.30	0.98	1.21	(0.08)	2.35	2.50	5.09	26.17
(2.67)	1.47	1.53	(1.25)	3.38	(2.19)	0.38	(1.94)	3.26	11.79
3.80	1.06	0.71	(1.43)	(1.41)	(1.08)	2.91	2.61	2.11	4.09
(1.52)	(0.87)	(1.38)	(1.23)	0.90	(0.22)	0.69	2.03	(2.42)	(3.25)
2.71	3.41	1.62	0.39	2.12	0.00	2.75	0.68	2.00	15.36
(2.14)	0.61	0.53	(2.73)	(0.50)	1.93	1.52	3.35	2.23	6.27
0.98	2.28	0.73	0.02	(0.82)	(4.58)	0.73	2.19	1.21	0.44
2.83	1.55	1.12	1.44	0.64	1.10	1.41	1.38	1.20	17.86
0.14	0.00	0.30	1.45	0.12	1.34	0.40	(2.22)	1.91	7.90
1.30	1.17	2.25	1.54	1.67	1.85	2.05	0.86	1.65	20.24
(0.25)	1.22	0.89	0.68	1.99	0.59	(0.26)	(0.22)	1.48	8.88
0.35	1.26	2.47	1.35	1.35	1.63	0.91	2.13	1.31	17.86
1.62	1.46	0.78	0.81	1.64	0.81	1.23	1.38	1.37	16.61
(0.70)	1.92	2.13	1.60	1.04	2.13	0.84	2.02	1.90	16.44
1.59	(0.60)	0.50	(0.57)	(5.69)	1.74	2.14	2.33	1.94	7.23
1.31	2.04	1.61	1.38	0.52	1.25	0.69	2.23	0.46	14.34
2.47	1.51	1.58	1.19	1.34	1.44	0.48	1.20	1.16	18.02
0.23	1.69	(0.84)	0.93	0.87	(2.72)	0.84	0.23	0.78	2.76
(0.04)	(0.25)	(1.23)	(1.90)	0.50	(0.44)	0.36	0.59	0.52	(0.87)
1.29	1.76	0.43	0.71	0.69	0.63	0.72	0.29	0.69	7.47
(0.85)	(0.14)	0.32	(1.02)	0.20	0.59	0.54	1.67	1.07	4.11
3.88	3.64	4.97	1.70	2.02	2.32	1.24	1.75	2.92	44.55
1.28	1.47	1.82	3.49	1.49	3.35	1.46	1.75	1.58	26.92
2.19	1.97	2.07	2.51	0.99	0.72	0.37	2.36	4.65	26.28
1.10	2.16	3.80	1.39	1.80	2.75	1.46	0.55	9.16	34.11
(1.65)	0.34	1.70	0.29	1.89	0.81	(1.90)	(3.97)	0.09	14.47
(1.61)	1.39	1.73	(1.45)	(0.02)	(2.09)	2.38	1.04	0.93	(1.72)
0.19	(1.73)	(0.19)	(0.35)	(0.91)	(1.17)	(1.30)	2.13	(2.39)	(5.49)
1.08	4.57	0.85	1.17	2.37	1.74	0.60	1.84	(0.43)	20.54
0.83	0.23	(0.35)	(1.30)	0.14	0.09	0.55	(0.17)	0.95	5.98
1.50	1.57	0.96	1.35	(0.46)	1.04	0.56	1.32	0.40	13.38
1.80	0.70	(0.45)	1.44	0.51	2.03	(0.51)	0.66	(1.19)	14.07
2.12	1.95	2.46	2.05	0.61	0.33	0.51	1.74	1.11	22.26
2.40	2.46	1.63	1.76	2.11	1.34	1.81	1.09	2.74	27.10
(0.42)	(0.14)	0.22	1.08	0.14	(0.28)	0.13	0.04	(0.06)	4.00
1.57	0.76	1.72	1.18	1.34	1.40	0.36	1.68	1.64	15.66

FUND	YEAR	JAN	FEB	MAR
Relative Value Arbitrage Index	1996	1.46	1.43	1.15
Relative Value Arbitrage Index	1997	1.38	1.09	(0.66)
Relative Value Arbitrage Index	1998	1.98	1.39	1.57
Relative Value Arbitrage Index	1999	2.61	0.11	0.57
Relative Value Arbitrage Index	2000	1.82	1.27	1.80
Relative Value Arbitrage Index	2001	2.04	1.05	0.26
Relative Value Arbitrage Index	2002	1.03	0.04	0.63
Relative Value Arbitrage Index	2003	1.03	0.70	0.71
Relative Value Arbitrage Index	2004	1.21	0.55	0.43
Sector (Total)	1990	(0.47)	0.73	6.56
Sector (Total)	1991	5.70	4.50	1.21
Sector (Total)	1992	5.32	1.91	(0.09)
Sector (Total)	1993	3.70	0.89	3.25
Sector (Total)	1994	2.57	(0.90)	(1.28)
Sector (Total)	1995	0.37	3.15	4.02
Sector (Total)	1996	5.14	2.88	1.72
Sector (Total)	1997	2.85	0.00	(4.53)
Sector (Total)	1998	(1.34)	3.67	2.18
Sector (Total)	1999	4.76	(3.62)	6.37
Sector (Total)	2000	3.04	17.86	(4.32)
Sector (Total)	2001	5.20	(8.97)	(4.82)
Sector (Total)	2002	(1.87)	(4.34)	3.26
Sector (Total)	2003	0.10	0.04	0.71
Sector (Total)	2004	3.46	1.13	0.11
Sector: Energy Index	1995	(1.52)	6.55	9.74
Sector: Energy Index	1996	2.33	6.47	10.29
Sector: Energy Index	1997	4.75	(7.98)	6.78
Sector: Energy Index	1998	(8.60)	1.96	3.81
Sector: Energy Index	1999	(1.98)	(3.68)	6.34
Sector: Energy Index	2000	2.10	3.78	19.83
Sector: Energy Index	2001	1.61	1.73	0.28
Sector: Energy Index	2002	(1.59)	0.82	3.62
Sector: Energy Index	2003	(1.74)	2.92	(0.86)
Sector: Energy Index	2004	2.13	3.84	1.46
Sector: Financial Index	1992	3.48	1.94	1.78
Sector: Financial Index	1993	4.53	4.42	3.47
Sector: Financial Index	1994	2.85	0.64	(1.14)
Sector: Financial Index	1995	2.42	4.27	1.73
Sector: Financial Index	1996	1.80	1.28	1.41
Sector: Financial Index	1997	5.73	5.40	(3.78)
Sector: Financial Index	1998	(2.81)	6.04	4.22
Sector: Financial Index	1999	0.11	0.63	(0.31)

APR	MAY	JUN	JUL	AUG	SEP	OCT	NOV	DEC	ANNUAL
2.04	1.74	0.99	(0.58)	1.53	0.80	0.17	1.02	1.89	14.49
1.30	1.83	1.93	1.57	1.43	1.86	0.96	1.31	0.90	15.93
1.93	0.30	0.16	(0.51)	(5.80)	0.19	(0.48)	1.66	0.63	2.81
2.80	1.17	1.37	0.83	0.80	0.48	0.53	1.08	1.51	14.73
1.41	0.68	2.18	0.93	1.59	0.91	(0.45)	(0.10)	0.64	13.41
0.76	0.93	(0.23)	0.70	0.85	0.24	0.85	0.54	0.60	8.92
0.59	0.21	(0.19)	(0.20)	0.68	0.29	0.41	1.12	0.70	5.44
1.39	0.98	0.48	0.04	0.37	0.86	1.06	0.48	1.23	9.72
(0.51)	(0.35)	0.16	0.65	0.83	0.36	0.31	1.06	0.68	5.50
1.30	(0.26)	6.41	0.40	3.42	(2.43)	3.66	5.21	4.08	32.09
0.64	1.21	(3.47)	1.38	2.93	0.59	3.62	(1.49)	4.78	23.40
1.04	3.65	(1.43)	7.98	2.51	4.36	3.99	5.43	4.47	46.47
0.29	3.14	1.92	2.86	3.89	3.37	3.87	(0.74)	3.09	33.71
(0.26)	2.57	0.59	0.75	2.87	1.55	0.38	(2.08)	1.08	7.98
3.10	1.94	4.60	5.47	4.83	2.48	(1.46)	2.95	2.62	39.65
4.72	4.13	(2.03)	(2.54)	3.97	3.27	0.62	3.12	2.39	30.68
(2.91)	7.27	1.46	4.16	1.03	6.38	(2.79)	(4.96)	(1.96)	5.21
2.48	(3.87)	1.45	(2.32)	(13.00)	5.52	2.40	6.65	5.21	7.62
5.71	(0.06)	5.62	1.00	3.04	0.35	3.70	10.42	16.53	67.00
(7.68)	(5.89)	10.50	(1.78)	8.00	(2.84)	(4.87)	(10.34)	2.29	0.31
5.17	1.20	0.47	(2.80)	(3.79)	(5.34)	3.89	4.45	1.58	(4.90)
(2.66)	(1.24)	(3.47)	(3.96)	0.56	(3.72)	2.07	4.37	(2.20)	(12.85)
4.42	6.82	1.47	2.08	2.42	0.63	3.38	1.04	1.98	27.93
(2.77)	0.34	0.76	(1.62)	0.11	2.52	1.49	3.72	1.79	11.39
8.42	2.48	(0.72)	3.88	8.00	0.53	(6.52)	5.18	12.49	58.45
6.84	(0.98)	(3.34)	(6.43)	4.26	2.43	16.24	3.15	7.57	58.37
(2.25)	13.81	5.23	14.20	4.75	15.69	2.14	(10.51)	(3.26)	47.45
6.71	(5.68)	(9.44)	(11.75)	(6.43)	0.00	(0.19)	10.68	(3.68)	(22.52)
15.20	(3.41)	4.19	4.21	3.85	(0.31)	(1.68)	1.16	0.49	25.51
(0.59)	10.30	(0.47)	(4.05)	8.04	4.15	(3.39)	(2.05)	11.86	58.36
3.21	1.15	(8.32)	(1.93)	(2.12)	2.35	1.07	(1.02)	2.93	0.37
1.69	(1.35)	(3.50)	(7.89)	2.04	(0.87)	2.38	2.68	1.06	(1.49)
2.27	11.80	(0.68)	(2.97)	4.48	(0.90)	2.92	1.15	8.17	28.83
(0.32)	(1.26)	4.60	1.95	(0.56)	7.89	2.51	8.64	0.52	35.63
1.75	5.08	(1.08)	1.60	(1.51)	1.47	3.38	4.60	4.12	29.82
(0.51)	0.39	3.20	5.22	2.28	2.93	1.09	2.68	4.08	39.31
0.52	4.64	5.24	(0.04)	2.97	1.12	(2.46)	(4.44)	1.14	11.14
2.56	3.19	4.14	4.87	4.64	1.65	1.03	2.16	1.53	39.96
0.87	0.90	0.65	0.65	4.09	4.13	2.60	4.36	0.96	26.31
0.84	4.38	5.20	6.18	0.61	8.44	1.34	1.34	5.73	49.35
2.29	(2.80)	0.96	0.07	(18.66)	(0.95)	(1.50)	3.89	(1.03)	(11.96)
5.12	0.34	3.07	(1.30)	(5.37)	(4.39)	7.40	(2.89)	(3.80)	(2.18)

FUND	YEAR	JAN	FEB	MAR
Sector: Financial Index	2000	(1.88)	(4.22)	8.64
Sector: Financial Index	2001	6.26	(0.23)	(0.53)
Sector: Financial Index	2002	0.58	1.05	3.52
Sector: Financial Index	2003	0.66	(0.66)	(0.00)
Sector: Financial Index	2004	1.67	1.46	(0.01)
Sector: Health Care/Biotechnology Index	1993	5.00	(4.71)	(1.36)
Sector: Health Care/Biotechnology Index	1994	4.38	0.42	(6.62)
Sector: Health Care/Biotechnology Index	1995	5.30	1.29	3.53
Sector: Health Care/Biotechnology Index	1996	8.13	1.37	(0.36)
Sector: Health Care/Biotechnology Index	1997	4.58	(1.86)	(5.75)
Sector: Health Care/Biotechnology Index	1998	(3.95)	4.87	2.20
Sector: Health Care/Biotechnology Index	1999	2.38	(4.31)	(2.22)
Sector: Health Care/Biotechnology Index	2000	14.38	42.20	(17.73)
Sector: Health Care/Biotechnology Index	2001	(3.95)	(6.79)	(7.14)
Sector: Health Care/Biotechnology Index	2002	(3.96)	(3.52)	3.59
Sector: Health Care/Biotechnology Index	2003	(0.33)	0.30	3.51
Sector: Health Care/Biotechnology Index	2004	5.31	1.24	0.70
Sector: Miscellaneous Index	1991	1.62	4.15	0.94
Sector: Miscellaneous Index	1992	1.99	1.66	(0.20)
Sector: Miscellaneous Index	1993	4.39	0.85	5.04
Sector: Miscellaneous Index	1994	1.32	0.51	(1.20)
Sector: Miscellaneous Index	1995	1.30	2.30	1.96
Sector: Miscellaneous Index	1996	2.43	2.43	2.14
Sector: Miscellaneous Index	1997	1.55	1.97	(0.13)
Sector: Miscellaneous Index	1998	0.53	1.92	3.28
Sector: Miscellaneous Index	1999	4.46	(1.58)	2.36
Sector: Miscellaneous Index	2000	(3.64)	0.05	0.95
Sector: Miscellaneous Index	2001	3.46	(2.32)	(1.41)
Sector: Miscellaneous Index	2002	(2.48)	1.61	2.36
Sector: Miscellaneous Index	2003	(0.33)	(0.56)	(1.37)
Sector: Miscellaneous Index	2004	(0.74)	1.20	2.54
Sector: Real Estate Index	1994	1.92	3.19	(1.03)
Sector: Real Estate Index	1995	(2.24)	0.15	1.84
Sector: Real Estate Index	1996	1.95	(0.01)	0.07
Sector: Real Estate Index	1997	2.28	1.92	0.49
Sector: Real Estate Index	1998	(0.88)	(0.54)	1.83
Sector: Real Estate Index	1999	(0.94)	(0.72)	0.29
Sector: Real Estate Index	2000	(0.61)	(1.21)	1.78
Sector: Real Estate Index	2001	0.45	(1.16)	0.71
Sector: Real Estate Index	2002	0.03	0.47	2.30
Sector: Real Estate Index	2003	(1.39)	(0.33)	0.32
Sector: Real Estate Index	2004	2.57	2.56	2.32

APR	MAY	JUN	JUL	AUG	SEP	OCT	NOV	DEC	ANNUAL
(2.94)	4.65	(0.51)	3.86	8.36	4.58	3.83	(2.88)	11.45	36.48
0.91	4.68	2.57	1.40	(1.96)	(1.83)	(1.58)	4.09	3.23	17.92
2.16	1.09	(0.91)	(6.21)	2.19	(5.27)	2.98	1.74	(0.41)	1.99
5.36	4.14	0.58	2.19	1.81	1.32	3.09	0.59	1.91	22.94
(2.45)	0.95	0.02	0.04	1.27	1.43	1.36	2.99	2.00	11.14
1.53	8.14	4.00	(1.34)	3.08	3.75	6.00	1.80	6.11	36.15
(2.60)	0.12	(2.05)	(4.04)	3.89	1.42	(2.26)	0.62	(3.56)	(10.34)
1.67	2.92	7.43	6.58	12.12	4.97	(0.33)	1.09	6.83	67.60
4.00	3.44	(2.91)	(4.75)	3.24	1.79	(0.96)	0.69	3.12	17.42
(7.31)	8.70	4.39	(0.33)	1.07	7.01	0.45	(5.91)	(2.36)	1.21
0.39	(4.14)	(1.69)	(2.32)	(13.07)	8.85	3.23	5.22	9.25	6.82
(2.81)	2.90	4.47	6.87	6.94	(4.00)	(1.85)	8.67	25.81	47.35
(6.83)	(6.14)	18.63	(1.42)	15.47	4.99	(3.81)	(9.37)	3.96	50.35
8.24	6.99	7.71	(4.52)	(1.45)	(6.59)	5.93	4.88	1.63	2.91
(5.07)	(2.97)	(5.83)	(3.20)	0.59	(4.31)	0.87	5.44	(3.58)	(20.45)
5.82	8.86	2.98	3.29	2.28	2.10	1.26	0.75	3.12	39.28
(0.10)	(1.12)	(0.90)	(2.35)	(0.15)	1.60	(0.70)	2.12	1.64	7.30
1.73	1.65	(3.67)	2.43	1.77	2.40	3.14	(2.11)	3.49	18.69
(1.03)	3.58	(1.86)	22.37	10.99	7.74	6.04	6.36	4.02	78.72
2.60	4.87	1.83	4.16	3.22	4.72	1.28	1.21	2.72	43.64
1.14	1.59	0.56	2.86	1.03	1.39	0.88	(1.28)	2.27	11.56
0.95	0.96	2.98	0.82	1.93	1.18	(0.85)	1.75	0.45	16.85
3.51	1.79	1.65	(1.84)	3.17	1.71	(0.02)	1.54	4.76	25.73
(0.84)	4.60	2.62	1.84	(0.23)	3.46	(0.90)	(0.15)	(0.69)	13.71
0.08	(0.32)	0.91	(3.28)	(5.74)	0.67	3.32	3.87	6.52	11.77
6.86	2.75	2.81	1.80	(3.08)	(0.45)	3.70	1.37	8.26	32.79
(7.57)	(2.35)	1.87	(0.03)	(0.62)	(1.44)	1.10	(4.52)	3.32	(12.61)
2.11	1.17	(1.09)	(1.94)	(1.80)	(3.13)	(1.21)	1.78	1.70	(2.89)
(0.08)	0.56	(1.04)	(4.06)	0.89	(1.74)	1.42	1.52	(1.31)	(2.52)
4.56	4.38	1.66	2.35	3.61	(1.13)	3.87	2.30	1.58	22.72
(8.86)	0.21	(0.51)	(2.26)	0.22	4.44	1.94	4.74	0.51	2.76
(0.07)	3.52	(0.32)	0.95	(0.66)	(0.94)	(1.01)	1.90	3.24	11.04
(0.02)	1.79	0.21	1.56	0.55	2.09	(1.05)	0.12	3.89	9.11
0.72	0.86	1.66	0.44	3.77	2.32	2.13	2.82	4.96	23.83
(0.71)	1.80	3.57	3.23	(1.48)	4.89	(2.50)	1.15	2.43	18.17
(0.66)	(0.28)	(0.66)	(1.36)	(7.29)	2.64	(1.65)	(0.12)	0.91	(8.08)
4.21	1.68	(0.16)	0.08	(0.92)	(1.41)	(1.46)	(2.18)	4.46	2.71
1.47	(0.47)	4.18	2.92	(0.68)	0.45	(2.24)	0.65	6.69	13.34
0.51	1.57	3.22	(0.63)	1.54	(1.80)	(1.42)	2.56	2.52	8.21
0.42	1.62	0.23	(0.05)	0.74	(1.62)	(0.28)	0.93	(0.28)	4.56
3.73	3.28	1.73	2.42	0.47	1.09	2.59	2.55	(0.35)	17.17
(6.07)	2.26	1.97	0.02	3.19	0.98	1.45	3.00	2.84	18.08

FUND	YEAR	JAN	FEB	MAR
Sector: Technology Index	1991	6.23	4.29	0.08
Sector: Technology Index	1992	12.94	3.84	(5.55)
Sector: Technology Index	1993	3.71	(3.34)	2.81
Sector: Technology Index	1994	2.53	(1.66)	(3.45)
Sector: Technology Index	1995	(0.24)	3.42	3.73
Sector: Technology Index	1996	2.45	3.32	0.87
Sector: Technology Index	1997	4.24	(7.24)	(6.91)
Sector: Technology Index	1998	(0.72)	5.57	0.10
Sector: Technology Index	1999	8.72	(4.33)	12.83
Sector: Technology Index	2000	3.13	21.00	(6.80)
Sector: Technology Index	2001	8.13	(13.10)	(6.00)
Sector: Technology Index	2002	(1.67)	(7.45)	3.14
Sector: Technology Index	2003	0.85	(0.33)	(0.06)
Sector: Technology Index	2004	4.22	(0.11)	(1.54)
Short Selling Index	1990	9.15	2.16	0.91
Short Selling Index	1991	(3.97)	(16.24)	(2.19)
Short Selling Index	1992	(2.78)	(2.56)	6.15
Short Selling Index	1993	(1.36)	6.06	(3.41)
Short Selling Index	1994	(4.87)	0.98	11.32
Short Selling Index	1995	2.37	(2.06)	(2.11)
Short Selling Index	1996	0.09	(4.26)	0.71
HFRI Short Selling Index	1997	(1.02)	5.75	6.75
HFRI Short Selling Index	1998	1.33	(4.98)	0.06
HFRI Short Selling Index	1999	(5.90)	6.97	(0.04)
HFRI Short Selling Index	2000	4.76	(21.21)	1.04
HFRI Short Selling Index	2001	(1.89)	11.77	7.14
HFRI Short Selling Index	2002	4.07	3.61	(4.19)
HFRI Short Selling Index	2003	1.07	1.43	0.19
HFRI Short Selling Index	2004	(1.89)	(0.46)	(0.22)

PLEASE NOTE: Figures for October 2004 to December 2004 are estimates.

Criteria for a fund to be included in the HFR Monthly Indices:
• Fund must report "net of all fees" performance returns • Fund must report its assets (in $US) on a monthly basis
Other important notes concerning the HFR Monthly Indices:
• All HFRI are fund weighted (equal weighted) • There is no required asset-size minimum for fund inclusion in the HFRI

APR	MAY	JUN	JUL	AUG	SEP	OCT	NOV	DEC	ANNUAL
(1.25)	2.07	(4.40)	1.58	2.96	(0.48)	7.90	(5.47)	4.89	18.97
(1.90)	0.92	(2.40)	1.67	0.12	4.86	4.13	4.90	4.77	30.74
0.93	3.53	2.49	2.51	7.61	3.78	4.87	(4.21)	2.90	30.61
(0.06)	(0.27)	(1.63)	2.75	2.58	0.99	6.72	1.14	0.35	10.05
3.34	1.74	9.02	10.11	2.74	4.15	(0.16)	5.66	(1.02)	50.91
9.62	8.59	(3.46)	(4.76)	2.71	5.56	(0.91)	4.94	(0.90)	30.56
(0.46)	11.85	(0.25)	9.08	0.73	6.72	(4.60)	(4.57)	0.16	6.89
3.46	(5.15)	8.35	(1.10)	(15.16)	7.87	5.44	10.40	9.30	28.46
6.95	(0.73)	7.99	(0.65)	5.57	3.13	7.43	17.99	21.56	124.26
(9.78)	(9.27)	12.02	(2.24)	7.66	(6.02)	(6.80)	(13.45)	(0.43)	(15.28)
5.51	(0.87)	(0.77)	(3.25)	(5.72)	(7.09)	5.40	5.37	1.04	(12.82)
(3.84)	(1.47)	(3.68)	(3.52)	(0.15)	(3.85)	2.69	5.61	(3.00)	(16.54)
3.88	6.40	1.26	2.14	2.56	(0.12)	4.85	0.87	0.80	25.41
(3.34)	1.13	1.25	(3.93)	(1.24)	1.32	2.42	2.72	2.58	5.24
5.15	(8.28)	6.64	6.62	4.82	11.91	3.64	(7.68)	(1.64)	36.22
(0.76)	(4.52)	8.73	(0.66)	(0.93)	3.65	(0.59)	8.83	(7.17)	(16.96)
7.64	1.86	7.80	(0.72)	2.93	1.42	(4.21)	(6.79)	0.06	10.05
4.17	(9.19)	0.16	3.35	(5.07)	(2.54)	(3.32)	3.81	0.67	(7.50)
3.33	2.28	12.04	(4.17)	(6.48)	0.52	0.43	4.70	(1.18)	18.53
(0.16)	(3.67)	(9.96)	(9.36)	1.05	(0.65)	7.66	(3.89)	3.54	(17.14)
(7.28)	(2.82)	9.26	9.00	(4.02)	(7.53)	6.47	(2.95)	1.08	(4.00)
(0.47)	(8.23)	(0.20)	(2.94)	(1.77)	(2.58)	4.60	2.21	2.69	3.86
(2.25)	8.16	1.16	3.04	19.40	(4.18)	(8.97)	(4.84)	(5.48)	(0.54)
(2.49)	(0.20)	(1.69)	(0.16)	4.38	3.18	(3.17)	(11.68)	(14.60)	(24.40)
22.84	9.68	(11.38)	7.30	(12.35)	13.42	8.66	16.16	0.42	34.63
(12.03)	(2.30)	0.99	5.93	8.27	8.52	(3.94)	(7.46)	(3.40)	8.99
4.34	4.08	5.23	6.41	1.05	6.80	(3.88)	(6.41)	5.90	29.17
(5.45)	(5.96)	(1.46)	(3.48)	(3.22)	1.62	(5.71)	(0.96)	(1.94)	(21.78)
3.74	(0.67)	(0.76)	4.34	0.01	(1.65)	(1.37)	(3.41)	(1.14)	(3.67)

• There is no required length of time a fund must be actively investing before inclusion in the HFRI • Both onshore and offshore funds are included in the HFRI • The trailing four months are left as estimates and are subject to change. All performance prior to that is locked and is no longer subject to change. • In cases where a manager lists mirrored-performance funds, only the fund with the larger asset size is included in the HFRI • The HFRI are updated three times a month (flash, mid, and end) • If a fund liquidates/closes, that fund's performance will be included in the HFRI as of that fund's last reported performance update.

GLOSSARY

Arbitrage. The simultaneous purchase and sale of a security or pair of similar securities to profit from a pricing discrepancy.

Average gain. The average percentage gain in periods with a positive return.

Average loss. The average percentage loss in periods with a negative return.

Beta. A measure of how much the value of a security or portfolio of securities moves in relation to the average performance of the stock market for a given period of time. In this book, beta is calculated by comparing the price movements of the HFR indices with the S&P 500 index of blue-chip stocks.

Boom-bust sequence. The process by which the value of an instrument or class of instruments is pushed to a valuation extreme, reverses itself, and crashes back to a more normal valuation.

Call feature. A feature that allows the issuer to redeem a bond before it matures.

Cash merger. A deal in which the acquiring company pays cash for the target company.

Catalyst. A near-term event, such as a press release or a new product launch, that will heighten investor interest in or change the market's perception of a company.

Collateral. Cash or very liquid securities that are held as a deposit on borrowed securities.

Conversion value. The value of a convertible bond if it were to be converted to common stock.

Convertible arbitrage. The simultaneous purchase of a convertible bond and sale of the underlying common stock to profit from a pricing discrepancy.

Convertible bond. A corporate bond issued with a corporate bond yield and a conversion feature that allows the holder to convert the bond into a fixed number of shares of the issuing company's common stock.

Core positions. Long-term positions in growth stocks from which managers derive the majority of their profits.

Coupon. A bond's fixed interest payment.

Distressed securities. The securities of companies that are experiencing financial or operational difficulties. Distressed situations include reorganizations, bankruptcies, distressed sales, and other corporate restructurings.

Duration. A measure of how sensitive a bond's price is to a shift in interest rates. In general terms,

$$\text{Duration} = \frac{(\text{Change in price})/\text{Price}}{\text{Change in interest rates}}$$

Emerging market. A market that is changing rapidly at the macroeconomic and company level, usually because it is restructuring on the free market model.

Equity-market-neutral portfolio. A portfolio composed of balanced exposure to long stock positions and offsetting short stock positions.

Event analysis. The process by which an analyst assesses the probabilities of all the possible outcomes of a corporate event.

Exit catalyst. An event on the horizon that the distressed securities specialist expects to change the market's perception of, and therefore the value of, the distressed company.

Far-from-equilibrium condition. An unusual macro situation characterized by persistent price trends or extreme price valuations of particular financial instruments.

Fixed-income securities. Securities that entitle the holder to a series of fixed payments at predetermined future dates.

Fundamental value. The intrinsic or "real" value of a security, which reflects both tangible and intangible company assets.

Gain period. The percentage of periods with positive or neutral returns.

Global investors. Investors who consider emerging markets to be one potential asset class, along with developed markets and fixed-income securities, and who allocate capital to each asset class when they believe that it offers attractive potential returns compared with other asset classes.

Growth stock. A stock that an invest or believes will appreciate because the company's output and earnings will grow.

Hedge ratio. The number of shares that the convertible arbitrage specialist decides to sell short out of the total number possible.

Hedging. The taking of positions to offset changes in economic conditions falling outside the core investment idea, such as purchasing a long position and a short position in similar stocks to offset the effect any changes in the overall level of the equity market will have on the long position.

High-period return. The highest rate of return for a one-month period.

Indicators. Financial data used to forecast the future performance of a company.

Inflection point. The point at which an extreme valuation reverses itself, usually marked or signaled by a major policy move.

Investment value. The value of the bond component of a convertible bond.

Leverage. The practice of borrowing to add to an investment position when one believes that the return from the position will exceed the cost of the borrowed funds. Both companies and investors can use leverage. A company that takes on more debt than its ability to generate cash warrants is said to be overleveraged.

Leveraged buyout. An often hostile situation in which the acquiring company buys out the target company by using borrowed funds.

Liquidation. The sale of assets for cash, sometimes to pay off debt.

Low-period return. The lowest rate of return for a one-month period.

Mark to market. To determine the price one can get today for currently owned securities.

Market exposure. The amount of portfolio that is exposed to market risk because it is not matched by an offsetting position.

Market inefficiencies. Pricing disparities caused by a lack of information about a market or company or by a distortion of the information that is available.

Market-neutral portfolio. A portfolio composed of equal dollar amounts of long stock positions and offsetting short stock positions.

Maturity date. The date on which a bond is redeemed (a 5-year bond comes to maturity five years after it is issued).

Maximum drawdown. The peak-to-valley percentage change in the value of some initial investment in a fund.

Mortgage-backed securities. Securities that represent an ownership interest in mortgage loans made by financial institutions (such as savings and loans, commercial banks, or mortgage companies) to finance the borrower's purchase of a home.

Net market exposure. The percentage of the portfolio exposed to market fluctuations because long positions are not matched by equal dollar amounts of short positions. In general terms,

$$\text{Market exposure} = \frac{\text{Long exposure} - \text{Short exposure}}{\text{Capital}}$$

One-period arithmetic standard deviation. The distribution of performance over any single period (one month) for a given set of noncompounded returns.

One-period geometric average. The hypothetical rate of return for a single period (one month), derived from the compounded geometric return of a time series.

Overleveraged company. A company that has a large amount of debt relative to its ability to pay interest on that debt.

Par value. The face value of a bond, or the amount that it is redeemed for at maturity.

Prepayments. Payments to repay a mortgage loan ahead of the scheduled repayment date.

Relative value. The value of a particular security relative to that of other similar or related instruments, such as the same company's other debt instruments.

Risk-free interest rate. The 3-month U.S. Treasury bill rate used in calculating the Sharpe ratio. The statistics in this book assume a 5 percent risk-free rate.

Sector. A group of companies or segment of the economy that is similar in either its product or its market, for example, health care, biotechnology, financial services, or information technologies.

Securities market infrastructure. The means of making investments and tracking financial information, including accounting standards, availability of trading and financial information, and sophistication of available financial instruments.

Senior debt. A class of debt securities whose holders a company is obligated to pay off before the holders of its other securities, in the case of bankruptcy.

Servicing debt. Paying the interest and principal due to bondholders.

Sharpe ratio. The reward-to-risk ratio, discounting for the risk-free interest rate. It is calculated as follows: Annualized geometric performance – Risk-free interest rate annual standard deviation.

Short interest rebate. The interest earned on the cash proceeds of a short sale of stock.

Short selling. The practice of borrowing a stock on collateral and immediately selling it on the market with the intention of buying it back later at a lower price.

Significant corporate events. Major public events, such as mergers, bankruptcies, and spin-offs, that have the potential to dramatically change a company's makeup and as a result the valuation of its debt and equity instruments.

Speculator. An investor who makes large directional bets on what financial markets will do next.

Spread. The difference between the prices of two comparable or related securities. Spreads are measured in basis points. One basis point equals 1/100 of a percent. For example, corporate bonds of a comparable maturity and comparable coupon rates will have higher yields than Treasuries to reflect greater default risk, so their yields are often quoted as a spread above the Treasury rate. The more risky the bond issue, the larger is the spread.

Static return. Returns, such as interest income from coupon payments and short interest rebates from short sales of stock, that are unaffected by price fluctuations of the underlying securities.

Stock selection risk. Exposure to uncertainty about the future valuation of a particular stock.

Stock swap merger. A deal in which the holders of the target company's stock receive shares of the acquiring company's stock rather than cash.

Strategic acquisition. A generally noncompetitive situation in which the acquiring company has a good business reason for the merger, such as expanding product capability.

Structural anomalies. Greater-than-expected price discounts that can be attributed to nonmarket or nonrational technical factors.

Systematic or market risk. Exposure to uncertainty about systematic rises and falls in stock market prices that affect the prices of all stocks in a market or sector.

Systematic risk factors. Factors, such as interest rates or the price of oil, that have the ability to affect systematically the valuation of a whole range of stocks if they change.

Time horizon analysis. The examination of the time frame for completion of a corporate event (if the event is going to happen, then when will it occur?).

Trading positions. Opportunistic positions designed to take advantage of short-term market mispricings and inefficiencies rather than hedge against market decline.

Warrant. The stock conversion component of a convertible bond.

Within the hedge. A phrase used to describe that portion of an equity hedge portfolio in which long positions are matched by equal dollar amounts of short positions.

Yield. The single investment rate that sets the present value of all a bond's future cash payments equal to the price of the bond.

NOTES

INTRODUCTION

1. All analysis and performance statistics provided in this book are based on Hedge Fund Research, Inc. Performance Indices. Appendix A explains the calculation methodology and provides definitions of important variables; Appendix B lists further resources, and Appendix C is Hedge Fund Research Performance Indices.

2. George Soros, *Soros on Soros: Staying Ahead of the Curve* (New York: John Wiley and Sons, 1995), 68.

CHAPTER 1

1. Carol J. Loomis, "The Jones Nobody Keeps Up With," *Fortune* (1962): 237–47.

CHAPTER 3

1. Chapter based on "Legal Issues in Connection with Investments by Tax-Exempt Entities in Hedge Funds, Other Investment Funds, and Managed Accounts" by Stephanie Breslow; Schultz, Roth and Zabel, L.L.P. (paper presented at the Hedge Fund Research, Inc. conference on Alternative Investments, University of Chicago, July 22, 1998).

CHAPTER 4

1. John Kerschner, Kent Fleming, and Dan Adler, Smith Breeden Associates, Inc., personal correspondence to author, December 10, 2004.

CHAPTER 5

1. Edward L. Finn, personal correspondence to author, July 22, 1998.

2. Sam Nathans, Martingale Asset Management, personal correspondence to author, December 10, 2004.

CHAPTER 6
1. Odell Lambroza, Advent Capital Management, personal correspondence to author, December 10, 2004.

CHAPTER 7
1. Seth Washburne, Washburne Capital Management, personal correspondence to author, December 10, 2004.

CHAPTER 8
1. Mickey Harley, Mellon HBV Alternative Strategies, personal correspondence to author, December 10, 2004.

CHAPTER 9
1. Karen Finerman, Metropolitan Capital Advisors, personal correspondence to author, December 10, 2004.

CHAPTER 10
1. Soros, 71–77.
2. Ray Dalio, Bridgewater Associates, personal correspondence to author, December 13, 2004.

CHAPTER 11
1. Source E.I.A.
2. Source MMS (minerals management service).
3. J.C. Frey, Kayne Anderson Capital Advisors, personal correspondence to author, December 10, 2004.

CHAPTER 12
1. David Fink, Matador Capital Management, personal correspondence to author, December 10, 2004.
2. Jeff James, Driehaus Capital Management, personal correspondence to author, December 10, 2004.

CHAPTER 13
1. Richard Giacomo, Gramercy Capital Management, personal correspondence to author, December 10, 2004.

INDEX

ABOUT BLOOMBERG

Bloomberg L.P., founded in 1981, is a global information services, news, and media company. Headquartered in New York, the company has sales and news operations worldwide.

Bloomberg, serving customers on six continents, holds a unique position within the financial services industry by providing an unparalleled range of features in a single package known as the BLOOMBERG PROFESSIONAL® service. By addressing the demand for investment performance and efficiency through an exceptional combination of information, analytic, electronic trading, and Straight Through Processing tools, Bloomberg has built a worldwide customer base of corporations, issuers, financial intermediaries, and institutional investors.

BLOOMBERG NEWS®, founded in 1990, provides stories and columns on business, general news, politics, and sports to leading newspapers and magazines throughout the world. BLOOMBERG TELEVISION®, a 24-hour business and financial news network, is produced and distributed globally in seven languages. BLOOMBERG RADIO^{SM} is an international radio network anchored by flagship station BLOOMBERG® 1130 (WBBR-AM) in New York.

In addition to the BLOOMBERG PRESS® line of books, Bloomberg publishes *BLOOMBERG MARKETS*® magazine. To learn more about Bloomberg, call a sales representative at:

London:	+44-20-7330-7500
New York:	+1-212-318-2000
Tokyo:	+81-3-3201-8900

ABOUT THE AUTHOR

Joseph G. Nicholas, J.D., is a leading authority on hedge funds, funds of funds, and alternative investment strategies. As founder and chairman of HFR Group, LLC and its affiliated companies, Nicholas pioneered the areas of hedge fund transparency and indexation. The HFR companies specialize in alternative investments, providing investment products and advisory and research services. HFR Group includes HFR Asset Management, LLC, an SEC-registered investment adviser based in Chicago, with offices in New York, London, and Tokyo, specializing in hedge funds, fund of funds, index funds, product structuring, trading manager selection, and risk management; and Hedge Fund Research, Inc., the industry's leading supplier of data and research on hedge funds, specializing in the construction and management of hedge fund indexes. In addition to *Investing in Hedge Funds,* Nicholas is author of *Hedge Fund of Funds Investing* (Bloomberg Press, 2004) and *Market-Neutral Investing* (Bloomberg Press, 2000), among other writings. He is a frequent lecturer on topics relating to alternative investments and has appeared on CNN and *Nightly Business Report.* Nicholas received a BS in Commerce from DePaul University and a JD from the Northwestern University School of Law.

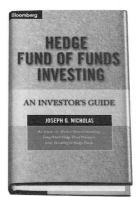